educated a... studied law. Since... a researcher and the... as a writer, broadcaster and journalis... principal writer of early editions of the board... Trivial Pursuit and has devised many televis... formats. He wrote an award-winning weekly column for the *Daily Express* and currently writes a weekly column for the *Sunday Express*. He has written over fifty books – including *Desert Island Discs: Flotsam & Jetsam*, and fifteen for children. He won the Blue Peter Best Book With Facts Award in 2010 and again in 2011.

In naming Mitchell as the friend he would phone (as a Phone-A-Friend) if he were appearing on *Who Wants To Be A Millionaire*, Chris Tarrant said: 'Mitch knows more totally useless things about useless subjects than anybody on earth'.

Also by Mitchell Symons

Adult Non-Fiction
Forfeit!
The Equation Book of Sports Crosswords
The Equation Book of Movie Crosswords
The You Magazine Book of Journolists (with John Koski. 4 books)
Movielists (with John Koski)
The Sunday Magazine Book of Crosswords
The Hello! Magazine Book of Crosswords (3 books)
How To Be Fat: The Chip And Fry Diet (with Penny Symons)
The Book of Criminal Records
The Book of Lists
The Book of Celebrity Lists
The Book of Celebrity Sex Lists
The Bill Clinton Joke Book
National Lottery Big Draw 2000 (with David Thomas)
That Book
This Book
The Other Book
The Sudoku Institute Sudoku (with David Thomas)
The Worst Noel (Contrib.)
Why Girls Can't Throw
How To Speak Celebrity
Where Do Nudists Keep Their Hankies
My Story (with Penny and Jack Symons)
Don't Get Me Started
The Ultimate Loo Book (the best of *That Book*, *This Book* and *The Other Book*)
Desert Island Discs: Flotsam & Jetsam
The Book of Poker Calls (with Jack Symons)

Adult Fiction
All In
The Lot
No Red Light Flashing

Children's Non-Fiction
How to Avoid a Wombat's Bum
Why Eating Bogeys Is Good For You
How Much Poo Does An Elephant Do?
Why Do Farts Smell Like Rotten Eggs?
Why Does Ear Wax Taste So Gross?
Mitchell Symons Diary 2010
At Your Age 8 (with Penny Symons)
At Your Age 9 (with Penny Symons)
Why You Need A Passport When You're Going To Puke
That's So Gross! Animals
That's So Gross! Creepy Crawlies
That's So Gross! History
That's So Gross! Human Body
Do Igloos Have Loos?
On Your Farts, Get Set, Go!
Don't Wipe Your Bum With A Hedgehog

THE BUMPER BOOK FOR THE LOO

THE BUMPER BOOK FOR THE LOO

MITCHELL SYMONS

CORGI BOOKS

TRANSWORLD PUBLISHERS
61–63 Uxbridge Road, London W5 5SA
A Random House Group Company
www.transworldbooks.co.uk

THE BUMPER BOOK FOR THE LOO
A CORGI BOOK: 9780552167116

First publication in Great Britain
Corgi edition published 2012

A CIP catalogue record for this book
is available from the British Library.

Addresses for Random House Group Ltd companies outside the UK
 can be found at: www.randomhouse.co.uk
The Random House Group Ltd Reg. No. 954009

The Random House Group Limited supports The Forest Stewardship Council (FSC®), the
leading international forest-certification organization. Our books carrying the FSC label are
printed on FSC®-certified paper. FSC is the only forest-certification scheme endorsed by
the leading environmental organizations, including Greenpeace. Our paper-procurement
policy can be found at www.randomhouse.co.uk/environment

Design by Hugh Adams, AB3 Design. Typeset in Frutiger.
Printed and bound by Clays Ltd, St Ives plc.

2 4 6 8 10 9 7 5 3 1

Acknowledgements

Now for some important acknowledgements: firstly, my fantastic editor Brenda Kimber, my wife and chief researcher Penny Symons.

In addition, I'd also like to thank the following people for their help, contributions and/or support: Gilly Adams, Hugh Adams, Marcus Berkmann, Paul Donnelley, Jonathan Fingerhut, Jenny Garrison, Pat Higgins, Bryn Musson, Muriel Ravenscroft, Nicholas Ridge, Mari Roberts, Jerry Sawyer, Charlie Symons, Jack Symons, Louise Symons, David Thomas, Martin Townsend, Clair Woodward, Rob Woolley and Stewart Wright.

Introduction

'Know your place' we are sometimes told. Well, I know mine: it's in the smallest room in the house. Hence the title of this book – and it's forebear, *The Ultimate Loo Book*.

Friends – and, remarkably, trivia devotees CAN have friends – often tell me in an embarrassed tone that they keep my books in their toilets. I tell them that that's great: I'd far rather they kept my books where they – and their guests – might actually read them than on some inaccessible shelf gathering dust.

Yup, I know who I am; I know where I belong.

This is a big book. So much so, that you might miss some great facts if (as you almost certainly will) you dip in and out of it. So please let me highlight a few of them.

There was once an internet rumour that Belgium doesn't exist.

Starbucks is named after Starbuck, Captain Ahab's first mate in the novel *Moby Dick*.

Banging your head against a wall uses 150 calories an hour.

Albania was the only European country occupied by the Axis powers (that's Germany and Italy) that ended World War 2 with a larger Jewish population than before the start of the War. Only one Jewish family was deported and killed during the Nazi occupation of Albania. Not only did the Albanians protect their own Jews, but they provided refuge for Jews from neighbouring countries.

There are only four clubs in the Football League with names starting and ending with the same letter: Liverpool, Charlton Athletic, Northampton Town and Aston Villa.

Diet Coke was invented in 1982. However, in 1379, a Mr and Mrs Coke of Yorkshire named their daughter 'Diot' (a short form of Dionisia, the modern-day name Denise).

The 19th-century French writer Guy de Maupassant hated the Eiffel Tower so much that he regularly used to eat lunch in the Tower's restaurant – because that was the one place in Paris he wouldn't have to look at it.

Dundee is the only British professional club with a name that doesn't contain any letters that appear in the word 'football'.

My favourite fact or story in the book is this one: It's a well-known fact that the record score for a British (professional) soccer match is Arbroath 36 Bon Accord 0. It's an *amazing* score but what's really incredible about it is that *on the very same day and in the very same competition* – 12 September 1885, the Scottish Cup – Dundee Harp beat Aberdeen Rovers 35–0. It was the Dundee Harp captain – a former Arbroath player – who got the news after he sent his former team a telegram to boast about the (what he thought was) record score. But the drama doesn't end there. According to the referee in the Dundee Harp v. Aberdeen Rovers game, the final score was 37–0 but the club secretary of Dundee Harp – the winning team, remember – reckoned that it was only 35-0 so the ref went with the lower figure.

Finally, People often ask me which one of my books I like the best – perhaps expecting me to come up with some tosh along the lines of 'They're all my babies: I love them all equally'. Er, no. I have absolutely no difficulty in choosing my favourite. Up till now, it was *The Ultimate Loo Book*. Well, now, I've got joint-favourites: that one and this one.

I hope you like it as much as I do.

Mitchell Symons
August 2012

Happy Birthday to you

Happy Birthday to you

FIRST THINGS FIRST

The **first** song to be sung in outer space was *Happy Birthday* – sung by the *Apollo 11* astronauts on 8 March 1969.

The **first** toothbrush was invented in China in 1498.

Bingo was **first** played in 1888.

The **first** Internet domain name to be registered was symbolics.com in March 1985.

The **first** man-made object to break the sound barrier was a whip.

The **first** blood transfusion was in 1668. The doctors used sheep's blood and the patient died. The **first** successful transfusion – using human blood this time – was in 1818.

Glenn Miller was the **first** recording artist or performer to receive a gold record. He received it for 'Chattanooga Choo Choo', in 1942.

In 1954, Richard Herrick received the **first** successful kidney transplant. It was donated by his twin brother Ronald Herrick.

The UK established the world's **first** speed limit. It was in 1903 and it was set at 20 miles per hour.

The **first** filmed sport was boxing in 1894.

Barbra Streisand's **first** performance was as a chocolate chip cookie.

The world's **first** contact lenses were worn in 1930.

Princess Eugenie was the **first** royal baby to have a public christening.

The **first** commercial text message was sent in December 1992.

Gold was the **first** metal to be discovered.

The **first** Burger King restaurant – called Insta Burger King – opened in Miami in 1954.

The **first** diet soft drink, called 'The No-Cal Beverage', was launched in 1952.

Britain's **first** Indian restaurant was opened more than 50 years before the first fish-and-chip restaurant.

Nottingham was the **first** city in the world to have Braille signs in its shopping malls.

When Iceland played Estonia in 1996, Eidur Gudjohnsen became the **first** player to replace his father (Arnor) in an international match. Between them, he and his dad helped Iceland to win 3–0.

The **first** automatic telephone exchange was invented in 1889 by an American undertaker who wanted to prevent telephone operators from advising his rivals of the death of local citizens.

The **first** instance of global electronic communications took place in 1871 when news of the Derby winner was telegraphed from London to Calcutta in under five minutes.

The world's **first** self-service restaurant, The Exchange Buffet, opened in New York in 1885. Only men were allowed to eat there.

King Louis XV (aka King Louis The Well-Beloved) was the **first** person to use a lift when in 1743 his 'flying chair' carried him between the floors of his Versailles palace.

Britain's very **first** mobile phone call was made on 1 January 1985 by Ernie Wise.

In 301 AD, Armenia became the **first** country to make Christianity the state religion.

Contrary to what you might read elsewhere, the world's **first** supermarket was not in France but in Memphis, Tennessee in the US. Opened in 1916, it was the first of a chain named (honestly) Piggly Wiggly.

However, France can boast the world's **first** department store: Le Bon Marché opened in Paris in 1838.

The **first** bagpipe was made from the liver of a dead sheep.

In 1620, Dutch inventor Cornelius van Drebbel launched the world's **first** submarine in the Thames. The first military submarine – *the Turtle* – was built in 1775.

The world's **first** scheduled passenger air service started in Florida in 1914.

The world's **first** newspaper was *Relation Aller Fürnemmen Und Gedenckwürdigen Historien*. It was published in 1605 in Strasbourg (now part of France but then an imperial free city in the Holy Roman Empire of the German Nation).

In 2004, Bhutan became the **first** country in the world to ban cigarettes.

The world's **first** airline was started in Germany in 1909.

Lego was **first** invented in Demark in 1949. The pieces were originally called Automatic Binding Bricks.

Coffee was **first** brewed in Ethiopia. The word coffee comes from Kefa, the name of a province in southern Ethiopia.

The area we now call Ethiopia is said to be where the very **first** human beings originated.

Germany was the **first** country to use Daylight Saving Time.

Mexico was the **first** country to produce chocolate on a large scale.

Russia was the **first** country to send a man into space (Yuri Gagarin in 1961) but the Russians also sent the first dog into space. In 1957, Laika, a stray, was launched into space on Sputnik 2. Alas, she died a few hours after launch from overheating, probably due to a malfunction in the thermal control system. However, the experiment proved that a living passenger could survive being launched into orbit and endure weightlessness. In 2008, the Russians unveiled a monument to Laika in Moscow.

Singapore is home to the world's **first** night zoo.

The Indian mathematician Aryabhatta **first** came up with the mathematical concept of zero at the end of the fifth century.

Sweden was the **first** country in the world to keep population statistics.

The world's **first** church was built in Turkey.

The **first** modern health resort opened in Spa in Belgium in the eighteenth century. Belgium was also the home of European's first casino (in 1763).

The **first** pull-top can was invented by Ermal Cleon Fraze in 1959, after he had to resort to using his car bumper to open a can of drink.

The **first** commercial vacuum cleaner was so large it was mounted on a wagon. People threw parties in their homes so guests could watch the new device do its job.

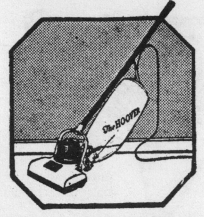

The **first** TV remote control – named Lazy Bones – was sold by Zenith in the US in 1950. It was connected to the set by a wire.

The **first** person killed in a car accident was Londoner Bridget Driscoll, who in 1896 was run over by a car travelling at the speed of 4 miles per hour.

Leonardo da Vinci was the **first** person to record that the number of rings in the cross section of a tree trunk revealed its age. He also discovered that the width between the rings indicated the annual moisture.

The **first** alarm clock could only ring at 4 a.m.

The **first** Michelin Man costume was worn by Colonel Sanders of Kentucky Fried Chicken fame.

Ties (as in neckties) were **first** worn at the time of the Thirty Years' War (1618–1648) when the traditional small, knotted neckerchiefs worn by Croatian mercenaries fighting for the French were adopted as ties by Parisians.

The **first** flight on earth was undoubtedly made by an insect.

In 1911, Bobby Leach, a British-born circus star, became the **first** man* to go over Niagara Falls in a barrel and survive (although he ended up in hospital for 23 weeks). Fifteen years later, he died ... after slipping on a piece of orange peel in New Zealand.

*... but not the **first** *person*. That was Annie Edson Taylor, a 63-year-old teacher, in 1901.

CELEBRITIES

Naomi Watts is the daughter of Pink Floyd's former sound engineer (and her mobile phone has *Money* as its ring tone).

Michael Sheen's father is a part-time professional Jack Nicholson lookalike.

Damon Albarn's father was the manager of Soft Machine.

Huey Lewis (of Huey Lewis and The News)'s grandfather invented the red wax sealant you find on certain cheeses.

Adrian Chiles holds the world record for the most number of kisses (78) received in one minute (air kisses didn't count).

Ozzy Osbourne's father used to have his milk delivered by Noddy Holder.

Kate Winslet had a block of flats named after her in Reading. A cinema was demolished to make way for it.

Kristen Stewart had to wear brown contact lenses for *Twilight* because she has naturally green eyes while Bella's eyes are supposed to be brown.

Eli Roth, the director of *Cabin Fever* and *Hostel*, can't stand the sight of real blood, saying it makes him sick to his stomach.

Mike Myers has a street named after him in Scarborough, Ontario: Mike Myers Drive. There is also a street named Wayne's World Drive in Draper, Utah.

Edward Norton's grandfather, James Rouse, is credited with being the inventor of the modern shopping mall.

Drew Barrymore used to hire a woman to come to her home and tickle her three times a week.

Prince Charles and **Prince William** never travel on the same aeroplane (as a precaution against both of them being involved in a plane crash).

Bill Gates was so clever at school that the school paid him to devise the school's timetable. He wrote it to ensure that he was put in classes that were mostly female. When he was fifteen, he designed a traffic control system for the city of Seattle.

Oprah Winfrey makes all her employees sign lifelong confidentiality agreements.

Janis Joplin sucked her thumb until the age of eight.

Sarah Palin won the 1984 Miss Wasilla beauty contest.

When **Sam Cooke** died, his widow, Barbara, married Bobby Womack. Cooke's daughter, Linda, later married Bobby's brother, Cecil.

Carey Mulligan went to school in Germany.

Loretta Lynn was a grandmother at the age of 29.

Stephen Hawking couldn't read until he was eight years old.

Kim Basinger puts sour cream and lemon juice in her bath water.

Jay Leno lived (at different times) with five women who were all born on 5 September.

Michael Keaton only ever wears cowboy boots. He has 70 to 80 pairs.

Rhona Cameron won a bronze medal in swimming in the 1998 Gay Games.

Sir Michael Gambon auditioned for the role of James Bond (after George Lazenby).

When **Pete Doherty** was 17, he won a competition and was chosen to travel with the British Council to Russia to perform his poetry.

Robert Downey Jr once worked as a piece of living art in a Soho nightclub in New York City.

Antwone Fisher was born in a women's prison (where his mother was an inmate).

PURE TRIVIA (1)

There's a river in Nicaragua called the Pis Pis river.

There was once an Internet rumour that Belgium doesn't exist.

Mozambique has all five vowels in it.

In 1961 the Museum of Modern Art in New York City hung Matisse's *Le Bateau* upside-down for 47 days before an art student noticed the error.

Beethoven took hay baths to remedy the swelling he used to get in his legs.

In 1969, a Finnish farmer was cutting wood when, in the middle of an aspen log, he found a dried fish.

In 1907, an ad campaign for Kellogg's Corn Flakes offered a free box of cereal to any woman who would wink at her grocer.

Native Americans used to name their children after the first thing the parent saw after the birth – hence such strange names as Crazy Horse and Sitting Bull.

The inventor of Vaseline ate a spoonful of his invention every morning.

Justin Timberlake's half-eaten French toast sold for more than £1,500 on eBay.

Medieval Welsh mercenary bowmen only wore one shoe at a time.

Ape's Laugh, Smoked Ox, Chimney-Sweep, and Dying Monkey were the names of sixteenth-century lipsticks.

Forty per cent of *Woman's Hour* listeners are men.

It cost $7 million to build the *Titanic* and $200 million to make a film about it.

The American games Advance to Boardwalk, Free Parking and Don't Go To Jail are all spin-offs from the game of Monopoly.

It's forbidden to take photographs at a Quaker wedding.

In the sixteenth century, a Turkish woman could divorce her husband if he failed to keep his family's pot filled with coffee.

When Rudyard Kipling was fired as a reporter for the *San Francisco Examiner*, his letter of dismissal said, 'I'm sorry Mr Kipling but you just don't know how to use the English Language. This isn't Kindergarten for amateur writers.'

The French critic Saint-Beuve, was involved in a duel. When asked to choose his weapons, he replied 'I choose spelling, You're dead.'

A couple named Richard and Carol Roble remarried each other 56 times.

In order for a deck of cards to be mixed up properly, it should be shuffled seven times.

The loudest sound that could be made in 1600 was on a pipe organ.

In its infancy, the Pepsi-Cola Company was declared bankrupt three times.

There is no living descendant of William Shakespeare.

People photocopying their buttocks are the cause of 23 per cent of all photocopier faults worldwide.

Before the sixteenth century, shoes didn't have heels. Queen Elizabeth I had them added to give the Royal family additional stature.

 **Eel-skin wallets have been known to demagnetize credit cards.**

Sir Walter Scott named his dog Hamlet.

A man named Giovanni Vigliotto married 104 women in 14 different countries between 1949 and 1981.

The longest recorded Monopoly game took 1,680 hours – more than 70 days.

Starbucks is named after Starbuck, Captain Ahab's first mate in the novel *Moby Dick*.

On average, 51 cars a year overshoot and drive into the canals of Amsterdam.

When Leonardo Da Vinci was young he drew a picture of a horrible monster and placed it near a window in order to surprise his father. Upon seeing the picture his father believed it to be real and set out to protect his family until the boy showed him it was just a picture. Da Vinci's father then enrolled his son in an art class.

When you open a new box of crayons, the scent you can smell is that of stearic acid – which is beef fat.

If done perfectly, any Rubik's cube combination can be solved in 17 turns.

If you go to the vet's and see the letters AMITO in your pet's notes – be annoyed: it stands for Animal More Intelligent Than Owner.

There are 294 steps in the Leaning Tower of Pisa.

All known mammals have tongues.

Statistically, couples are more likely to break up on 12 January than on any other day of the year.

Ghosts appear in four Shakespeare plays: *Julius Caesar, Richard III, Hamlet* and *Macbeth*.

Henry Ford produced the Model T Ford in black only because the black paint available at the time was the fastest to dry.

Counting at one digit per second it would take over eleven and a half days and nights of non-stop counting to reach one million.

In Britain, about ten people a week go to hospital because of injuries suffered while playing Wii games.

American tobacco auctioneers can speak at up to 400 words per minute.

According to Beatles producer George Martin, the 1960s *Batman* theme song inspired George Harrison to write the hit song *Taxman*.

The longest rendering of a national anthem was *God Save the King*, performed by a German military band on the platform of Rathenau railway station in Brandenburg, on 9 February, 1909. King Edward VII was struggling inside the train to get into his German Field-Marshal uniform, so the band had to play the anthem 17 consecutive times.

PEOPLE WHO WERE BORN ON SIGNIFICANT DAYS IN HISTORY

Tom O'Connor – the day the Battle of Britain ended.

Brian Lara – the day that the *QE2* sailed from Southampton on her maiden voyage.

Lance Bass – the day that Margaret Thatcher became Prime Minister.

Stevie Nicks – the day that apartheid began in South Africa.

Keith Allen – the day that Queen Elizabeth II was crowned.

Andrew Flintoff – the day that South Africa granted 'independence' to Bophuthatswana.

Sienna Miller, British actress – the day that the first American test-tube baby was born.

George Clooney – the day Spurs won the FA Cup to achieve the Double.

Helena Bonham Carter – the day that Guyana became independent.

Naomi Campbell – the day that the South African cricket tour of England was cancelled.

Nelson Mandela – the day that the second Battle of the Marne was fought.

Jennifer Lopez – the day that *Apollo 11* splashed down safely in the Pacific Ocean.

Gary Oldman – the day that the London Planetarium opened.

Billy Joel – the day that Britain's first laundrette opened.

Norah Jones – the day that Airey Neave was killed by a car bomb planted by the Irish National Liberation Army.

Joss Stone – the day that the London Agreement was secretly signed between Israel and Jordan.

Andy Serkis – the day that BBC2's launch was halted by a power cut.

Prince William – the day that John Hinckley was found not guilty by reason of insanity for the attempted assassination of US President Ronald Reagan.

Pixie Lott – the day that an act of the US Congress authorized the use of military force to drive Iraq out of Kuwait.

Phil Neville – the day that President Jimmy Carter pardoned nearly all American Vietnam War draft evaders.

Fergie (the singer) – the day that construction of the Trans-Alaska Pipeline System began.

Charlie Watts – the day that clothes rationing began in the UK.

Usain Bolt – the day that carbon dioxide gas erupted from volcanic Lake Nyos in Cameroon, killing 1,800 people within a 20-kilometre range.

John Bishop – the day that Barbados became independent from the UK.

Miranda Hart – the day that Eugene Cernan became the last person to walk on the moon.

Jamie Cullum – the day that the East Coast Main Line rail route between England and Scotland was restored.

Anne Hathaway – the day that Lech Wałesa, the Polish Solidarity leader, was released from prison.

Conrad Black – the day that Paris was liberated by the Allies.

Margaret Hodge – the day the first V2 rocket bombs landed in London.

Stella McCartney – the day that the Attica Prison revolt ended.

Nicole Richie – the day that Belize was granted full independence from the UK.

Nicky Haslam – the day that Poland surrendered to Germany.

Ben Fogle – the day that NASA launched the *Mariner 10* toward Mercury (the first space probe to reach that planet).

Lord Douglas Hurd – the day that Mahatma Gandhi began his campaign of civil disobedience.

Gail Porter – the day that Bangladesh proclaimed its independence from Pakistan.

Dr Miriam Stoppard – the day of King George VI's coronation.

Konnie Huq – the day that an American *Apollo* and a Soviet *Soyuz* spacecraft docked with each other in orbit making the first such link-up between spacecraft from the two nations.

Owen Hargreaves – the day that Ronald Reagan was inaugurated as US President.

Monty Panesar – the day that Israel completed its withdrawal from the Sinai Peninsula as per the Camp David Accords.

Retief Goosen – the day that Yasser Arafat was appointed leader of the Palestine Liberation Organization (PLO).

Jono Coleman – the day that Pakistan became an Islamic republic.

Dennis Bergkamp – the day that the battle in the Vietnam War that became known as Hamburger Hill was fought.

THE HUMAN CONDITION (1)

All mammals have jaws but only humans have chins.

On one square centimetre of our skin there are 8 million microscopic animals.

Human bones can withstand being squeezed twice as hard as granite can. Bones can also stand being stretched four times as hard as concrete can.

The spinal chord is as flexible as a rubber hose.

The longest recorded leg hair is 10cm long.

If you are right-handed you tend to chew your food on the right side of your mouth. If you are left-handed you tend to chew on the left.

The largest known kidney stone weighed 1.36 kilograms.

Sight accounts for 90 to 95 per cent of all sensory perceptions.

The substance that human blood resembles most closely in terms of chemical composition is sea water.

There are more bacteria in your mouth than there are people in the world.

Women smile more than men do.

Humans can distinguish between 3,000 and 10,000 different smells.

The tongue is the fastest-healing part of the body.

The average person's field of vision is at an angle of 200 degrees.

The eye muscles are the most active muscles in the whole body.

Your tongueprint is as unique as your fingerprints.

If you yelled for eight years, seven months and six days, you would have produced enough sound energy to heat enough water for one cup of tea.

The human heart has enough pumping pressure to squirt blood 9 metres.

We shed about 20 kilograms of dead skin in a lifetime.

When we blush, our stomach lining also turns red.

Eating beetroot can turn your urine red.

Vitamin B2 can turn it bright yellow.

Certain blue dyes (typically found in cheap sweets) can turn it blue-green.

Rhubarb can turn it slightly pink.

Drinking turpentine is said to make urine smell like roses.

Our eyes don't freeze in very cold weather because of the salt in our tears.

Babies can breathe and swallow at the same time until they're six months old.

Rubbing the groove between your lips and your nose in a circular fashion is said to help get rid cravings for sweets and chocolates.

Humans are the only animals to sleep on their backs.

It is possible to cough your guts up.

On average, people can hold their breath for one minute. The world record is seven-and-a-half minutes.

Over the last 150 years the average height of people in wealthy countries has increased by 10cm.

The loss of just 15 per cent of the body's water can be fatal. If the amount of water in your body is reduced by just 1 per cent, you'll feel thirsty.

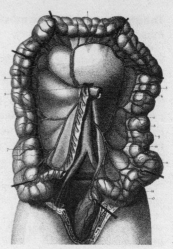

On average a bout of hiccups lasts five minutes.

The bones in your body are not white – they range in colour from beige to light brown. The bones you see in museums are white because they have been boiled and cleaned.

Banging your head against a wall uses 150 calories an hour.

The average person has 100,000 hairs on his or her head – but redheads have fewer and blondes have more.

The hardest substance in your body is the enamel in your teeth.

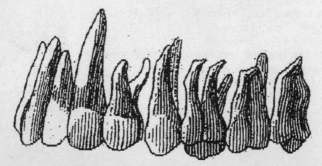

An infant cries without tears until it's three months old.

Taste is 75 per cent smell.

There are four basic tastes: sweet, salty, sour and bitter.

Red blood cells, created in the bone marrow, go round the body 250,000 times before returning to the bone marrow to be destroyed.

Within a tiny droplet of blood, there are some 5 million red blood cells.

An olfactory receptor cell is something that helps us to smell smells. The average human has 40 million of these cells. The average rabbit has 100 million. The average dog has 1 billion.

A human being can taste one gram of salt in 500 litres of water.

The average person will spend some six months of their lives on the toilet.

In terms of mortality, the safest age is ten years old.

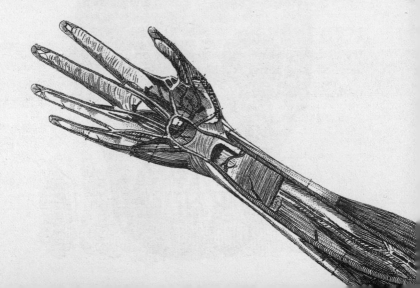

The hand with the larger and squarer thumbnail is likely to be your dominant hand.

Until the age of about twelve, boys cry as often as girls.

The common cold will delay a child's growth for the duration of the cold.

A quarter of all children have one or more sleepwalking episodes before the age of twelve.

Twenty-two per cent of twins are left-handed. In the non-twin population the number is just under ten per cent.

Too much Vitamin A can kill you.

The colour green is said to be effective in relieving homesickness.

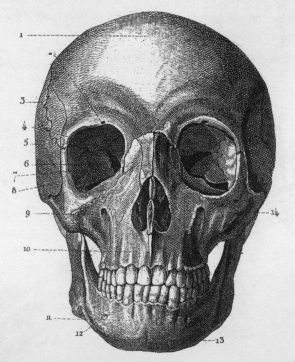

The average human eye can distinguish about 500 different shades of grey.

The period between the hours of 4 and 6 in the afternoon is when people are the most irritable.

Drinking water after eating reduces the acid in your mouth by more than 60 per cent.

While we're resting, the air we breathe passes through our noses at 4 miles per hour which means that every hour we breathe over 1,500 litres of air.

While reading a page of print, our eyes don't move continuously across the page. Instead, they move in a series of jumps, called 'fixations', from one clump of words to the next.

Whispering is more wearing on the voice than speaking. Shouting also stretches the vocal cords.

THINGS THAT ARE NOT WHAT THEY SEEM

Rice paper contains no rice.

Great Danes come from Germany not Denmark.

Polecats aren't cats, they're weasels.

Koala bears aren't bears, they're marsupials.

Mountain goats aren't goats, they're small antelopes.

Fireflies aren't flies, they're beetles.

The funny bone isn't a bone, it's a nerve.

 **Jackrabbits aren't rabbits, they're hares.**

Shooting stars aren't stars, they're meteors.

Prairie dogs aren't dogs, they're rodents.

Guinea pigs aren't pigs, nor are they from Guinea; they're South American rodents.

Lead pencils contain graphite, not lead.

Glow-worms aren't worms, they're beetles.

Horned toads aren't toads, they're lizards.

Silkworms aren't worms, they're caterpillars.

Bombay duck isn't duck, it's dried fish.

Black-eyed peas aren't peas, they're beans.

The French poodle originated in Germany.

The Jerusalem artichoke isn't an artichoke and doesn't come from Jerusalem. It's from America and is part of the sunflower family.

Bald eagles aren't bald. The top of the eagle's head is covered with slicked-down white feathers, which makes it look bald.

The Caspian Sea is a lake.

The grey whale is black.

Petit Suisse cheese is made in France not in Switzerland.

Panama hats come from Ecuador – not Panama.

Female blackbirds aren't black, they're brownish-grey.

The flying fox isn't a fox, it's a bat.

Catgut isn't made from cats, it's made from sheep.

Turkish baths originated in Ancient Rome, not in Turkey.

There wasn't a single pony in the Pony Express, only horses.

Banana oil doesn't come from bananas: it's made from petroleum.

FISH

Fish can taste with their fins and tails as well as with their mouths.

Atlantic salmon can leap 4.5 metres into the air.

The fastest fish in the sea is the swordfish, which can reach speeds of 68 miles per hour.

Fish can drown if there isn't enough oxygen in the water, which can happen if the water is polluted.

The slowest fish is the seahorse, which moves along at about 0.01 mph.

When seahorses want to stay in one place, they wrap their tails round some seaweed.

The largest species of seahorse is 20 centimetres tall.

Giant Antarctic cod grow up to 2 metres long, weigh up to 90 kilograms and live up to 30 years.

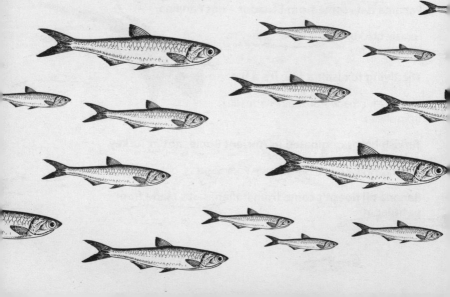

Most tropical marine fish could survive in a tank filled with human blood.

The average cod deposits between 4 and 6 million eggs at a single spawning.

Sturgeon can live as long as 100 years. Mature females will produce millions of eggs every two to three years.

The African lungfish, which is a freshwater fish, can live without water. If there is a drought, it buries itself under a duvet of slime and earth, leaving a small opening for breathing. The earth dries and hardens, and the fish is protected. When rain comes, the earth dissolves and the lungfish swims away.

The flying fish builds up speed in the water then leaps into the air to escape predators. Once in the air, it can stay airborne for up to 100 metres.

Fish cough.

Flatfish (halibut, flounder, turbot and sole) hatch like any other normal fish. But as they grow, they turn sideways and one eye moves round so they have two eyes on the side that faces up.

Minnows have teeth in their throats.

Saltwater fish, such as flounder and cod, have thicker bones than freshwater fish, such as catfish and trout.

The lethal lion's mane jellyfish is the largest known species of jellyfish. The largest specimen ever – found washed up on the shore of Massachusetts Bay in 1870 – had a bell (body) with a diameter of 2.3 metres and its tentacles reached 36.5 metres, making it longer than a blue whale, which is commonly considered to be the largest animal in the world.

Fish that live more than half a mile below the surface of the sea don't have eyes.

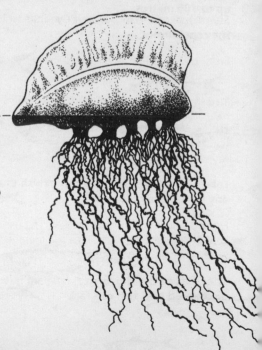

Many reptiles can replace limbs or tails if they're lost or damaged but only the aquatic newt has the ability to regenerate the lens of its eye.

The sea cucumber, a relative of the starfish, has the incredible ability to change from solid to fluid in order to escape predators.

More than 90 per cent of all fish caught are caught in the northern hemisphere.

The oldest known goldfish was Goldie who lived for 45 years after being won at a fairground in 1960.

There are about 21,000 varieties of fish on Earth.

The Dover sole uses the sound of the wind above the waves to tell where it is and where it's going.

The mudfish can survive in mud for a year until the rain comes.

If a goldfish is exposed to a loud noise, it can take a month for its hearing to go back to normal.

Three-quarters of the average caught fish is eaten – the rest is used to make things such as glue, soap, margarine and fertilizer.

Swordfish can heat up their eyeballs to help them see when they go hunting.

Even though cuttlefish are colour-blind they can change colour to camouflage themselves.

The bream, a freshwater fish, hatches its eggs in its mouth.

The pla buek is the biggest freshwater fish in the world, measuring up to 3 metres in length and weighing about 300 kilograms. It can be found in the Mekong river.

Lake Malawi has more species of fish than any other lake on earth.

Fish fighting is very popular in Laos. The fish are kept hungry and then put in a tank together where they fight each other.

Scientists at the University of Guam have discovered that fish can fart.

PEOPLE WHO WERE IN FILMS

Jools Holland – *Spiceworld The Movie* (1997)

Sir Yehudi Menuhin – *The Magic Bow* (1946)

James Taylor – *Funny People* (2009)

Lech Wałesa – *Man of Iron* (1981)

Billy Idol – *Trigger Happy* (1996)

Pablo Picasso – *The Testament of Orpheus* (1960)

Buffalo Bill Cody – *The Indian Wars* (1914)

Donald Trump – *Zoolander* (2001)

Earl Haig – *Remembrance* (1928)

Bianca Jagger – *The Great American Success Company* (1980)

Koo Stark – *Star Wars* (1977)

Ty Cobb – *Angels In The Outfield* (1951)

Shakira Caine – *The Man Who Would Be King* (1975)

Sir Arthur Conan Doyle – *The $5,000,000 Counterfeiting Plot* (1914)

Colonel Harland Sanders (of KFC) – *The Big Mouth* (1967)

Woodrow Wilson – *The Adventures of A Boy Scout* (1915)

Gore Vidal – *Bob Roberts* (1992)

Quentin Crisp – *Orlando* (1992)

Thomas Keneally – *The Devil's Playground* (1976)

Allen Ginsberg – *Ciao. Manhattan* (1972)

Patty Hearst – *Cry Baby* (1990)

Robbie Robertson – *Carny* (1980)

Peter Benchley – *Jaws* (1975)

André Previn – *Pepe* (1960)

Jomo Kenyatta – *Sanders of The River* (1935)

Suzanne Lenglen – *Things Are Looking Up* (1935)

Osvaldo Ardiles – *Escape To Victory* (1981)

Mario Andretti – *Speed Fever* (1979)

Fats Domino – *Every Which Way You Can* (1980)

Cecil B. De Mille – *Sunset Boulevard* (1950)

Timothy Leary – *Fatal Skies* (1990)

Billy Graham – *Two A Penny* (1970)

Buzz Aldrin – *The Boy In The Plastic Bubble* (1976)

Damon Runyon – *The Great White Way* (1924)

Jean-Paul Sartre – *La Vie Commence Demain* (1952)

Mickey Spillane – *Ring of Fear* (1954)

William Burroughs – *It Don't Pay to be an Honest Citizen* (1984)

G.K. Chesterton – *Rosy Rapture* (1915)

Norman Mailer – *King Lear* (1987)

Clive James – *Barry McKenzie Holds His Own* (1974)

Andrew Neil – *Dirty Weekend* (1993)

Richard Dimbleby – *Libel* (1959)

Joan Bakewell – *The Touchables* (1968)

Debbie Harry – *Videodrome* (1982)

Adam Ant – *Slamdance* (1988)

Tina Turner – *Mad Max Beyond Thunderdome* (1986)

Bob Geldof – *The Wall* (1982)

Marie Helvin – *The Children* (1990)

Joe Louis – *Spirit of Youth* (1938)

Jack Dempsey – *The Prizefighter And The Lady* (1933)

Primo Carnera – *A Kid for Two Farthings* (1955)

Tony Bennett – *Bruce Almighty* (2003)

Johnny Cash – *Five Minutes to Live* (1961)

Cyndi Lauper – *Vibes* (1988)

Mama Cass – *Pufnstuf* (1970)

Abbie Hoffman – *Born On The Fourth of July* (1989)

Martin Bashir – *Mike Bassett: England Manager* (2001)

Kylie Minogue – *Moulin Rouge* (2001)

Adrian Chiles – *Sex Lives Of The Potato Men* (2004)

Princess Beatrice – *The Young Victoria* (2009)

ROYALTY

In 1830, King Louis XIX ruled France for 15 minutes.

King Philip II of Spain had a palace with 2,673 doors.

King Charles I's dog accompanied him to his execution.

Queen Isabella of Castile, who dispatched Christopher Columbus to find the Americas, boasted that she had only two baths in her life – at her birth and before she got married.

King Henry III kept a quartet of lions in the Tower of London.

Queen Anne banned the wearing of spectacles, inappropriate wigs and the smoking of pipes from St James's Palace.

A man attempted to assassinate Queen Mary I by climbing St James's Palace and using a large lens to focus the sun's rays on her while she was walking below. It failed.

As a result of King Edward VIII's abdication, the year 1936 saw three different kings on the throne: his father, George V, himself and his brother George VI. There are two other years when this has happened: 1066 (Edward The Confessor, Harold and William The Conqueror) and 1483 (Edward IV, Edward V and Richard III).

King James VI banned the use of the surname MacGregor.

Russian Tsarina Elizabeth, who ruled from 1741 to 1762, never wore a dress twice. She left fifteen thousand dresses in her wardrobe when she died.

Queen Victoria banned the colour black from her funeral and left instructions for her mourners to wear white.

Queen Elizabeth I wasn't buried until five weeks after her death.

Queen Anne is said to have died from a fit of apoplexy, due to overeating, while at an outdoor supper party at Kensington Palace.

King James I introduced a swear box to St James's Palace, and all the money was given to the poor.

King Charles II was a keen tennis player and would weigh himself before and after every game to see how much weight he had lost.

Louis IV of France had a stomach the size of two regular stomachs.

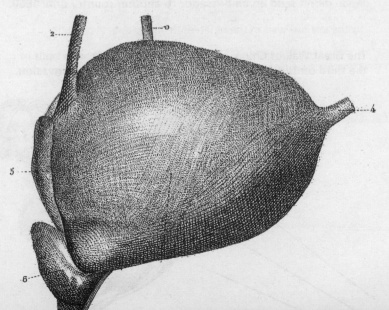

HISTORY (1)

In 1778 Prussia and Austria fought the Potato War, in which each side tried to starve the other by consuming their potato crop.

In 1765, the British Government paid £70,000 for the Isle of Man.

For a long time, Ethiopia was ruled by women. That explains why Alexander the Great stopped at the border: he didn't want to be defeated by women.

French women didn't get the vote until 1945. Before 1964, when the Matrimonial Act was passed, French women couldn't open a bank account or start a business without their husband's permission.

The US bought Alaska from the Russians in 1867 for two cents per acre ($7.2 million in total).

Japan didn't send an ambassador to another country until 1860.

Austria lost five wars in the nineteenth and twentieth centuries.

The Great Wall of China, all 6,000 kilometres of it, was built in the third century BC to protect China's heartland from invasion.

Cleopatra tested the efficacy of her poisons by giving them to her slaves.

Napoleon Bonaparte finished bottom of his class at military school.

Stalin's left foot had webbed toes.

Paul Gauguin was a labourer on the Panama Canal.

Ludwig van Beethoven was once arrested for being a tramp.

In ancient Greece, women counted their age from the date they were married.

Between 1947 and 1959, 42 nuclear devices were detonated in the Marshall Islands in the Pacific Ocean.

To save costs, the body of Shakespeare's friend and fellow dramatist, Ben Jonson, was buried standing up in Westminister Abbey, London in 1637.

During a typical medieval siege, missiles thrown by catapults occasionally included rotten food, dead horses and even captured soldiers.

Portugal is Britain's oldest ally. Dating back to the fourteenth century, it is the longest standing alliance in the world.

The Pacific Ocean was so named by Ferdinand Magellan because it was calmer (more pacific) than the Atlantic.

During the American Civil War, the Vatican was the only political entity to grant official recognition to the Confederate States of America.

The shoelace was invented in England in 1790. Prior to this time, all shoes were fastened with buckles.

Archduke Karl Ludwig, brother of the Austrian emperor, was a man of such piety that on a trip to the Holy Land in 1896, he insisted on drinking from the river Jordan, despite warnings that it would make him fatally ill. He died within a few weeks.

US Civil War General Stonewall Jackson died when he was accidentally shot by one of his own men.

Albert Einstein was once offered the presidency of Israel. He declined, saying he had no head for problems.

There were 57 countries involved in World War 2.

During the fifteenth century, sick people were often dressed in red and surrounded by red objects because it was believed that the colour red would help them to get better.

Benjamin Franklin's peers decided not to give him the assignment of writing the Declaration of Independence because they feared he would conceal a joke in it.

Alfred Nobel invented dynamite; his father Emmanuel invented plywood.

In Sweden in the Middle Ages, a mayor was once elected by a louse. The candidates rested their beards on a table and the louse was placed in the middle. The louse's chosen host became mayor.

During World War 2, the American automobile industry produced just 139 cars.

During the Crusades, the difficulty of transporting bodies off the battlefield for burial was resolved by taking a huge cauldron on to the battlefield, boiling down the bodies and taking away the bones.

In the 1600s, thermometers were filled with brandy instead of mercury.

An earthquake on 16 December 1811 caused parts of the Mississippi river to flow backwards.

The Ottoman Empire once had seven emperors in seven months. They died of (in order): burning, choking, drowning, stabbing, heart failure, poisoning and being thrown from a horse.

When the railway was first invented, some people believed that anyone travelling faster than 12 mph risked mental problems.

The Anglo-Saxons believed Friday to be such an unlucky day that they ritually slaughtered any child unfortunate enough to be born on that day.

After the French Revolution of 1789 selling sour wine was considered against the national interest and the merchant was promptly executed.

During the American revolution, many brides used to wear the colour red instead of white as a symbol of rebellion.

Before World War 2, it was a sacrilege to touch an emperor of Japan.

The electric razor was invented by Jacob Schick. During World War 1, he was in the US army and was in an Alaskan army base. Tired of breaking the layer of ice that formed in the washbasin so that he could shave, he developed the first hand-held motor, which he patented in 1923. In 1931, he finished his razor and it was on the market for $25. By 1937, he sold nearly 2 million.

When Leonardo da Vinci's *Mona Lisa* was stolen from the Louvre in 1912, six replicas were sold as the original, each at a huge price, in the three years before the original was recovered.

Auguste Rodin died of frostbite in 1917 when the French government refused him financial aid for a flat, yet they kept his statues warmly housed in museums.

In 1816, J R Ronden tried to stage a play that didn't contain the letter 'a'. The Paris audience was offended, rioted and refused to allow the play to finish.

Benito Mussolini would ward off the evil eye by touching his testicles.

The river Nile has frozen over twice – once in the ninth century, and again in the eleventh century.

Playing cards that were issued to British pilots in World War Two could be soaked in water and unfolded to reveal a map in the event of capture.

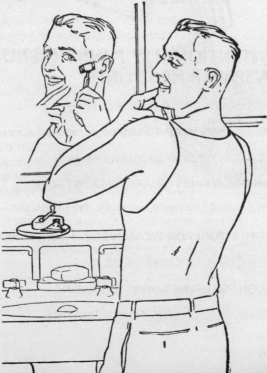

UNINTENTIONALLY FUNNY (GENUINE) NEWSPAPER HEADLINES

ALCOHOL ADS PROMOTE DRINKING

AMERICAN SHIPS HEAD TO LIBYA

BANK DRIVE-IN WINDOW BLOCKED BY BOARD

BRITISH UNION FINDS DWARFS IN SHORT SUPPLY

CHEF THROWS HIS HEART INTO HELPING FEED FRENZY

CORONER REPORTS ON WOMAN'S DEATH WHILE RIDING HORSE

CRIME: SHERIFF ASKS FOR 13.7% INCREASE

DEAF COLLEGE OPENS DOORS TO HEARING

DEFENDANT'S SPEECH ENDS IN LONG SENTENCE

DOG THAT BIT 2 PEOPLE ORDERED TO LEAVE TOWN

ENRAGED BULL INJURES FARMER WITH AXE

FACTORY ORDERS DIP

FLAMING TOILET SEAT CAUSES EVACUATION AT HIGH SCHOOL

GAS RIG MEN GRILLED BY VILLAGERS

GIRL KICKED BY HORSE UPGRADED TO STABLE

GRANDMOTHER OF EIGHT MAKES HOLE IN ONE

HERE'S HOW YOU CAN LICK DOBERMAN'S LEG SORES

HOSPITALS SUED BY SEVEN FOOT DOCTORS

IF STRIKE ISN'T SETTLED QUICKLY, IT MAY LAST A WHILE

INFERTILITY UNLIKELY TO BE PASSED ON
IRAQI HEAD SEEKS ARMS

IS THERE A RING OF DEBRIS AROUND URANUS?

JURY SUSPECTS FOUL PLAY IN DEATH OF MAN SHOT, BURNED &
BURIED IN SHALLOW GRAVE

JUVENILE COURT TO TRY SHOOTING DEFENDANT

KICKING BABY CONSIDERED TO BE HEALTHY

KIDS MAKE NUTRITIOUS SNACKS

KILLER SENTENCED TO DIE FOR SECOND TIME IN 10 YEARS

L.A. VOTERS APPROVE URBAN RENEWAL BY LANDSLIDE

LARGER KANGAROOS LEAP FARTHER, RESEARCHERS FIND

LAWMEN FROM MEXICO BARBECUE GUESTS

LAWYERS GIVE POOR FREE LEGAL ADVICE

LEGISLATOR WANTS TOUGHER DEATH PENALTY

LIVING TOGETHER LINKED TO DIVORCE

LOW PAY REASON FOR POVERTY, STUDY SAYS

LUNG CANCER IN WOMEN MUSHROOMS

MAGISTRATES ACT TO KEEP THEATRES OPEN

MAN DENIES HE COMMITED SUICIDE

MAN FOUND BEATEN, ROBBED BY POLICE

MAN FOUND DEAD IN CEMETERY

MAN IS FATALLY MURDERED

MAN MINUS EAR WAIVES HEARING

MAN RECOVERING AFTER FATAL ACCIDENT

MAN ROBS, THEN KILLS HIMSELF

MAN RUN OVER BY FREIGHT TRAIN DIES

MAN STRUCK BY LIGHTNING FACES BATTERY CHARGE

MINERS REFUSE TO WORK AFTER DEATH

NEW VACCINE MAY CONTAIN RABIES

NO WATER SO FIREMEN IMPROVISED

NUNS FORGIVE BREAK-IN, ASSAULT SUSPECT

OFFICIAL: ONLY RAIN WILL CURE DROUGHT

PASSENGERS HIT BY CANCELLED TRAINS

PATIENT AT DEATH'S DOOR – DOCTORS PULL HIM THROUGH

PLANE TOO CLOSE TO GROUND, CRASH PROBE TOLD

PLOT TO KILL OFFICER HAD VICIOUS SIDE

POLICE BEGIN CAMPAIGN TO RUN DOWN JAYWALKERS

POLICE MOVE IN BOOK CASE

POLICE NAB STUDENT WITH PAIR OF PLIERS

POLICE RECOVER STOLEN HAMSTER, ARREST 3

POLICE SEARCH FOR WITNESSES TO ASSAULT

POSTMEN AWARDED A £2 MILLION PAY RISE

PRISONERS ESCAPE AFTER EXECUTION

PROPERLY DRAFTED WILL REDUCES ANXIETY AFTER DEATH

PROSTITUTES APPEAL TO POPE

PROTESTERS MARCH OVER ILLEGAL IMMIGRANTS

QUARTER OF A MILLION CHINESE LIVE ON WATER

RED TAPE HOLDS UP NEW BRIDGES

SCHIZOPHRENIC KILLED HERSELF WITH TWO PLASTIC BAGS

SCHOOL CHILDREN MARCH OVER NEW TEACHERS

SHELL FOUND ON BEACH

SLIM-FAD GIRL, 17, VANISHES

SQUAD HELPS DOG BITE VICTIM

STAR'S BROKEN LEG HITS BOX OFFICE

STOLEN PAINTING FOUND BY TREE

STUDY REVEALS THOSE WITHOUT INSURANCE DIE MORE OFTEN

SUDDEN RUSH TO HELP PEOPLE OUT OF WORK

SUICIDE BOMBER STRIKES AGAIN

SUPERTRAIN TALKS

TEACHER DIES; BOARD ACCEPTS HIS RESIGNATION

**TEENAGE GIRLS OFTEN HAVE BABIES FATHERED BY MEN
THIEVES STEAL BURGLAR ALARM**

THUGS EAT THEN ROB PROPRIETOR

THREATENING LETTERS – MAN ASKS FOR LONG SENTENCE

THREE AMBULANCES TAKE BLAST VICTIM TO HOSPITAL

TRAFFIC DEAD RISE SLOWLY

VOLUNTARY WORKERS STRIKE FOR HIGHER PAY

**WHATEVER THEIR MOTIVES, MOMS WHO KILL KIDS STILL
SHOCK US**

WOMAN OFF TO JAIL FOR SEX WITH BOYS

AMERICANS AND AMERICA

All the earthworms in America weigh 55 times what all the people weigh.

Americans eat more bananas than any other fruit.

The United States has 5 per cent of the world's population, 25 per cent of the world's prisoners and 70 per cent of the world's lawyers.

Fifty per cent of Americans live within 50 miles of where they were born.

Fried chicken is the most popular meal in American restaurants.

Twenty per cent of Americans think that the sun orbits the Earth.

7 per cent of Americans claim they never bathe at all.

The total number of Americans killed in the Civil War is greater than the combined total of Americans killed in all other wars.

About 18 per cent of American pet owners share their beds with their pets.

Thirty-two per cent of all the land in the US is owned by the government.

For four years in the 18th century, there was a state called Franklin (named after Benjamin Franklin). Later it was incorporated into Tennessee.

The average American bank teller loses about $250 every year.

There are more Irish in New York City than in Dublin, Ireland; more Italians in New York City than in Rome, Italy; and more Jews in New York City than in Tel Aviv, Israel.

The White House, in Washington DC, was originally grey, the colour of the sandstone it was built out of. After the War of 1812, during which it had been burned by Canadian troops, the outside walls were painted white to hide the smoke stains.

In the US just three people can be accused of rioting; in the UK, there have to be at least twelve people to constitute a riot.

One in every five New Yorkers was born in another country.

The Procrastinators' Club of America sends news to its members in 'last month's newsletter'.

Florida's beaches lose 20 million cubic yards of sand annually.

The US State of Louisana was named after King Louis XIV of France.

It is estimated that two hundred million M&Ms are consumed each day in the US.

There are over sixty towns in US where the word turkey appears in the name.

Fifty-eight per cent of American men say they are happier after divorce.

Eighty-five per cent of American women say they are happier after divorce.

The largest object ever found in the Los Angeles sewer system was a motorcycle.

In the US, murder is committed most frequently in August and least frequently in February.

Every year in the US, more people are killed by deer than by any other animal.

A survey disclosed that twelve per cent of Americans believe that Joan of Arc was Noah's wife.

There is enough water in American swimming pools to cover the whole city of San Francisco to a depth of more than 2 metres.

About 7 million cars are junked each year in the US.

In 2006, an American man named Eric Dogan left Amanda Newkirk, a waitress, a tip of $973.65 on a $24.35 bill.

The US has the highest number of marriages and remarriages.

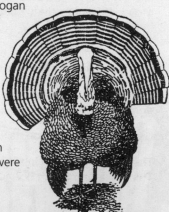

In 1976, doctors in Los Angeles went on strike because of the rising cost of malpractice insurance. All non-emergency surgery and medical attention were cancelled. During the strike, there were 18 per cent *fewer* deaths than usual.

Sometimes, the number of hot dog sales at a baseball stadium exceeds the number of spectators – though, typically, hot dog sales at ballparks average 80 per cent of the attendance.

Every citizen of the State of Alaska over the age of 6 months receives an oil dividend check of about $1000 per year.

More than 1 million dogs and cats have been made the main beneficiaries in US wills.

The state of Oregon has one city named Sisters and another called Brothers. Sisters got its name from a nearby trio of peaks in the Cascade Mountains known as the Three Sisters. Brothers was named as a counterpart to Sisters.

The exact geographic centre of the United States is near Lebanon, Kansas.

An old law in Bellingham, Washington, made it illegal for a woman to take more than three steps backwards while dancing.

In Michigan, there was a law forbidding a woman to cut her own hair without her husband's permission.

The average American eats at McDonalds more than 1,800 times in their life.

At 21, the United States has the highest minimum drinking age in the world.

The United States has never lost a war when donkeys were used.

Nine out of ten New York taxi drivers were born outside of the US.

The deepest canyon in the world is Hell Canyon in Idaho, US. The maximum depth is 2,400 metres.

Mailing an entire building has been illegal in the US since 1916 when a man mailed a 40,000-ton brick house across Utah to avoid high transport costs.

There have been more Americans deaths in car accidents than in ALL the wars in which the US has fought since independence.

The world's first outdoor miniature golf courses were built on rooftops in New York City in 1926.

In 1982, an American man named David Grundman was killed by a cactus after firing two shots from his shotgun at a giant saguaro cactus that ended up falling on top of him.

 Americans eat the most meat, drink the most fizzy drinks and buy the most toys.

America spends the largest amount of money per person on healthcare, and on foreign and military aid to other countries.

America, which is only 33 per cent forested, produces the world's most timber but it also has all the world's tallest trees, mostly in its national parks.

America has more dentists per person than any other country.

American Highway patrolmen carry gallons of cola in their vehicles and they use it to remove blood from the road after an accident.

Every year, over a thousand people are bitten by other people in New York City.

On average, one American drowns in their own bath every day. More Americans, however, simply freeze to death (just under twice as many). Thirty-five Americans die every year from falls.

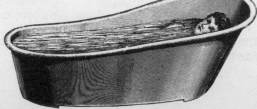

BIRDS (1)

The chicken is the closest living relative of tyrannosaurus rex.

Male cockatoos can be taught to speak, but females can only chirp and sing.

The longest recorded chicken flight is 13 seconds.

The albatross can glide on air currents for several days at a time.

Homing pigeons use roads in their route-finding. Some pigeons even fly around roundabouts before choosing the exit that leads them home.

Ospreys return to the same nest each year, repairing any damage caused by the weather since they last used it.

Wild turkeys can fly, but farmed turkeys cannot.

Wild turkeys are docile, while farmed ones are aggressive.

The kiwi, national bird of New Zealand, can't fly. It lives in a hole in the ground, has very poor sight and lays only one egg a year.

Parrots can have a vocabulary of up to 20 words.

Condors in the Andes of South America can live for 70 years.

Flamingoes can live for 50 years.

Vultures often eat so much that they're too heavy to fly. So they have to throw up to make themselves light enough to get up in the air again.

Wandering albatrosses devote a full year to raising their young.

An owl can see a mouse 50 metres away in light no brighter than a candle-flame.

Wild turkeys are capable of running at speeds of over 30 mph.

The male wren builds several nests as part of his courtship ritual. Once the nests are completed, his potential bride looks them all over, then selects one in which to lay her eggs.

Similarly, the male weaverbird, found in Africa and India, builds elaborate nests. The female weaverbird will refuse to mate with a male if his nest is not good enough. If she rejects the nest, he must take it apart and rebuild it.

The raven tricks its rival into thinking there's food elsewhere and then sneaks back to eat what it wanted in the first place.

Grebes plunge as deep as 30 metres and can stay underwater for as long as three minutes. There, they snare fish, which they swallow alive, head first.

A flock of starlings flies in loose formation – until a falcon appears. Then the flock tightens up so the falcon doesn't have a single bird to strike at.

Migrating geese fly in a V-formation to conserve energy. The wings churn the air and create a current. In the flying wedge, each bird is in position to get a lift from the current created by the bird ahead. It is easier going for all, except the leader. During a migration, geese take turns in the lead position.

 The female condor lays one egg every two years.

Only ten of the ten thousand bird species have been domesticated.

Pigeons process visual information three times quicker than we do.

The hummingbird, the kingfisher and the grebe are all birds that can't walk.

Turkeys can have heart attacks.

The Moa bird of New Zealand, which became extinct four hundred years ago, was over 3 metres tall.

Bald eagles build the largest nests of any bird – up to three metres wide and 6 metres deep.

Size for size, birds live longer than mammals.

There are around seventy common breeds of chicken.

The Emperor penguin can hold its breath for twenty minutes.

In Ireland, geese used to be used to sweep chimneys. They would be pulled up chimneys by a rope tied to their legs and then the beating of their wings would dislodge the soot.

On a clear day, a gobbling turkey can be heard a mile away.

The penguins that inhabit the tip of South America are called jackass penguins.

Emus lay emerald-coloured eggs.

Fossil finds show that some of the earliest bird species had four wings rather than two.

The male cockerel makes noises pretending that he's found food as a way of luring (female) hens.

Birds don't have sweat glands so their bodies cool down by flight or, when at rest, by panting.

The broad-tailed hummingbird drinks five times its own body weight in nectar every day.

At 24 billion, there are more chickens in the world than any other bird.

Mallee fowl chicks are born buried alive and have to burrow their way out of the sand.

ABOUT AVERAGE

In a lifetime, the average person will ...

... shed 57 litres of tears.

... eat three thousand meals of Spaghetti Bolognese.

... eat over thirteen thousand eggs.

... eat ten thousand chocolate bars.

... eat 36 pigs, 36 sheep, eight cows and over five hundred chickens.

... have 7,163 baths.

... walk 100,000 miles.

... blink 500 million times.

DINOSAURS

The first dinosaur appeared around 225 or 230 million years ago. It was called the Staurikosaurus and it survived for about 5 million years.

The first dinosaur to be given a name was the Iguanodon, found in Sussex in 1823. It was not the first dinosaur to be found.

Dinosaurs didn't eat grass: it didn't exist then.

Dinosaurs lived on Earth for more than 150 million years. That's about 75 times longer than humans have lived on Earth.

Some dinosaurs had tails 12 or 13 metres long.

The brachiosaurus's nostrils were on the top of its head. It also had teeth shaped like chisels (and a very small brain).

The dinosaur noises in *Jurassic Park* came from elephants, geese and slowed-down horses.

Most dinosaurs lived to be more than a hundred years old.

Argentina is home to some of the oldest known dinosaur fossils and a dinosaur which was the largest land animal that ever existed: the Argentinosaurus.

Lesothosaurus is a dinosaur named after the country of Lesotho where its fossilized remains were found. It was 1 metre long and lived around 200 million years ago. In fact, dinosaur footprints can be found in many places in Lesotho.

The fiercest, most aggressive dinosaur was the velociraptor, but as it only grew to be about 2 metres long, it would have been no match for the tyrannosaurus rex ('Tyrant Lizard King') which grew to 13 metres and weighed 68,000 kg. The tyrannosaurus rex had huge pointy teeth, which could rip anything to shreds.

THE RECORD FOR RUNNING A MILE

Roger Bannister of Great Britain was the first person to run a mile in under 4 minutes – in 3 minutes 59.4 seconds, to be exact. Other runners have since beaten his record. Here is the complete list.

Time	Name	Place (date)
3:59.4	Roger Bannister (Great Britain)	Oxford, UK (6 May 1954)
3:58.0	John Landy (Australia)	Turku, Finland (21 June 1954)
3:57.2	Derek Ibbotson (Great Britain)	London, UK (19 July 1957)
3:54.5	Herb Elliott (Australia)	Dublin, Ireland (6 August 1958)
3:54.4	Peter Snell (New Zealand)	Wanganui, New Zealand (27 January 1962)
3:54.1	Peter Snell	Auckland, New Zealand (17 November 1964)
3:53.6	Michel Jazy (France)	Rennes, France (9 June 1965)
3:51.3	Jim Ryun (USA)	Berkeley, USA (17 July 1966)
3:51.1	Jim Ryun	Bakersfield, USA (23 July 1967)
3:51.0	Filbert Bayi (Tanzania)	Kingston, Jamaica (17 May 1975)

Time	Name	Place (date)
3:49.4	John Walker (New Zealand)	Gothenburg, Sweden (12 August 1975)
3:49.0	Sebastian Coe (Great Britain)	Oslo, Norway (17 July 1979)
3:48.8	Steve Ovett (Great Britain)	Oslo, Norway (1 July 1980)
3:48.53	Sebastian Coe	Zurich, Switzerland (19 August 1981)
3:48.40	Steve Ovett	Koblenz, Germany (25 August 1981)
3:47.33	Sebastian Coe	Brussels, Belgium (28 August 1981)
3:46.32	Steve Cram (Great Britain)	Oslo, Norway (27 July 1985)
3:44.39	Noureddine Morceli (Algeria)	Rieti, Italy (5 September 1993)
3:43.13	Hicham El Guerrouj (Morocco)	Rome, Italy (7 July 1999)

THE FIRST EUROPEAN COUNTRIES TO HAVE McDONALD'S

Germany (Munich, in 1971)

Holland (Voorburg, in 1972)

Sweden (Stockholm, in 1973)

UK (Woolwich, London, in 1974)

Switzerland (Geneva, in 1975)

Ireland (Dublin, in 1977)

Austria (Vienna, in 1977)

Belgium (Brussels, in 1978)

France (Strasbourg, in 1979)

Spain (Madrid, in 1981)

MONEY

The worst inflation ever occurred in post-Second World War Hungary, in July 1946, when the rate of inflation was a mind-numbing 41,900,000,000,000,000 per cent – the equivalent of prices doubling every 13½ hours. The largest banknote ever issued was the 1946 Hungarian 100 quintillion pengo note. That's a ten with twenty zeros.

In a survey, between 7 and 42 per cent of all paper money contained 'revolting bacteria'.

The United States Treasury Department maintains a fund known as 'The Conscience Fund,' which accepts money sent in anonymously by taxpayers who think they've cheated the government. The money is used for the department's expenses.

Stone wheels a metre or so in diameter were once used as currency by the Yap Islanders of Micronesia.

In 1985, Argentian changed its currency from the peso to the austral. In 1992, the government replaced the austral with the nuevo peso argentino.

Spanish doubloons were legal tender in the US until 1857.

Australia pioneered the use of bank notes made of plastic (polymers). They last four times as long as regular paper notes and provide greater security against counterfeiting.

In 2008, inflation in Zimbabwe went over 2 million percent.

The US has more billionaires than any other country in the world.

Many ships are registered in Liberia because it is financially advantageous to the ships' owners.

In Croatia in 1994, the kuna replaced the dinar as the national currency. The Croatian kuna is an indigenous animal whose pelt was used as a means of currency in Croatia during the Middle Ages.

The Brazilian real is an interesting-looking currency because on one side the image is horizontal but on the other side it's vertical.

Until the twentieth century, some Ethiopians still used an ancient form of currency called amole, which are salt bars. The system arose because salt was scarce.

Malaysia's currency is called the Ringgit which is the Malay word for 'jagged'. This is supposed to be a reference the jagged edges of the Spanish silver dollars that used to be used in this region.

Tulip bulbs were a form of currency in the seventeenth century in the Netherlands.

The vatu currency of Vanuatu can't be broken down into smaller units like cents or pence.

In Togo, it's customary to use the right hand when giving or receiving money.

The dollar symbol ($) is a U combined with an S.

Until the ninteenth century, blocks of tea were used as money in Siberia.

Cocoa beans were used as money in ancient Guatemala. Counterfeiters were at work even in those days: some people removed the insides of the beans and filled them with clay.

Luxembourg's the richest country in the world. It's also the most generous country in the world.

The largest ocean liners pay a $250,000 toll for each trip through the Panama Canal. The canal generates one-third of Panama's entire economy.

Walter Hunt owed a friend $15, which was a large amount of money in 1849. The friend offered to cancel the debt in return for an item made by Walter from a piece of wire. Walter had invented the first safety pin, and it made his friend into a millionaire.

In Ancient Rome, if a man owed money to a lot of people, they were all allowed to take a knife and cut slices off him.

Market research has found that light purple makes customers feel like spending money.

At Chinese funerals people sometimes burn paper money so that the dead person will be rich in the afterlife.

THE SEVEN WONDERS OF THE ANCIENT WORLD

The Pyramids of Giza
(in Egypt – the only one of the Seven Wonders still in existence)

The Mausoleum of Halicarnassus

The Hanging Gardens of Babylon

The Statue of Zeus at Olympia

The Colossus of Rhodes

The Temple of Artemis at Ephesus

The Pharos (or Lighthouse) at Alexandria

ENGLISH COUNTIES AND THEIR VARIETIES OF APPLE

Kent: Kentish Fillbasket, Mabbott's Pearmain, Gascoyne's Scarlet, Golden Knob

Yorkshire: Green Balsam, Flower of The Town, French Crab, Acklam Russett

Hereford: King's Acre Pippin, Herefordshire Beefing, Lord Hindlip, Yellow Ingestrie

Lancashire: Golden Spire, Roseberry, Scotch Bridget, Proctor's Seedling

Surrey: Claygate Pearmain, Cockles Pippin, George Carpenter, Joybells, Scarlet Nonpareil

Devon: Michaelmas Stubbard, Crimson Costard, Devonshire Quarrenden, Star of Devon

Sussex: Crawley Beauty, Forge, Lady Sudeley, First And Last, Wadhurst Pippin

Hertfordshire. Lane's Prince Albert, Golden Reinette, Bushey Grove

Cornwall: Cornish Gilliflower, Glass Apple, Cornish Pine, Tommy Knight

AROUND THE WORLD (1)

Belgium produces more comic books per square mile than any other nation on Earth.

Those born in San Marino remain citizens and can vote no matter where they live.

At 979 metres tall with a clear drop of 807 metres, the world's highest waterfall is the Angel Falls in Venezuela. It's twenty times taller than Niagara Falls. The height of the falls is so great that before getting anywhere near the ground, the water is turned into mist by the wind. The Angel Falls are named after the American Pilot, Jimmy Angel, whose plane got stuck at the top of the waterfall in 1937. It took him and his companions 11 days to climb down the side of the waterfall and that's why the falls are named after him.

There's an island off the coast of Tanzania called 'Mafia'.

There are 1,040 islands around Britain, one of which is the smallest island in the world: Bishop's Rock.

The Sahara desert expands by about 1 kilometre a month.

The smallest island with country status is Pitcairn in Polynesia.

Five hundred million years ago, Antarctica was on the equator.

The English Channel grows about 300 millimetres each year.

No building is taller than the tallest palm tree anywhere in the South Pacific.

Half of all adult Dutch people have never flown in a plane.

There are more cows in the world than there are cars: 1.5 billion cows compared to 1 billion cars.

The world spends more than $2 billion a day on weaponry.

By the end of this year, approximately 22 billion rolls of toilet paper will have been used around the world.

The Ainu – native Japanese people – believe that the world is supported on the back of a giant trout. For this reason, they also have a fear of large lakes.

Starbucks buys up 2 per cent of the world's coffee.

Hurricanes and tornadoes always go clockwise in the southern hemisphere and counterclockwise in the northern hemisphere.

When flowers are given for romantic reasons in Russia, they're always in odd numbers as an even number of flowers is given at funerals.

The Mexican Hat Dance is the official dance of Mexico.

The deepest mine in the world is Western Deep Levels near Charletonville, South Africa. It is 4.2 kilometres (2.6 miles) deep.

Eighty per cent of millionaires drive second-hand cars.

There is a cash machine at McMurdo Station in Antarctica, which has a population of one thousand people.

The country with the highest density of natural blondes in Finland.

Dutch and Israeli soldiers aren't required to salute officers.

Every year in France there is a 'Thieves Fair' where people are encouraged to try to steal things from the stalls.

Until 1984, Belgians had to choose their children's names from a list of 1,500 drawn up in the days of Napoleon.

More than a hundred cars can drive side by side on the Monumental Axis in Brazil, the world's widest road.

All pilots on international flights identify themselves in English, regardless of their country of origin.

Seventy per cent of computer virus writers work under contract for organized crime syndicates.

Twenty-seven per cent of all journeys taken in the Netherlands are on a bicycle (this compares to just 2 pe cent of journeys in the UK).

Sixty-seven per cent of the world's illiterate adults are female.

Workers at the Matsushita Electric company in Japan beat dummies of their foremen with bamboo sticks to let off steam.

In Irian Jaya, there's a tribe of people who use parrots to warn them against intruders.

If you fly from Tokyo to Honolulu at 7.00 a.m., you'll arrive at your destination at 4.30 p.m. the previous day.

Australia has more British migrants than any other country.

Every day is a holiday somewhere in the world.

There is enough stone in the Great Wall of China to build a 2.43-metre wall encircling the globe at the equator.

Sahara means 'desert' in Arabic.

Finland has more islands than any other country: 179,584.

The town of Churchill in Manitoba, Canada, has a 20-cell prison for polar bears that cause trouble. The most frequent reason for imprisonment is scavenging in the town's rubbish dump. When a bear is released from prison, a green button is tagged behind its ear. If the bear returns, it's given a red button. If a red-buttoned bear attempts to come back into the town, it's shot on sight.

The largest iceberg ever recorded was larger than Belgium. It was 200 miles long and 60 miles wide.

Canada derives its name from a Native American word meaning 'big village'.

As a result of snowfall, for a few weeks every year K2 is bigger than Everest.

China has more borders with other countries than any other country.

India has more post offices than any other country.

The Tibetan mountain people use yak's milk as a form of currency.

Volk's Electric Railway which runs along Brighton's seafront is the oldest operating electric railway in the world.

The oldest republic in the world is San Marino, located in Europe. It has been a republic more than 1,700 years, since 301.

Nine out of ten Canadians live within 100 miles of the US border.

For the Berbers in the Atlas mountains of northern Morocco, the liver, not the heart, is the source of love. When a girl falls in love, she says, 'Darling, you have stolen my liver.'

Hundreds of years ago in Japan, anyone attempting to leave the country was executed.

A Dutch court ruled that a bank robber could deduct the 2,000 Euros he paid for his pistol from the 6,600 Euros he had to return to the bank he robbed.

In Bhutan, all citizens officially become a year older on New Year's Day.

The largest McDonald's in the world is in Beijing, China.

At one time it was against the law to slam car doors in Switzerland.

Japanese and Chinese people die on the fourth of the month more often than any other dates. The reason may be that they are 'scared to death' by the number four. The words for four and death sound alike in both Chinese and Japanese.

On average in the West, people move house every seven years.

The annual global trade in counterfeit goods is worth an estimated $340 billion.

Worldwide there are more statues of Joan of Arc than of anyone else. France alone has about forty thousand.

Japan has 24 recorded instances of people receiving serious or fatal skull fractures while bowing to each other in the traditional greeting.

Australians are the heaviest gamblers in the world (an estimated eighty-two per cent of Australians bet regularly).

Of all the world's land that's owned, just one percent is owned by women.

Tristan da Cunha is the world's most remote settlement being 2,334 km away from its nearest neighbours.

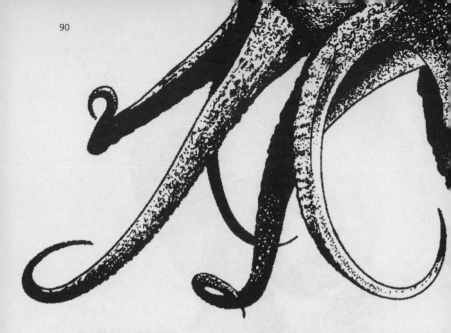

CINEMA SNACKS

Popcorn and sweets are the most popular cinema snacks in Britain but elsewhere in the world they eat other things.

In China they prefer salted plums, or chunks of tofu in a spicy sauce.

In Japan they like fried squid pancakes or octopus kebabs.

In Indonesia they eat dried fish and cuttlefish.

In Korea they like to chew on roasted octopus tentacles – including the suckers.

THE SEVEN VIRTUES

Charity

Courage

Faith

Hope

Justice

Prudence

Temperance

THE SEVEN DEADLY SINS

Anger

Avarice

Envy

Gluttony

Lust

Pride

Sloth

FOOD

Chocolate chip cookies were first made by mistake when the chocolate in the biscuit didn't melt properly.

In Guatemala, lemons are green and limes are yellow.

Pork is the world's most widely eaten meat.

A 340g jar of peanut butter contains about 548 peanuts.

Milk chocolate was invented by Daniel Peter, who sold the concept to his neighbour Henri Nestlé.

In the 1950s, 80 per cent of chickens in Europe and the US were free-range. By 1980, it was only 1 per cent. Today, the number has gone back up to about 13 per cent.

Lettuce is 97 per cent water.

Rice, the main food for half of the people of the world, is grown on more than 10 per cent of the Earth's farmable surface.

Lobster used to be poor people's food.

The world's oldest existing restaurant opened in Kai-Feng, China in 1153.

The Brazil nut is the most naturally radioactive food.

Every year, more than 150 million avocados are sold in the UK.

Carpaccio, thin strips of raw beef, is named after the painter Vittore Carpaccio, who used a lot of red in his paintings.

Spanish people call a plain omelette an English omelette. What we call a Spanish omelette they call a peasant's omelette.

Ketchup was originally made from fish broth and mushrooms. Tomatoes were added later.

Cornish pasties – pies containing meat, potato, swede and onion – were given a milled sealing edge to make them easier for tin miners to hold with dirty hands.

Salt is one of the few spices that is all taste and no smell.

All of an egg's vitamins A, D and E are in the yolk. Egg yolks are one of the very few foods naturally containing vitamin D.

Chop suey, Russian dressing, and hamburgers all originated in the US.

Cadbury's Dairy Milk is Britain's most popular chocolate bar with 500 million produced annually.

The average ear of corn has 800 kernels arranged in 16 rows.

Chillies have been eaten since at least 7000 BC in South America, and at one point were used as currency.

Almonds are the oldest nuts in the world.

In Ancient Egypt, the apricot was called the egg of the sun.

About 27 per cent of food in developed countries is wasted each year. It's simply thrown away.

An onion, apple and potato all have the same taste. The differences in flavour are caused by their smell.

You can make yoghurt from camel's milk but you can't make butter.

Women are twice as likely as men to be vegetarians.

Chocolate is the number one foodstuff flavour in the world, beating vanilla and banana by three-to-one.

Many Hondurans grow pineapples in their gardens. Every part of the pineapple is used for something. The skin is used to make tea or vinegar for preserving vegetables. The fruit is used to make juice, jam or pies. The tops are put in buckets of water until they sprout roots and can be replanted in the garden.

The Danish eat the most frozen food.

Doughnuts originated in Holland.

In Iceland, hot dogs are usually made of lamb rather than beef or pork.

The average French person eats 800 grams of garlic a year.

More chocolate is sold at Brussels airport than anywhere else in the world.

The durian fruit is the smelliest fruit in the world. In fact, it's so smelly that in those countries to which it's native (Brunei, Indonesia and Malaysia) there are markets and restaurants which have special rooms for people who want to enjoy the fruit without its smell disturbing other people.

US soldiers' dried food rations can be rehydrated with urine.

The British eat more baked beans than the rest of the world combined.

All M&Ms taste the same – whatever their colour.

There are more than two thousand different types of cheese in the world.

The powder on chewing gum is finely ground marble.

The Journal of Consumer Research reports that, contrary to what you might have expected, healthy choice options on a menu actually make people more likely to order 'unhealthy' foods.

There are 300 distinct different types of honey.

Sushi is actually named after the rice that is used to make it. The Japanese term for raw fish is sashimi.

Two million different combinations of sandwiches can be created from a SUBWAY menu.

It takes 10 kilograms of milk to make 1 kilogram of cheese.

Turkey has about 60 companies that manufacture chewing gum.

In 1868, a banquet was held in London. The main course was horse – more than 130 kilos of it.

ANIMALS (1)

The average koala sleeps 22 hours a day.

Bull (male) giraffes forage higher in trees than cow (female) giraffes, which reduces food competition between the sexes.

A baby caribou is so swift, it can outrun its mother when it is only three days old.

The definition of a 'mammal' is that the female animal feeds her young on milk she has produced.

Most monkeys can cling with their tails, except for the marmoset, whose tail cannot grip.

A giraffe can kill a lion with just one kick.

The golden bamboo lemur eats half a kilo of bamboo every day. This contains more than enough cyanide to kill a human being.

Unusually for carnivores, hyena clans are dominated by females.

All living cheetahs are as close as identical twins as they're descended from a very small gene pool.

The heart of a giraffe is 60 centimetres long, and can weigh as much as 10 kilograms.

The arctic fox often follows the polar bear, feeding on the abandoned carcass of its kill.

Hyenas produce an unusually high number of twins but the twins often end up killing one another.

Giraffes can live without water for longer than camels can.

Thinking that its parents were a camel and a leopard, Europeans once called a giraffe a 'camelopard'.

A hedgehog's heart beats 190 times a minute. This drops to 20 beats per minute during hibernation.

A giraffe can clean its ears with its 50cm tongue.

The red kangaroo of Australia can leap more than 8 metres in one bound.

Beaver teeth are so sharp that Native Americans once used them as knife blades.

The stomach of a hippopotamus is 3 metres long.

Kangaroos can't walk backwards.

The South American giant anteater eats more than 30,000 ants a day.

Camel milk does not curdle.

A grasshopper needs a minimum air temperature of 16°C before it's able to hop.

There are no furry animals native to Antarctica.

Skunk litters are born in April.

More than 99.9 per cent of all the animal species that ever lived on Earth were extinct before the arrival of man.

A horse eats about seven times its own weight a year.

Sheep can recognize faces.

A sloth will spend 75 per cent of its life asleep but can move twice as fast in water as it can on land.

It takes a sloth up to six days to digest the food it eats.

A rhinoceros's horn is made of compacted hair.

Armadillos can be house-trained.

You can smell the unpleasant odour of a skunk from a mile away.

A dairy cow produces four times its weight in manure each year.

A hippopotamus is born underwater.

The male moose sheds its antlers every winter and grows a new set the following year.

The hump of a starving camel may flop over and hang down the side of its body because the fat in it has been used up.

A tiger's night vision is six times better than ours.

Reindeer have scent glands between their hind toes. The glands help them leave cheesy-smelling scent trails for the herd to follow.

An armadillo can walk under water.

A baby beaver stays with its parents for two years.

The oldest horse in the world lived to be sixty-two years.

BORN ON THE VERY SAME DAY AS ANOTHER CELEBRITY

Mark Lamarr & Nick Clegg (7.1.1967)

Tim Vine & Sam Taylor-Wood (4.3.1967)

Jane McDonald & Graham Norton (4.4.1963)

Professor Niall Ferguson & Bez (18.4.1964)

David Tennant & Samantha Cameron (18.4.1971)

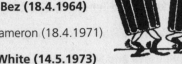

Natalie Appleton & Julian White (14.5.1973)

Olly Murs & Nigel Reo-Coker & Mark Zuckerberg (14.5.1984)

Fabien Barthez & Louise Bagshawe (28.6.1971)

Jeremy Guscott & Jeremy Kyle (7.7.1965)

Angela Griffin & Benedict Cumberbatch (19.7.1976)

Wayne Bridge & Sophie Winkleman (5.8.1980)

Evander Holyfield & Tracy Chevalier (19.10.1962)

Boris Becker & Mark Ruffalo (22.11.1967)

Ben Stiller & David Laws (30.11.1965)

Christian Bale & Jemima Khan (30.1.74)

Ben Elton & Neil Pearson (3.5.59)

Richard E. Grant & Peter Howitt (5.5.57)

Pierce Brosnan and Christian Lacroix (16.5.51)

Courtney Love and Gianluca Vialli (9.7.64)

Garth Brooks and Eddie Izzard (7.2.62)

Kenny Dalglish and Chris Rea (4.3.51)

Ernie Els and Wyclef Jean (17.10.69)

David Threlfall and Les Dennis (12.10.53)

Aretha Franklin and Richard O'Brien (25.3.42)

Nick Price and Frank Skinner (28.1.57)

Alan Rickman and Tyne Daly (21.2.46)

Steven Norris and Priscilla Presley (24.5.45)

Darcey Bussell and Mica Paris (27.4.69)

Paul Azinger and Nigella Lawson (6.1.60)

Ainsley Harriott and John Turturro (28.2.57)

Justin Hayward and Lesley Joseph (14.10.46)

Fiona Bruce & Hank Azaria (25.4.1964)

Lightning & Dido (25.12.1971)

Jenny McCarthy & Toni Collette (1.11.1972)

Mikey Graham & Ben Affleck (15.8.1972)

Carol Decker & Colin Firth (10.9.1960)

OTHER COUNTRIES THAT DRIVE ON THE LEFT

South Africa, Australia, Sri Lanka, Mauritius, Nepal, Cyprus, India, Lesotho, Indonesia, Singapore, Bangladesh, Namibia, Surinam, Pakistan, Uganda, Fiji, Barbados, Japan, Malaysia, The Seychelles, Brunei, The Bahamas, The British Virgin Islands, Kenya, Tanzania, Papua New Guinea, Swaziland, Mozambique, Zambia, Guyana, Malta, Ireland, Jamaica, Thailand, Malawi, New Zealand, Nauru, Botswana, Trinidad and Tobago, Dominica Grenada, St Lucia, Western Samoa, St Vincent, Zimbabwe.

THE BRAIN

The human brain is about 85 per cent water.

When you stub your toe, your brain registers the pain in 1/50th of a second.

We actually do not see with our eyes – we see with our brains. The eyes basically are the cameras of the brain. One-quarter of the brain is used to control the eyes.

Aristotle thought that blood cooled the brain.

Male human brains are about 10 per cent heavier than female brains.

Brain-wave activity in humans changes when we catch the punch line of a joke.

Your brain will stop growing in size when you are about 15 years old.

The human brain is capable of recording more than 86 million bits of information per day.

The creature with the largest brain relative to its body is the ant.

A sparrow's brain is 4 per cent of its total body weight (ours is 2 per cent).

Parrots have the largest brains in relation to their body size than any other bird.

The brain is not sensitive to pain; if it is cut into, the person feels nothing. Headache originates in the nerves, muscles and tissues surrounding the brain. This explains how brain surgery is sometimes performed on patients who are fully conscious (necessarily so since the surgeon gains valuable information by the patient's responses).

The human brain continues sending out electrical wave signals for up to 37 hours following death.

The brain of a sperm whale weighs 7.8 kilograms, but that is only 0.02 per cent of its body weight.

Primates called tarsiers have brains smaller than their eyeballs.

Scientists have performed brain surgery on cockroaches.

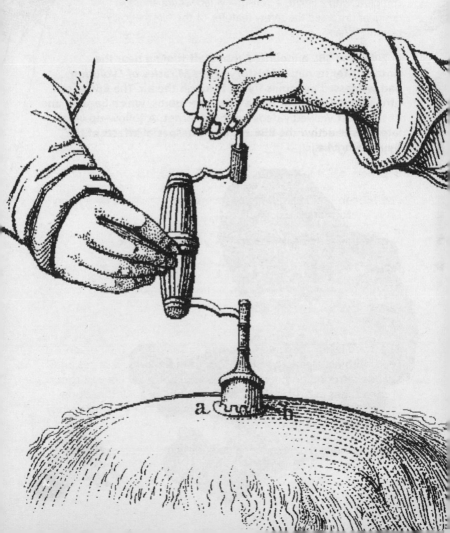

APRIL FOOLS' DAY PRANKS

In 2011, IKEA Australia announced their latest product as the 'IKEA Hundstol', aka a highchair for dogs. News of the product was placed on IKEA Australia's Facebook page, complete with a link to a YouTube video where an IKEA designer discussed the safety features of the 'aesthetically pleasing' chair.

In 2008, the BBC announced that staff filming near the Antarctic for its natural history series *Miracles of Evolution* had witnessed penguins flying through the air. The BBC even offered a video clip of these flying penguins, which became one of the most viewed videos on the internet. A follow-up video later showed how the BBC created the special effects of the flying penguins.

In 2007, an illusion designer (for magicians) posted on his website images illustrating the corpse of an unknown 8-inch creation – purporting to be the mummified remains of a fairy. He later sold the 'fairy' on eBay for £280.

In 2006, a Norwegian newspaper devoted an entire page to 'raindrop power' – an alternative to oil as a primary energy source. Readers were invited to write to the energy company to receive the power generated for free.

In 2005, Peter Jackson, the director of *King Kong*, aided by cast members, crew members, and even a studio representative, announced that *King Kong* would be followed by a sequel, *Son of Kong*, which would see Kong's offspring battle Nazis with shoulder-mounted machine guns. Jackson went so far as to have fake production drawings and computer animation test footage created for the film.

In 2002, an Australian radio station announced that Athens had lost the 2004 Summer Olympics because they couldn't be ready in time and that Sydney would have to host it again.

In 2000, the *Daily Mail* announced that Esporta Health Clubs had launched an innovative new type of socks which could help people lose weight. Dubbed FatSox, these revolutionary socks could suck body fat out of the feet if they were made to sweat.

In 1998, the Channel 4 show *The Big Breakfast* showed video footage of the Millennium Dome on fire.

In 1998, Burger King ran an ad in *USA Today* saying that people could get a Whopper for left-handed people with condiments designed to drip out on the right-hand side.

In 1998, the newsletter of New Mexicans for Science and Reason declared that the Alabama Legislature had voted to change the value of the mathematical constant pi from 3.14 to its 'Biblical value' of 3.0.

In 1997, an email message went round the world announcing that the internet would be shut down for cleaning for twenty-four hours from March 31 until April 2. This cyber-cleaning was said to be essential to clear out the 'electronic flotsam and jetsam' that had accumulated in the network and was threatening to block it completely. The cleaning would be done by five very powerful Japanese-built multi-lingual Internet-crawling robots. All dead websites and emails would be purged. During this period, all users were warned to disconnect all devices from the internet. The message supposedly originated from the 'Interconnected Network Maintenance Staff, Main Branch, Massachusetts Institute of Technology.' This joke was an updated version of an old joke that used to be told about the telephone system. For many years, gullible phone customers had been warned that the phone systems would be cleaned on April Fool's Day. They were cautioned to place plastic bags over the ends of the phone to catch the dust that might be blown out of the phone lines during this period.

In 1996, the fast-food outlet Taco Bell took out a full-page ad in *The New York Times* announcing that they had purchased the Liberty Bell to 'reduce the country's debt' and renamed it the 'Taco Liberty Bell'. When asked about it, the White House press secretary Mike McCurry joined in the prank by saying that the Lincoln Memorial had also been sold and would henceforth be known as the Ford Lincoln Mercury Memorial.

In 1995, *Discover* magazine reported that the highly respected wildlife biologist Dr Aprile Pazzo had discovered a new species in Antarctica: the hot-headed naked ice borer. This fascinating creature had a bony plate on its head which could become burning hot, allowing the animals to bore through the ice at high speeds. By this method, they were able to hunt penguins, melting the ice beneath the penguins and causing them to sink down into the slush where they could be caught. *Discover* received more letters in response to this article than they had received for any other article in their history.

In 1987, a Norwegian newspaper announced that 10,000 litres of illegally smuggled wine had been confiscated and that it would be distributed to the people of Bergen at a local department store. Some two hundred people turned up with bottles and buckets.

In 1986, *Le Parisien* newspaper stunned its readers when it reported that the Eiffel Tower was to be dismantled and reconstructed in the new Euro Disney theme park to the east of Paris.

In 1981, the *Daily Mail* ran a story about an unfortunate Japanese long-distance runner, Kimo Nakajimi, who had misunderstood the rules of the London Marathon and thought that he had to run for 26 days, not 26 miles. Reportedly, the blissfully unaware Nakajimi was somewhere out there still running, determined to finish the race. Various people had spotted him still running, but nobody had been able to flag him down.

In 1980, *Soldier* magazine reported that the black fur on the bearskin helmets worn by the Irish guards while on duty at Buckingham Palace kept growing and needed to be regularly trimmed. The article quoted a Major Ursa who said: 'Bears hibernate in the winter and the amazing thing is that in the spring the skins really start to sprout'. An accompanying photo showed guardsmen sitting in an army barbershop having their helmets trimmed. A national newspaper fell for the report and ran it as a straight story.

In 1979, the BBC TV programme *That's Life* featured an Old English sheepdog that could drive a car.

In 1975, An Australian news programme announced that the country was planning a conversion to 'metric time' in which there would be 100 seconds to the minute, 100 minutes to the hour, and 20-hour days. In addition, seconds would become millidays, minutes would become centidays, and hours would become decidays. The town hall in Adelaide was shown with a new 10-hour metric clock face. The programme received many calls from viewers who believed the story.

In 1965, BBC TV featured an interview with a professor who, it was claimed, had just invented a device called 'smellovision' which enabled viewers to experience smells from the television studio. The professor proceeded to offer a demonstration by brewing coffee and slicing up some onions. A number of viewers called in claiming that they had experienced these scents as if they were right there in the studio with him.

In 1965, a Danish newspaper reported that the Danish parliament had passed a new law requiring all dogs to be painted white. Why? To improve safety on the roads by enabling drivers to see any dogs that were out and about at night.

In 1962, there was only one TV channel in Sweden – and that was broadcast in black and white. The station's technical expert, Kjell Stensson, came on the news bulletin and announced that, thanks to new technology, viewers could now convert their existing TV sets to colour. All they had to do was to pull a nylon stocking over their TV screens ... something he proceeded to demonstrate on screen. Thousands of people were taken in. Regular colour broadcasts in Sweden started eight years later: on 1 April – yes, honestly – 1970.

In 1959, the residents of Wellingborough, Northamptonshire, woke up to find that someone had left a trail of white footprints painted all along the main street. When the footsteps stopped they found the words, 'I must fly.'

On 1 April, 1915, in the middle of World War 1, a French aviator flew over a German military camp and dropped what appeared to be a huge bomb. The German soldiers scattered in all directions, but the bomb didn't go off. Very nervously, the soldiers tiptoed towards the bomb which, in fact, *wasn't* a bomb but a large football with a note tied to it reading 'April Fool'.

BORN ON APRIL FOOL'S DAY

David Gower, Ali MacGraw, Phillip Schofield, Michael Praed, Chris Evans, Susan Boyle, Kris Marshall, Stephen Fleming, Bijou Phillips, Hannah Spearritt.

FORMER FLATMATES

Marc Bolan and James Bolam

Rory Bremner and Jeremy Hardy

Arabella Weir and David Tennant

William Hague and Alan Duncan

Sienna Miller and Hannah Sandling

Ronnie Wood and Jimi Hendrix

CHILDHOOD NICKNAMES

Jennifer Lopez – The Supernova

Keith Urban – Suburban

Sienna Miller – Squit

Tyra Banks – Olive Oyl, Lightbulb Head, Fivehead and Froggy.

Sir Alan Sugar – Mopsy

THE DARWIN AWARDS HONOUR 'THOSE WHO DO A SERVICE TO HUMANITY BY PERMANENTLY REMOVING THEMSELVES FROM THE GENE POOL'. HERE ARE SOME PAST DEEDS WHICH HAVE BEEN 'RECOGNISED' BY THE JUDGES

An American man shot himself while explaining gun safety to his wife. He placed a .45-calibre pistol he thought was unloaded under his chin and pulled the trigger.

Two men robbed a store in South Carolina and then fled, but they couldn't flee from their own stupidity. One of them had disguised himself by painting his face gold. The noxious paint fumes gave him breathing difficulties and he died wheezing shortly after the robbery took place.

A young man was kicked out of a Florida bar for fighting. He sneaked back in and leapt off a staircase, aiming a kick at another man, but was killed when he landed on his head.

Two South African muggers were running away from their victims. One of them spotted a fence and leapt over it ... into the Bengal tiger cage at Bloemfontein Zoo. The tigers had just been fed so they didn't eat him: they simply tore him apart instead.

Two Belgian bankrobbers died in an explosion when they overestimated the quantity of dynamite needed to blow open a cash machine.

A pack of thieves attempted to steal scrap metal from an abandoned factory in the Czech Republic. Unfortunately for them, they selected the steel girders that supported the factory roof. When the roof supports were dismantled, the roof fell, fatally crushing two thieves and injuring three others.

An Iraqi terrorist didn't put enough postage on a letter bomb and it came back marked 'return to sender.' He opened the package and was blown up.

Two German animal rights activists protesting against cruelty to pigs released 2,000 of them and were promptly trampled to death.

An American man tried stealing the office safe but was crushed to death when it fell on top of him while he was taking it down the stairs. To make matters worse, the 600-lb safe was empty.

A keen American hunter was having a row with his girlfriend and so used the butt of his shotgun to bash in her windshield. His loaded gun accidentally discharged into his stomach and killed him.

A German man attempting to impress his wife with his unbelievable strength climbed over the balcony of their seventh-floor flat, clung to the outside of the parapet, and began a set of pull-ups. After a few pull-ups, he was exhausted and couldn't pull himself back on to the balcony. He fell to his death, impaling himself on a thornbush.

Matthew was sliding down a Mammoth Mountain ski run on a yellow foam pad when he crashed into a lift tower and died. He would have been fine but the yellow foam designed to protect skiers had been stolen … by Matthew for his makeshift sledge.

PEOPLE WHO HAD STATIONS NAMED AFTER THEM ON THE PARIS METRO

King George V, Charles de Gaulle, François Mitterrand, Victor Hugo, Georges Clemençeau, Michelangelo, Pierre Curie, Simón Bolívar, Alexandre Dumas, Emile Zola, Voltaire, Cardinal Richelieu.

ROCK PEOPLE WHO WERE MURDERED

Sam Cooke (the great American singer whose hits included *Only Sixteen, Twistin' The Night Away, Wonderful World* and *Cupid* – was shot dead in 1964, when he was 33, by the manageress of a motel who claimed that he had attempted to assault her.)

Al Jackson Jnr (Jackson, a founder member of Booker T. & The MG's who had worldwide hits with *Green Onions* and *Time Is Tight*, was shot dead in 1975 at the age of 39 by an intruder at his home in Memphis. This was only three months after he survived being shot in the chest by his wife.)

Harry Womack (One of the six Womack brothers who made up The Valentinos, Womack was stabbed to death by his wife in 1974 when he was 28. His elder brother, Bobby, is a famous singer-songwriter who wrote the Rolling Stones hit *It's All Over Now.*)

Mal Evans (The former Beatles roadie who had been with the group right from the start was shot dead by the LAPD in 1976, when he was 40, because he refused to give up a gun he was brandishing. It later transpired that the gun wasn't loaded.)

Carlton Barrett (A former member of Bob Marley's Wailers, Barrett, 36, was shot dead by person(s) unknown in 1987 in Jamaica. Interestingly, Bob Marley himself survived an assassination attempt before his death from cancer.)

Peter Tosh (In 1987, only a few months after Barrett's murder, his more famous fellow-Wailer was murdered by burglars in his home in Jamaica.)

Felix Pappalardi (In 1983, Pappalardi, 43, the former manager and producer of Eric Clapton's band, *Cream*, was shot dead by his wife. As well as being the group's manager, he also played keyboards on several of their songs, including *Badge* and later played bass with the rock group Mountain.)

Marvin Gaye (The legendary soul singer who brought us *What's Going On* and *I Heard It Through The Grapevine* was shot dead by his father in 1984 during a violent argument. Marvin Gaye had become increasingly mentally disturbed and his father was charged with manslaughter and was sent to jail for five years.)

Jaco Pastorius (Pastorius, a founder member of Weather Report, is reckoned by many to have been the greatest bass player of all time. In 1987 at the age of 35, while suffering from alcoholism and mental illness, he was beaten to death by a bouncer outside a nightclub in his home town of Fort Lauderdale, Florida.)

John Lennon (By Mark David Chapman in 1980.)

CELEBRITIES AND THE NAMES THEY GAVE TO THEIR PETS

CELEBRITY	PET	NAME
Russell Brand	Cat	Morrissey
Jim Carrey	Iguana	Houston
Angelina Jolie	Rat	Harry
John Lennon	Cat	Elvis
Venus Williams	Dog (Yorkshire Terrier)	Pete (named after Pete Sampras)
Jose Mourinho	Yorkshire Terrier	Gullit
Paris Hilton	Dog (Chihuahua)	Tinkerbell
Miley Ray Cyrus	Dogs	Loco, Juicy and Minnie Pearl
Fearne Cotton	Cats	Tallulah and Keloy
Anthony Horowitz	Dog (Labrador)	Lucky
Zac Efron	Dogs (Australian Shepherds)	Dreamer and Puppy
	Siamese cat	Simon
Ashley Tisdale	Dog (Teacup Poodle)	Maui
Connie Fisher	Guinea Pig	Mister Ruffles
Kristen Stewart	Dogs	Oz, Jack and Lily
	Cat	Jella.
Ozzy Osbourne	Dog (Bulldog)	Baldrick
Ringo Starr	Dogs	Ying and Yang
Brad Pitt	Dog	Saudi

CELEBRITY	PET	NAME
Sylvester Stallone	Dog (Boxer)	Gangster
Princess Beatrice	Dog (Terrier)	Wat
Dustin Hoffman	Dog	Maggie
The Duke of Kent	Dog	Muff
Rob Lowe	Dog	Spot
Prince William	Dog	Widgeon
Charisma Carpenter	Dog (Golden Retriever)	Sydney
Robbie Williams	Dogs	Little Wallee and The Poops
Mira Sorvino	Dog	Deer
Wolfgang Joop	Dogs (Pomeranians)	Otto, Willy and Wolfie
Marc Jacobs	Dog (Dalmatian)	Tiger
Davina McCall	Dog	Chloe
Princess Stephanie of Monaco	Giraffe.	Aisha
Louise Redknapp	Dog	Winston
Melissa Joan Hart	Dogs	Holly Ochola and Permani Pele
Jake Gyllenhaal	Dog	Atticus (after a character in his favourite book, *To Kill A Mockingbird*)
Jenny Frost	Dog	George Michael

WONDERFULLY NAMED
CHARLES DICKENS CHARACTERS

Doctor Neeshawts (*The Mudfog Papers*), Oswald Pardiggle (*Bleak House*), Paul Sweedlepipe (*Martin Chuzzlewit*), Doctor Soemup (*The Mudfog Papers*), Mortimer Knag (*Nicholas Nickleby*), Augustus Moddle (*Martin Chuzzlewit*), Quebec Bagnet (*Bleak House*), Simon Tappertit (*Barnaby Rudge*), Mercy Pecksniff (*Martin Chuzzlewit*), Morleena Kenwigs (*Nicholas Nickleby*), Chevy Slyme (*Martin Chuzzlewit*), Dick Swiveller (*The Old Curiosity Shop*), Conkey Chickweed (*Oliver Twist*), Sophy Wackles (*The Old Curiosity Shop*), Minnie Meagles (*Little Dorrit*), Canon Crisparkle (*The Mystery of Edwin Drood*), Peepy Jellyby (*Bleak House*), Nicodemus Boffin (*Our Mutual Friend*), Count Smorltork (*The Pickwick Papers*).

THE UK

The Queen has the right to any sturgeon caught off the British coast.

Four per cent of British house sellers admit to removing the house number when they leave.

Mayfair – the most expensive property on the Monopoly board – derives its name from an annual fair which was held every May until the eighteenth century.

The Royal Mail uses 342 million rubber bands a year to bundle up letters.

There are some two thousand Cornish speakers in Britain.

Four per cent of Britons actually believe in the Loch Ness Monster.

There are some 600,000 vegans in the UK.

Twelve per cent of Britons believe that they have seen ghosts.

Ten per cent of Britain's perfume sales take place at Heathrow.

In Britain, it's reckoned that every time broadband grows by 1 per cent, newspaper sales decline by 0.2 per cent.

Eight is the average age at which a British child gets a mobile phone.

Nine out of ten British households have microwaves.

In a contest held by a British magazine to try to discover who had the worst boss, many people agreed with the statement that their boss could be replaced by a hamster and no one would notice.

Ten per cent of British adults admit to wearing the same item of underwear three days in a row.

There are six times as many sheep in the UK as there are in the US.

The oldest city in Britain is Ripon which received its original charter in 886.

There are more than 4 million CCTV cameras in Britain, 1 for every 14 people. It's reckoned that only China and Malaysia spy more on their people than the British do.

The UK has the highest number of botanical gardens and zoos in the world (relative to its size).

Only 7 per cent of British people say that they trust their neighbours.

Sixty-two per cent of British people speak no other language than English.

Forty-five per cent of Britons reckon they don't get enough sleep.

Fifty-five per cent of British workers say that they never take a lunch break.

Twenty-nine per cent of British women cut off the size labels from their clothes.

Twelve per cent of married British men claim to do most of the housework (the rest of us tell the truth).

Only 29 per cent of British families sit down to eat a meal together more than once a week.

There are nearly 11 million cows in the UK.

There are 21,000 black cab taxis in London (taking 85 million fares per year, mostly in London and around Heathrow) and 40,000 minicabs.

There's a village in Somerset named Curry Mallet.

Five million Britons have more than one job.

About 7 per cent of the adult UK population are vegetarians.

Every year in Britain, some 250 people are killed or injured on motorway hard shoulders.

Every year, the Isles of Scilly Wildlife Trust pays Prince Charles a single daffodil in rent.

ACTORS WHO WON NON-ACTING OSCARS

Matt Damon & Ben Affleck (Best Original Screenplay 1997: *Good Will Hunting*).

Clint Eastwood (Best Director 1992: *Unforgiven*; Best Director 2004, Best Film 2004: *Million Dollar Baby*).

Julian Fellowes (Best Original Screenplay 2001: *Gosford* Park).

Sofia Coppola (Best Original Screenplay 2003: *Lost In Translation*).

Robert Redford (Best Director 1980: *Ordinary People*).

Keith Carradine (Best Song 1975: *I'm Easy* from *Nashville*).

Emma Thompson (Best Adapted Screenplay 1995: *Sense and Sensibility*).

Kevin Costner (Best Director 1991: *Dances With Wolves*).

Michael Douglas (Best Producer 1975: *One Flew Over The Cuckoo's Nest*).

Mel Gibson (Best Director 1995: *Braveheart*).

Richard Attenborough
(Best Director 1982: *Gandhi*).

**Warren Beatty
(Best Director 1981: *Reds*).**

SPORT (1)

Charlie Chaplin was a fine table-tennis player who thought he'd be able to beat Maxwell Woosnam, a champion, who was using a butter knife in place of a bat. Woosnam won and then chucked Chaplin into his own swimming pool.

C.B. Fry must surely lay claim to being the greatest sporting all-rounder. He captained England at cricket, played for England at football and held the world long-jump record. After retiring from sport, he was offered the throne of Albania but turned it down.

Ten-pin bowling used to be done with nine pins. A law was passed in colonial Connecticut making 'bowling at nine pins' illegal. So keen bowlers added another pin to make it 'bowling at ten pins' which was, of course, legal.

Dr James Naismith invented basketball (or 'indoor rugby' as it was originally called) in 1891 as something to occupy students between the football and baseball seasons. It was one of the game's early players who started calling it basketball because of the peach baskets that acted as the original goals.

Rudyard Kipling attributed Britain's failure to win the Boer War to 'Britain's obsession with sport'.

When a baseball is hit really hard, it momentarily changes shape by as much as 25 per cent.

With one pitch, baseball player Babe Ruth could throw two balls simultaneously, and they would stay parallel all the way to the catcher.

The heaviest sumo wrestler wasn't Japanese but Hawaiian. At his heaviest, Konishiki – known as the Dump Truck – weighed 630 lbs (286 kilos). He was once said to have drunk more than a hundred beers and eaten 70 pieces of sushi in a single meal.

At the age of 101, Larry Lewis ran the 100 yards in 17.8 seconds – setting a new world record for runners 100 years old or older.

Americans spend more than $630 million a year on golf balls.

The man who won the Indianapolis 500 in 1915 had to get out and push his broken car for the last mile of the race.

At 120 miles per hour, a Formula One car generates so much downforce that, in theory, it could be driven upside-down on the roof of a tunnel.

Until the 1870s, baseball was played without the use of gloves.

Racehorses have been known to wear out new shoes in just one race.

When the Olympics were held in France, in 1900, the winners were given a valuable piece of art instead of a medal.

From a complete stop, a human is capable of outrunning a Formula One race car for about ten metres.

In 1991, the Grand National was sponsored by Seagram and, completely coincidentally, the winner was called Seagram. The following year's winner was almost

as felicitous: Party Politics won just five days before the General Election.

There were five one-eyed men in the 1920 France–Scotland rugby union match. One of them was the remarkable Prop Marcel-Frederic Lubin-Lebrere who, just a few years earlier in the first World War, had lost an eye and had also had 23 pieces of shrapnel removed from his body. He later became Mayor of Toulouse.

In the 1936 Swathling Cup table tennis match, Alex Ehrlich of Poland and Paneth Farcas of Rumania played a 2-hour-and-12-minute-rally for the first point.

Chris Balderstone once played first-class cricket and professional football on the very same day. On 15 September 1975, he played championship cricket for Leicestershire against Derbyshire at Chesterfield (11.30 a.m. to 6.30 p.m.) and then soccer for Doncaster Rovers against Brentford at Doncaster (7.30 p.m. to 9.10 p.m.).

All major league baseball umpires must wear black underwear (in case their black trousers split).

William Webb Ellis of Rugby School was credited with inventing the sport of rugby. It was another former pupil of Rugby, Tom Wills, who invented the sport of Australian Rules Football.

No high jumper has ever been able to stay off the ground for longer than a second.

The US diver, Harry Prieste, got more enjoyment out of his Olympic medal than any other medallist ... well, he certainly enjoyed it the longest. Born in 1896, he won the bronze medal in the platform diving at the 1920 Games in Antwerp. He then lived for more than another 80 years – dying in 2001 at the age of 104.

At the opposite end of that scale was the Swiss rower Gottfried Kottmann. At the 1964 Tokyo Games he won the bronze medal in the single sculls rowing event on his 32nd birthday. However, just 22 days later, he died in a car accident.

In 2005, a British man named Dave Cornthwaite took up skateboarding. The following year, he became the first person to skate from John O'Groats (at the top of Scotland) to Land's End (at the bottom of England).

In the 1904 Olympic marathon, the American runner, Fred Lorz, dropped out after 9 miles and was given a lift back to the stadium by his manager. When he was seen trotting over the finish line (to retrieve his clothes), the officials thought he had won the race. Lorz played along with it until he was found out shortly after the medal ceremony. He was banned for a year.

But that wasn't the only extraordinary occurrence in the race. A Cuban postman named Felix Carbajal decided to join in – running in street clothes that he cut around the legs to make them look like shorts. He stopped off in an orchard on the way and ate some apples for a snack. Alas, they turned out to be rotten and made him ill, forcing him to lie down and take a nap. Despite all this, he finished in fourth place.

Meanwhile, Thomas Hicks (a Briton running for the United States) was the first to cross the finish line legally – but only after receiving several doses of strychnine

sulphate mixed with brandy from his trainers who also physically helped him to cross the finishing line. In fact, Hicks was in such a bad state that he had to be carried off the track and might very well have died in the stadium had he not been treated by several doctors. Still, he was awarded the gold medal.

When Andy Murray was called up to play doubles for Great Britain's Davis Cup team in March 2005, he became Britain's youngest ever Davis Cup player.

Table tennis was banned in the USSR in the 1930s and 1940s because it was believed that it harmed people's eyes.

Michael Jordan was dropped from his high school basketball team.

Stanislawa Walasiewicz – or Stella Walsh as she was known in her adopted country of America – ran the 100 metres in 1932 and in 1936 for her native Poland but only because the US couldn't support her financially. However, when the athlete was shot dead in Cleveland in 1980, the autopsy revealed that she was actually a man.

ALL THE KINGS AND QUEENS OF ENGLAND AND THE UNITED KINGDOM SINCE 1066

House of Normandy

1066–1087 William I

1087–1100 William II

1100–1135 Henry I

1135–1154 Stephen

House of Plantagenet

1154–1189 Henry II

1189–1199 Richard I

1199–1216 John

1216–1272 Henry III

1272–1307 Edward I

1307–1327 Edward II

1327–1377 Edward III

1377–1399 Richard II

House of Lancaster

1399–1413 Henry IV

1413–1422 Henry V

1422–1461 Henry VI

House of York

1461–1483 Edward IV

1483 Edward V

1483–1485 Richard III

House of Tudor

1485–1509 Henry VII

1509–1547 Henry VIII

1547–1553 Edward VI

1553 Lady Jane Grey (9 days)

1553–1558 Mary I

1558–1603 Elizabeth I

House of Stuart

1603–1625 James I

1625–1649 Charles I

1649–1653 Commonwealth/protectorate

1653–1658 Protectorate of Oliver Cromwell

1658–1659 Protectorate of Richard Cromwell

House of Stuart restored

1660–1685 Charles II

1685–1688 James II

1689–1694 William III and Mary II (jointly)

House of Orange

1694–1702 William III (sole ruler)

1702–1714 Anne

House of Hanover

1714–1727 George I

1727–1760 George II

1760–1820 George III

1820–1830 George IV

1830–1837 William IV

1837–1901 Victoria

House of Saxe-Coburg

1901–1910 Edward VII

House of Windsor

1910–1936 George V (a Saxe-Coburg until 1917)

1936 Edward VIII

1936–1952 George VI

1952– Elizabeth II

CROSS-CHANNEL SWIMMING

Captain Matthew Webb (1848–83) became the first person to swim the English Channel when, on 25 August 1875, he swam from Dover to Calais. It took him just under 22 hours.

It wasn't until 1923 – 48 years later – that Enrico Tiraboschi made the first crossing of the English Channel from France to England.

As of 2011, Alison Streeter had swum the Channel 43 times. Her fastest time is just under nine hours. She is the first (and so far only) woman to swim the Channel three ways non-stop. Think about that for a second. Three ways non-stop. The three crossings (in 1990) took 34 hours and 40 minutes.

Only two men have achieved that feat – one slower (Jon Erikson in 1981 in a time of 38 hours and 27 minutes) and one faster (Philip Rush in 1987 in a time of 28 hours and 21 minutes).

This is one area where women compete on equal terms with men. Indeed, Alison Streeter's closest rival – Kevin Murphy – has swum the Channel fewer times than Alison: 34 (including three double-Channel swims).

The fastest swim (by a man) was 6 hours 57 minutes (by the Bulgarian Petar Stoychev in 2007) while the fastest swim (by a woman) was 7 hours 25 minutes (by Yvetta Hlavacova of the Czech Republic).

The oldest person to swim the Channel was the 70-year-old American George Brunstad and the youngest person was Thomas Gregory, a British boy of just under twelve. The youngest girl – Samantha Druce, also British – was just over twelve.

The most famous cross-Channel swimmer is probably the comedian, David Walliams, who astonished the world when he completed the crossing in the very fast time of 10 hours and 34 minutes. It was in 2006 for Sport Relief and he raised over £1 million in donations.

But what of brave Captain Webb, the pioneer of cross-Channel swimming? He retained his passion for dangerous swims and, in 1883, he decided to swim through the Whirlpool Rapids below Niagara Falls. Alas, it was a feat too far and he died. In 1909, Webb's brother Thomas unveiled a memorial in Dawley, Shropshire which bore the inscription 'Nothing great is easy'.

SWEETS – AND WHEN THEY WERE INTRODUCED

Cadbury Eclairs – 1974 launched nationally in the UK (around non-nationally since 1960s)

Cadbury Caramel, Double Decker, Yorkie and Lion Bar – 1976

Drifter – 1980

Wispa – 1983

Boost – 1985

Twirl – 1987

Cadbury's White Buttons – 1989

Timeout – 1992

Fuse – 1996 (40 million bars sold in the first week)

Maverick – 1997

Cadbury's Miniature Heroes, Cadbury's Giant Buttons, Kit-Kat Chunky – 1999

Cadbury's Brunchbar, Dream, Snow Flake – 2001

Kit-Kat Kubes – 2003

Fruity Smarties, Kit-Kat Editions – 2004

DRINK

Beethoven was so particular about his coffee that he always counted out 60 beans for each cup.

The world's costliest coffee is *kopi luwak* (civet coffee), which is produced from the droppings of an animal that eats only the very best coffee beans and then excretes them partially digested.

Frederick the Great had his coffee made with champagne and a bit of mustard.

The French philosopher, Voltaire, drank 50 cups of coffee a day.

When it originally appeared in 1886, Coca-Cola was advertised as an 'Esteemed Brain Tonic and Intellectual Beverage'.

The teabag was introduced in 1908 by Thomas Sullivan of New York.

It costs 10,000 times more to produce a litre of bottled water than a litre of tap water.

Tea is said to have been discovered in 2737 BC by a Chinese emperor when some tea leaves accidentally blew into a pot of boiling water.

Wine has been made for at least 7,000 years.

Adding sugar to coffee is believed to have started in 1715, in the court of King Louis XIV of France.

According to a study from Harvard University, regular coffee drinkers have about one-third fewer asthma symptoms than non-coffee drinkers.

The world's biggest ever teabag was 4 metres by 3 metres, and made 11,000 cups of Earl Grey. It was made in 2003 to celebrate Twining's three-hundredth Birthday.

When consumed with a meal, orange juice helps the body absorb iron.

Bananas grow pointing upwards.

After the decaffeinating process, processing companies no longer throw the caffeine away but sell it to pharmaceutical companies.

Syria has one of the highest rates of sugar consumption in the world. Syrian soft drinks are the sweetest in the world.

In Germany, there are 5,000 different types of beer.

Tea is the national drink of Afghanistan.

In France the average person drinks over 25 gallons of wine per year.

In Somalia, some nomads drink a fermented beverage which is made by burying camel's milk in a leather flask for a week.

In Mexico, chocolate, which comes from a bean of the cacao tree, was known as the drink of the gods, because by law only the nobility could drink it.

In Costa Rica, babies are allowed to drink coffee.

Goat's milk is used more widely throughout the world than cow's milk.

In the US, 12 per cent of Coca-Cola is consumed with or for breakfast.

Pepsi-Cola was originally called 'Brad's drink'.

PEOPLE AND THEIR FEARS OR PHOBIAS

Eminem (Owls)

Sophie Ellis-Bextor (Owls)

Reese Witherspoon (Spiders)

Tobey Maguire (Spiders)

Jackie Chan (Water)

Keanu Reeves (The dark)

Sigourney Weaver (Lifts)

Nicole Kidman (Butterflies)

Chevy Chase (Snakes)

Justin Timberlake (Spiders, snakes and sharks)

Christopher Walken (Going too fast in cars)

Declan Donnelly (Pigeons)

Robson Green (Wasps)

Harry Connick Jnr (Heights and rats)

Angela Merkel (Dogs)

Frank Skinner (Water)

Pamela Anderson (Mirrors)

Daniel Radcliffe (Clowns)

Orlando Bloom (Pigs)

Scarlett Johansson (Cockroaches)

Uma Thurman (Confined spaces)

Carmen Electra (Water)

Sarah Michelle Gellar (Graveyards)

Christina Ricci (Indoor plants)

Jennifer Love Hewitt (The dark)

David Bowie (Death)

Stephen King (Death, deformity, rats, beetles and all flying insects)

Lyle Lovett (Cows)

Anne Rice (The dark)

Ant McPartlin (Spiders)

Julia Roberts (Spiders)

Fiona Bruce (Garden worms)

Jenny Eclair (Fish – live ones, not on a plate)

Leonardo DiCaprio (Needles)

Barbra Streisand (Public toilets. She often travels in a fully-equipped Winnebago so she never has to sit on a public toilet seat. She also scatters rose petals in the toilet bowl before going.)

Frank Bruno (Mice)

NUMBERS

1,274,953,680 uses all the digits 0–9 and you can divide it exactly by any number from 1 to 16.

If you multiply 1,089 by 9 you get 9,801. It's reversed itself. This also works with 10,989 or 1,099,989 and so on.

The number 2,520 can be divided precisely by 1, 2, 3, 4, 5, 6, 7, 8, 9, and 10.

There is a way of writing the number 1 by using the numbers from 0–9 once each: 148/296 + 35/70 = 1.

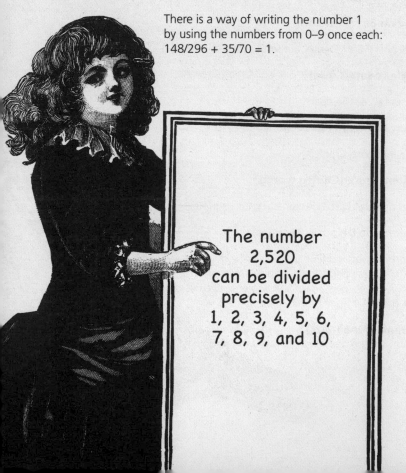

The number 2,520 can be divided precisely by 1, 2, 3, 4, 5, 6, 7, 8, 9, and 10

Acetwothreefourfivesixseveneightninetenjackqueenking ... If you add up the letters in all the names of the cards in the deck, the total number of letters is 52, the same as the number of cards in the deck.

111,111,111 x 111,111,111 = 12,345,678,987,654,321.

Six is a perfect number. The numbers that go into six – 1, 2 and 3 – add up to 6.

One year is 31,557,600 seconds long.

These are all the prime numbers (a prime number is one that can only be divided by itself or by 1) below 100: 2 3 5 7 11 13 17 19 23 29 31 37 41 43 47 53 59 61 67 71 73 79 83 89 97

Chimps can be taught to understand the different values of numbers and remember them years later.

Medical researchers found that volunteers stopped shivering when they were given lists of numbers to add up.

One year is 31,557,600 seconds long.

THE PIRATE CODE

This varied from ship to ship but this, from the eighth century, was a fairly typical set of rules:

Everyone shall obey orders.

Booty shall be shared as follows: half goes to the captain, a quarter is shared by the gunner, boatswain and master carpenter, and the remaining quarter is divided among all the ordinary sailors.

Anyone attempting to desert will be marooned. He will be left with a flask of gunpowder, a bottle of water and a gun with one bullet.

The punishment for hitting a man is 40 lashes on the bare back.

Failure to keep weapons clean will lead to the loss of a share of the booty.

Everyone has a vote on all important decisions.

Everyone gets a share of captured drink and fresh food.

Anyone found stealing from another member of the crew will have his ears and nose split open and be set ashore.

Gambling is forbidden.

The penalty for bringing a woman aboard in disguise is death.

No one may leave the crew until each man has made £1,100.

The compensation for losing a limb is 800 silver dollars.

Pirates still exist. These days, they use speedboats and carry automatic weapons but are just as merciless as the pirates of old. But don't worry if you're crossing the English Channel. Most pirates nowadays are in the China Sea or around the coast of Africa and Brazil.

THE WAY WE LIVE (1)

Fifty-five per cent of women apply lipstick daily.

Lipstick outsells all other cosmetics four to one.

It's estimated that you will spend one year of your life looking for things you've lost.

When left alone with a tea cosy, 98 per cent of men will put it on their heads.

A can of Spam is opened every four seconds.

The rate of heart attacks among people who live near airports is 18 per cent higher than people who don't. Similarly, the rate of crime-related deaths and suicides is double, while people over the age of 75 are twice as likely to have accidents.

An estimated 300,000 accidents a year are caused by satnavs.

Soldiers avoid marching in step across some bridges so as not to set up a vibration that could destabilize it.

Experiments conducted in Germany and at the University of Southampton in England show that even small noises cause the pupils of the eyes to dilate. It is believed that this is why surgeons, watchmakers, and others who perform delicate manual operations are so bothered by noise. The sounds cause their pupils to change focus and blur their vision.

Fingernails grow four times faster than toenails.

Because of their elasticity, human lungs are a lot easier to blow up than a balloon.

Human bones can withstand being squeezed twice as hard as granite can.

Most people button their shirts upwards.

According to research, women are enticed to buy more if they hear the sound of heels clicking on the floor.

Men have more car accidents than women, but drive more miles. Women have more accidents per mile driven.

Athlete's foot is the most common skin infection. It's caused by a fungus which causes the skin between the toes to peel off.

Children between the ages of two and seven spend an average of 28 minutes a day colouring.

A person is more likely to eat twice as much in the company of others as when eating alone.

For every mile travelled, death is 140 times more likely in a car than in a plane. However, cars are actually safer than planes on a per journey basis.

Brushing your teeth with the water on wastes almost twenty litres of water.

If the entire population of Earth was reduced to exactly 100 people, 50 per cent of the world's currency would be held by 6 people.

Four per cent of the food you eat will be eaten in front of the refrigerator with its door open.

The average British person eats 2.8 unhealthy snacks a day.

The average Briton spends more than 400 hours a year shopping.

It is estimated that 60 per cent of home smoke detectors in use do not work because they either don't have batteries in them or because batteries are dead.

A quarter of British adults have no savings at all.

Men are almost twice as likely as women to take a day off work claiming to have flu.

The average person keeps magazines for 29 weeks before throwing them out.

Eighty-six per cent of women and 72 per cent of men look at price tags when they shop.

Sixty-eight per cent of Britons say they believe in the existence of ghosts and/or spirits.

The average Briton spends 2 hours and 44 minutes a day on the internet.

The average person throws away seven times their body weight in rubbish every year.

On average, 78 people die each year playing Twister.

CHRISTMAS

The average Briton devotes 15 hours a year to Christmas shopping. Around 25 per cent of that time is spent in queues.

The Christmas song 'Jingle Bells' was originally composed in 1857 as a Thanksgiving song.

The Queen and the Duke of Edinburgh send some 850 Christmas cards a year.

The reason why robins are associated with Christmas is because postmen who wore red were known as robins and so many Christmas cards depicted robins delivering cards.

Santa Claus is called Babbo Natale in Italy.

It's St Francis of Assisi we have to thank for introducing Christmas carols to church services.

It wasn't until 440 that December 25th was first celebrated as the birthday of Christ.

The average British mother spends 13 days preparing for Christmas.

Two-thirds of office workers receive corporate Christmas cards from people they don't know.

In the nineteenth century, Christmas cards were delivered on Christmas day itself.

More than 8 million Christmas trees were sold in Britain last year.

Holly is associated with Christmas because the sharply pointed leaves symbolized the thorns in Christ's crown and the red berries his blood.

Christmas pies – aka mince pies – were banned by Oliver Cromwell and the Puritans in 1657.

There are 178 legs in the song *The Twelve Days of Christmas*: 1 partridge, 2 doves, 3 hens, 4 colly birds, 6 geese, 7 swans, 8 maids with a cow each, 9 ladies, 10 lords, 11 pipers and 12 drummers.

The commercial phenomenon of retailers exploiting the commercialized status of Christmas earlier and earlier every year is known as 'Christmas Creep'.

The Christmas Day 1986 edition of *EastEnders* attracted a record audience of 30.15 million people.

Around 16 million turkeys were sold in the UK last Christmas.

The world's first Christmas stamp was issued by Austria in 1937.

In about 1597, William Shakespeare gave *The Merry Wives of Windsor* to Queen Elizabeth I for Christmas.

Rudolph the Red-Nosed Reindeer was created in 1939, in Chicago, for the Montgomery Ward department stores for a Christmas promotion. The lyrics were written as a poem by Robert May, but weren't set to music until 1947. Gene Autry recorded the hit song in 1949.

In Belgium, it's officially against the law for children to chuck bananas at policemen on Christmas Eve and for policemen to chuck bananas at children on Christmas Day.

In Ukraine, it's considered good luck to find a spider's web in the house on Christmas morning.

During Christmas Eve dinner in Slovakia, people save food for carol singers and visitors. In the old days, Slovakian peasants used to take a little of each Christmas dish and give it to the domestic animals.

WHAT PEOPLE AROUND THE WORLD EAT FOR THEIR CHRISTMAS DINNER

Hungary – Fish soup and fried fish

Romania – Bread-based Christmas cake

Iceland – Smoked lamb

Jamaica – Curried goat, rice and gungo peas

Latvia – Sausage, cabbage and brown peas in a pork sauce

Nicaragua – Chicken stuffed with fruit and vegetables

Ukraine – Meat broth

Denmark – Roast duck

Finland – Turkey casserole with carrots, macaroni, potatoes and swede

Germany – Roast goose

Greenland – Seabirds wrapped in the skin of a seal

Luxembourg – Venison, hare and black pudding

Norway – Cod or haddock and Christmas meatloaf

Brazil – Turkey marinated in rum and ham, with coloured rice

Czech Republic – Fish soup, salad, carp and eggs

Portugal – Salted codfish and potatoes

Russia – Goose and suckling pig

Sweden – Herring, ham and meatballs

SPIDERS

There are more than 30,000 species of spiders.

Relative to its size, the ordinary house spider is eight times faster than an Olympic sprinter.

The silk of a spider's web is the strongest natural fibre known to man. Its ability to bear weight is greater than that of steel (relative to its size). However, spider silk is only about 1/200th of a millimetre in diameter and is so light that if a spider could spin a strand around the world it would weigh less than 200 grams.

Spiders cannot be farmed to produce silk commercially – in the way that silkworms can – because they are too antisocial.

When a female spider dies, she is eaten by her babies.

There are some species of spiders where newly-born children eat their mother's legs. Scientists think the mothers sacrifice their legs to stop their children from eating each other.

The black widow spider can devour as many as 20 'mates' in a single day.

The average spider will spin more than 4 miles of silk in a lifetime.

All spiders are carnivorous – that's to say meat-eating. They're also cannibals and will eat other spiders. Their usual diet is flies. A large fly can take up to 12 hours to eat.

The world's biggest spider is the Goliath bird-eating spider. This spider weighs 100 grams and has legs that can grow up 25cm long.

The water spider lives underwater. It uses special hairs to trap air around its body and help it to breathe. The female water spiders build underwater 'diving bell' webs which they fill with air and use for digesting prey.

Spiders can't eat solid food so they have to liquefy their prey before consuming it

Spiders make new webs every day. They don't waste the old ones, though – they roll them up into balls and eat them.

No two spider webs are exactly the same.

As well as web-building and prey-catching, spiders also use their silk to make parachutes as a means of transport.

The weight of insects eaten by spiders every year is greater than the total weight of the entire human population.

The banana spider from Central and South America produces enough venom to kill six adults.

The female black widow spider kills its male mating partner after it's finished with it.

The female nursery web spider sometimes attempts to eat the male after mating. To reduce the risk of this, the male will often present the female with a gift – something like a fly – in the hope that this will satisfy her hunger and that she won't kill him.

The biggest spider in the world weighed 122 grams.

When surprised, a barn spider will bounce up and down in the middle of its web – probably in an attempt to look bigger and therefore more threatening.

All spiders spin silk, but not all make webs.

The female golden silk orb-weaver spider is five times bigger than the male.

Adult cave spiders live in darkness because they can't stand the light. Incredibly, though, their children are strongly attracted to light. It's thought that this has evolved out of necessity to ensure the spread of the species to new areas.

A woman who had recently visited the South America rainforests began to experience severe pains in her left ear, accompanied by headaches, dizziness and constant rustling sounds. It became so serious that exploratory surgery was required, which revealed that a spider had become trapped in her ear. It had eaten through her eardrum and was living within the aural cavity. The rustling sounds were from the spider crawling around inside her skull. The spider's egg sac was also removed.

Unlike other spiders, the crab spider doesn't build webs to trap its prey. Instead, it hunts by ambushing its prey. It'll sit on – or among – flowers, bark, fruit or leaves and wait for visiting insects. Then it pounces.

The bolas spider eats moths but catches them in an unusual way: it fishes for them. Using a sticky strand of silk covered with a substance similar to the pheromone that moths use to attract mates, it dangles its 'line' until moths get stuck to it.

THE NEWEST STATES IN THE USA

Hawaii (joined the Union in August 1959)

Alaska (January 1959)

Arizona (February 1912)

New Mexico (January 1912)

Oklahoma (November 1907)

Utah (January 1896)

Idaho (July 1890)

Wyoming (July 1890)

Montana (November 1889)

Washington (November 1889)

ALL THE LANDLOCKED COUNTRIES IN THE WORLD

Afghanistan, Andorra, Armenia, Austria, Azerbaijan, Belarus, Bhutan, Bolivia, Botswana, Burkina Faso, Burundi, Central African Republic, Chad, Czech Republic, Ethiopia, Hungary, Kazakhstan, Kyrgyzstan, Laos, Lesotho, Liechtenstein, Luxembourg, Macedonia, Malawi, Mali, Moldova, Mongolia, Nepal, Niger, Paraguay, Rwanda, San Marino, Slovakia, Swaziland, Switzerland, Tajikistan, Turkmenistan, Uganda, Uzbekistan, Vatican City, Zambia, Zimbabwe.

SOME BRITISH CHEESES

Ribblesdale Blue Goat

Black Bevon Welsh

Balcombe Brown Ring

Coquetdale

Kidderton Ash

Lord of the Hundreds

Rothbury Red

Village Green Goat

Coverdale

Blacksticks Blue

Goosnargh Gold

Farmhouse Llanboidy

Fine Fettle Yorkshire

Goldilocks

Black Eyed Susan

Golden Cross

Netting Hill Cheese

Dunsyre Blue

Brinkburn

Innkeepers Choice

Radden Blue

Cotherstone

Bonchester

Katy's White Lavender

FRIENDSHIP

'It's not the people you meet in the world – it's the friendships you make on the way.' (Nicole Kidman).

'Friendship is born at that moment when one person says to another: What. You too? I thought I was the only one.' (C.S. Lewis).

'Love demands infinitely less than friendship.' (George Jean Nathan).

'Rare as is true love, true friendship is rarer.' (Jean De La Fontaine).

'Your friends will know you better in the first minute you meet than your acquaintances will know you in a thousand years.' (Richard Bach).

'I always felt that the great high privilege, relief and comfort of friendship was that one had to explain nothing.' (Katherine Mansfield).

'Friendship should be a responsibility, never an opportunity.' (Unknown).

'Be slow to fall into friendship; but when thou art in, continue firm and constant.' (Socrates).

'Friendship is like money, easier made than kept.' (Samuel Butler).

'Friendship is a sheltering tree.' (Samuel Taylor Coleridge).

'Every man passes his life in the search after friendship.' (Ralph Waldo Emerson).

'A friend to all is a friend to none.' (Aristotle).

THE VICTORIA CROSS

The Victoria Cross was first issued on 29 January 1856, in recognition of acts of valour during the Crimean War of 1854–5. It is the highest award for bravery that any British or Commonwealth soldier can receive.

The VC is awarded for 'acts of valour in the face of the enemy'. However, between 1858 and 1881, six were awarded for brave acts 'under circumstances of extreme danger' (rather than 'in the face of the enemy').

The honour for acts of valour that weren't 'in the face of the enemy' is the George Cross, which ranks second to the VC.

Awards of the Victoria Cross are always announced in the pages of the *London Gazette*.

Famously, all VCs are cast from the two bronze cannon that were captured from the Russians at the siege of Sebastopol. However, in his 2006 book, *Bravest of The Brave: The Story of The Victoria Cross*, the historian John Glanfield reveals that this is not true: 'I was astonished,' he has said. 'There was an accepted legend and no one had researched whether it was true. When something has been the belief for 150 years it becomes accepted as the truth.'

A total of 1,355 Victoria Crosses have been awarded since 1856. Three people were awarded the VC twice: Noel Chavasse, Arthur Martin-Leake, both members of the Royal Army Medical Corps, and New Zealander Charles Upham.

Before 1905, the VC couldn't be awarded posthumously. Only one in ten VC recipients in the twentieth century is reckoned to have survived the action for which they received the VC.

Before the twentieth century, it couldn't be awarded to Indian or African troops. Khudadad Khan became the first Indian soldier to get one in 1914.

The largest number of VCs awarded on a single day was 24 on 16 November 1857, for the relief of Lucknow.

The largest number of VCs awarded in a single action was 11 at Rorke's Drift on 22 January 1879 (famously recorded in the film *Zulu*).

The largest number of VCs awarded in a single war or conflict was 634 during World War 1.

Since 1945, the VC has been awarded just 12 times. Four were awarded during the Korean War, one in the Indonesia–Malaysia confrontation in 1965, four to Australians in the Vietnam War, two during the Falklands War in 1982, and one in the Second Gulf War in 2005 (to Private Johnson Beharry).

Flying Officer Lloyd Trigg was the only person ever to be awarded a Victoria Cross on evidence provided *solely* by the enemy (in World War 2). There were no surviving Allied witnesses and the recommendation was made by the captain of the German U-boat sunk by Trigg's aeroplane.

A VC was awarded to the American Unknown Soldier (while the US Medal of Honor was awarded to the British Unknown Warrior).

VCs are highly prized by collectors and can fetch more than £200,000 at auction. The British businessman and former Conservative Party chairman, Lord Ashcroft, has amassed the largest private collection of about one hundred VCs.

IN ANCIENT CHINA

Doctors were paid only if the patient stayed well. If the patient's health got worse, the doctor had to pay the patient.

People committed suicide by eating a pound of salt.

Mouse meat was considered a delicacy.

Anyone caught drunk in public was put to death.

If a monk broke the law, he'd have his neck pierced with a heavy chain which he'd then have to drag behind him.

Any person who attacked a traveller had his nose cut off. This was also the punishment meted out to prisoners-of-war. In fact, it was so common that the Chinese became the first people to go in for plastic surgery to reconstruct noses.

WIMBLEDON

Wimbledon is the world's original tennis tournament.

Two hundred spectators turned up to watch the first championship in 1877, paying one shilling each. The first champion, Spencer Gore, won 12 guineas.

It is Europe's largest single annual sporting catering operation. Some 1,600 catering staff will be on duty.

The crowds consume 17,000 bottles of champagne, 300,000 cups of tea and coffee and 250,000 bottles of water during the fortnight.

Fred Perry (in 1936) was the last Briton to win the Men's Singles Championship – but the UK still holds the record (35) for the most wins.

In World War 2, a bomb fell on Centre Court destroying most of the seating. The Club remained open but was also used by various organizations including the Home Guard.

Only five years have been entirely rain free: 1931, 1976, 1977, 1993 and 1995.

Court 2 is known as 'The Graveyard' because it's proved to be the place where many seeded players have been knocked out.

The club colours, dark green and purple, were introduced in 1909.

Full seeding began in 1927.

Brame Hillyard, in 1930, was the first man to play wearing shorts.

Yellow balls were first used in 1986.

Apart from jumpers/tracksuits etc., all players' clothing at the Wimbledon championships must be predominantly white. No other Grand Slam tournament has such a strict dress code for players.

Every morning of the fortnight, one hour before the gates open, Hamish the hawk is released to ward off the local pigeons.

In 1985, 17-year-old Boris Becker of Germany became the youngest player, the first unseeded player and the first German to win the Men's Singles.

Martina Navratilova holds the record for the most matches played by a woman (326).

Jean Borotra holds the record for the most matches played by a man (223). In 1964, he took part in the Men's Doubles at the age of 65.

Since 2003, the only members of the Royal Family to whom players leaving the court have had to bow or curtsey are the Queen or the Prince of Wales.

In 1952, Frank Sedgman became the first man to be top seeded in all three events (Men's Doubles and Mixed Doubles).

Chairs were first provided for players to sit in between changing ends in 1975.

Since 1949, Singles champions have received miniature versions of the trophies.

Some 42,000 balls are used at the Wimbledon tennis tournament each year. The balls are stored at 20ºC.

There are more than 50,000 shrubs and plants planted in the All England Club grounds.

Jimmy Connors was seeded a record seventeen times between 1973 and 1989 in the Singles championships.

Lindsay Davenport, 1999 Ladies Singles Champion, is the tallest lady to compete at Wimbledon at 6'2". At 4' 9", Gem Hoahing, who played in the late 1930s, was the shortest.

The first TV coverage of a Wimbledon match was in 1937.

In 1920, the French tennis player Suzanne Lenglen won all three Wimbledon titles (the singles, the doubles and the mixed doubles) without dropping a single set.

There are 375 full members of the All England Lawn Tennis and Croquet Club, plus a number of honorary members, including past Singles Champions.

Margaret Court, Chris Evert, Steffi Graf, Billie-Jean King, Suzanne Lenglen, Helen Wills Moody and Martina Navratilova are the only women listed as 'legends' on Wimbledon's offical web site.

Roger Federer (1998), Pat Cash (1982), Ivan Lendl (1978) and Björn Borg (1972) all won Boys' Singles titles.

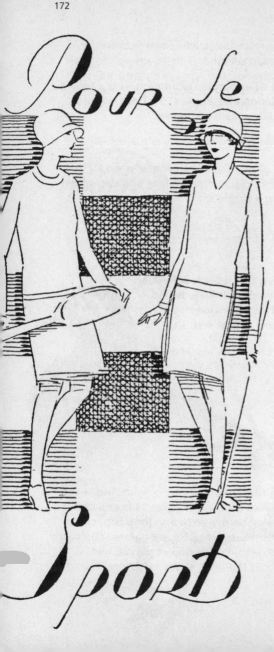

Martina Hingis (1994), Annabel Croft (1984), Tracy Austin (1978) and Ann Jones (as Ann Haydon in 1956) all won Girls' Singles titles.

In 2001, Goran Ivanisevic became the first wild-card entrant to win a singles' title.

There are 375 full members of the All England Lawn Tennis and Croquet Club, plus a number of honorary members, including past Singles Champions.

St Leger Goold was runner-up in the 1879 Wimbledon Men's Singles Championship. In 1907, he was convicted of a brutal murder and sent to the notorious Devil's Island penal colony off French Guiana where he died two years later.

In 1946, the French tennis player Yvon Petra was extremely fortunate to find himself playing at

Wimbledon – or, indeed, anywhere. He had been seriously wounded during the war and seemed likely to lose his leg but for the skill of a German surgeon (he had been captured) who saved the limb. Incredibly, Petra recovered from that injury and not only competed at Wimbledon in 1946 but actually won that year's Men's Singles Championship.

Richard Williams survived the sinking of the *Titanic* in 1912 and went on to win the Wimbledon Men's Doubles title in 1920.

A wooden racket was last used at Wimbledon in 1987.

Although men had worn shorts at Wimbledon since 1930, in 1933, the British tennis player Bunny Austin became the first man to wear shorts (albeit very long shorts) on Centre Court.

The world's longest competitive tennis match took place at Wimbledon in 2010 when the American player John Isner beat the Frenchman Nicolas Mahut after playing for 11 hours and 5 minutes over 3 days. The reason it went on so long is because in the final set, a player must win by two clear games. The score in their final set was 70–68 – that's 138 games played over 8 hours 11 minutes – making it the longest set in history in both time and games.

TRANSPLANT FIRSTS

First cornea transplant: 1905

First liver transplant: 1963

First pancreas transplant: 1966

First heart transplant: 1967

First heart–liver transplant: 1984

First heart–liver–kidney transplant: 1989

First hand transplant: 1998

First face transplant: 2005

SOME ALTERNATIVE COMPUTER ACRONYMS

WWW – World Wide Wait

EMAIL – Endure Mailshots And Idiotic Letters

MICROSOFT – Most Intelligent Consumers Realize Our Software Only Fools Toddlers

APPLE – Arrogance Produces Profit-Losing Entity

WINDOWS – Will Install Needless Data On Whole System

ISDN – It Still Does Nothing

CD-ROM – Computer Device – Rendered Obsolete in Months

MSN – Massive Spamming Network

IBM – I Blame Microsoft

NAMES WALT DISNEY CONSIDERED AND REJECTED FOR SNOW WHITE'S DWARFS

Gloomy, Wheezy, Shirty, Sniffy, Woeful, Weepy, Lazy, Snoopy, Puffy, Shorty, Baldy, Biggo-Ego, Burpy, Gabby, Jumpy, Nifty, Stubby, Stuffy.

ELEPHANTS

Elephants sleep for about two hours per day.

An elephant's trunk has 40,000 muscles but no bone.

Elephants are not afraid of mice.

Botswana has the largest population of elephants in the world.

Elephants are an important part of Sri Lankan culture. They are decorated for religious processions and their images appear in temples and palaces.

There's an elephant orphanage in Sri Lanka.

Elephants eat their mother's dung, which contains essential gut flora.

Elephant polo is played in Nepal, Sri Lanka, India and Thailand.

Elephants walk on tiptoe – the back of the foot is made up of fat and no bone.

The brain of an African elephant weighs 7.5 kilograms – which is 0.15 per cent of the animal's total body weight. The brain of an adult human weighs 1.3–1.4 kilograms, which is about 2 per cent of total body weight.

Elephants are covered with hair. You cannot see it from a distance, but at close range it is possible to see the thin coat of light hairs that covers the animal's body.

An African elephant eats more than 200 kilograms of twigs, leaves, grass and fruit a day.

Elephant herds post their own sentries. When danger threatens, the sentry raises its trunk and the rest of the herd is alerted.

Elephants communicate in sound waves below the frequency that humans can hear.

Elephants are 70 per cent water.

An elephant produces about 20 kilos of dung a day.

At birth an Asian elephant weighs around 200 kilograms, and an African elephant weighs 264 kilograms. By adulthood, both types of elephants will weigh close to 4 tons.

An elephant's ears weigh more than 45 kilograms each.

An elephant's trunk is strong enough to tear a tree out of the ground, nimble enough to untie a knot and sensitive enough to smell water 3 miles away.

Both male and female African elephants have tusks, but only male Asian elephants do.

The elephant's closest relative is the hyrax, which is found in the Middle East and Africa. The tiny creature is about 30cm long. Like its gigantic cousin, the hyrax has hoofed toes and a two-chambered stomach for digesting a vegetable diet.

Elephants use leafy branches and plant stalks as fly swatters.

Tusks grow throughout an elephant's life.

To keep from damaging its skeleton, which is supporting as much weight as it can, an African elephant has to move sedately, never jumping or running. The 'charge' of these animals is a fast walk, at about 15 miles per hour.

Elephants greet returning members of their group by spinning round, flapping their ears and trumpeting.

Besides humans, the only animal that can stand on its head is the elephant.

TRIAL AND PUNISHMENT (ELEPHANT)

In 1903, Topsy was a tame elephant that worked at the circus in Coney Island. However, she killed three men (one of whom was a cruel trainer who'd tried to feed her a lit cigarette). Topsy's owners decided that she should be killed. This would be unremarkable but for the fact that they also decided to execute her as a murderer (or, I suppose, murderess).

Having made that decision, they then had to work out how to carry it out. At first, they thought of hanging her but the American Society for the Prevention of Cruelty to Animals (the equivalent of our RSPCA) protested, and so they settled on electrocution, a means of execution used on human murderers since 1890.

So, in front of a crowd of over a thousand people, poor old Topsy was fed carrots laced with poison before more than 6,000 volts were sent through her body. She was dead in seconds. There was even a film made of the whole grisly event.

When Coney Island burned down in 1911, the fire was referred to as 'Topsy's Revenge'.

In 2003, a memorial for Topsy was put up at the Coney Island Museum.

BORN ON THE VERY SAME DAY AS ANOTHER CELEBRITY DIED

Heath Ledger and Ali Bhutto – 4.4.1979

Dougray Scott and Dame Myra Hess – 25.11.1965

Richie McCaw and Marshall McLuhan – 31.12.1980

Emma Watson and Greta Garbo – 15.4.1990

Ian Poulter and Howlin' Wolf – 10.1.1976

Daniel Carter and John Belushi – 5.3.1982

Channing Tatum and Dame Cicely Courtneidge – 26.4.1980

François Steyn and Rita Hayworth – 14.5.1987

Lionel Messi and Jackie Gleason – 24.6.1987

Julian Assange and Jim Morrison – 3.7.1971

Robin Söderling and J.B. Priestley – 14.8.1984

Tom Hollander and Paul Muni – 25.8.1967

Stacey Solomon and Graham Chapman – 4.10.1989

Stephen Fry and Ronald Knox – 24.8.1957

Donnie Wahlberg and Mies van der Rohe – 17.8.1969

Davy Crockett and Frederick the Great – 17.8.1786

Richard Stilgoe and Sergei Rachmaninov – 28.3.1943

Billie Jean King and Lorenz Hart – 22.11.1943

Laura Dern and Billy Rose – 10.2.1966

Bryan Ferry and Bela Bartok – 26.9.1945

Georges Seurat and John Brown – 2.12.1859

Kevin Costner and George Morrow – 18.1.1955

Kian Egan and Sir Alfred Hitchcock – 29.4.80

Rutger Hauer and Edvard Munch – 23.1.1944

Phil Collins and C.B. Cochran – 31.1.1951

Peter Willey and Leadbelly – 6.12.1949

Colin Jackson and Robert Oppenheimer – 18.2.1967

Debra Winger and James Agee – 16.5.1955

Candice Bergen and Booth Tarkington – 19.5.1946

Mark Goodier and Carl Jung – 6.6.1961

Mike Tyson and Margery Allingham – 30.6.1966

Peter De Savary and Lucien Pissarro – 11.7.1944

Alan Mullery and P.C. Wren – 23.11.1941

Julio Iglesias and Elinor Glyn – 23.9.1943

Chris Cowdrey and Jack Buchanan – 20.10.1957

Daniel Ortega and Jerome Kern – 11.11.1945

Jack Simmons and Virginia Woolf – 28.3.1941

Anthea Redfern and Ernest Bevin – 14.4.1951

Che Guevara and Emmeline Pankhurst – 14.6.1928

Christina Aguilera and Ben Travers – 18.12.80

Julia Ormond and T.S. Eliot – 4.1.65

Imogen Stubbs and Percy Grainger – 20.2.61

Rosemarie Ford and George Formby – 6.3.61

Jerome Flynn and William Henry Beveridge – 16.3.63

Clyde Barrow and J.M. Synge – 24.3.09

Srinivas Venkataraghavan and John Maynard Keynes – 21.4.46

Cheryl Gillan and Sir Stafford Cripps – 21.4.52

Jane Goldman and Alexander Kerensky – 11.6.70

Valerie Brisco-Hooks and Aneurin Bevan – 6.7.60

Georgi Kinkladze and Otto Klemperer – 6.7.73

Mickey Rourke and Hilaire Belloc – 16.7.53

Andi Peters and Sir John Barbirolli – 29.7.70

Anna Massey and Edith Wharton – 11.8.37

Jonathan Powell and Bertolt Brecht – 14.8.56

Gus Macdonald and Leon Trotsky – 20.8.40

Jarvis Cocker and Sir David Low – 19.9.63

Janeane Garofalo and Harpo Marx – 28.9.64

Ann Widdecombe and Max Planck – 4.10.47

Oliver North and Margaret Radclyffe Hall – 7.10.43

George Cohen and Zane Grey – 23.10.39

Stephen Rea and Max Reinhardt – 31.10.43

Larry Mullen Jr and Augustus John – 31.10.61

Leonardo DiCaprio and Cyril Connolly – 11.11.74

**Robert F. Kennedy and
Queen Alexandra – 20.11.25**

Mary Archer and Harry Langdon – 22.12.44

**Christopher Frayling and
W.C. Fields – 25.12.46**

Jay Kay and Trygve Lie – 30.12.68

LEFT SCHOOL WITHOUT ANY QUALIFICATIONS

Jack Osbourne

Tamara Beckwith

Robert Carlyle

Catherine Zeta-Jones

Jonathan Cainer

Delia Smith

Max Clifford

Debbie Moore

Sir Philip Green

Sam Torrance

Pete Waterman

Richard Briers

Sir Peter Ustinov

SOCCER (1)

It's a well-known fact that the record score for a British (professional) soccer match is Arbroath 36, Bon Accord 0. It's an amazing score but what's *really* incredible about it is that *on the very same day and in the very same competition* – 12 September 1885, the Scottish Cup – Dundee Harp beat Aberdeen Rovers 35–0. It was the Dundee Harp captain – a former Arbroath player – who got the news after he sent his former team a telegram to boast about the (what he thought was) record score. But the drama doesn't end there. According to the referee in the Dundee Harp vs Aberdeen Rovers game, the final score was 37–0 but the club secretary of Dundee Harp – the winning team, remember – reckoned that it was only 35–0 so the ref went with the lower figure.

In 1908, a Newcastle United fan named Gladstone Adams drove all the way down to Wembley to see his team play in the FA Cup final. It was such a novelty to see a car in those days that it was put into a car showroom window while he was at the game because so many people wanted to see it. On the long way home, snow kept getting on the windscreen which meant that Adams had to keep getting out of the car to clear it. This experience led him to invent the windscreen wiper which he patented three years later.

Antonio Carbajal, the Mexican goalkeeper, is the only man to play in five World Cups (in the final stages) – from 1950–1966. It earned him the nickname 'El Cinco Copas' (The Five Cups).

A yo-yo club is one that's always getting promoted and then relegated again soon afterwards. According to statistics, Birmingham City have been promoted and relegated to and from the top division more times than any other English club with 12 promotions (1894, 1901, 1903, 1921, 1948, 1955, 1972, 1980, 1985, 2002, 2007 and 2009) and 11 relegations (1896, 1902, 1908, 1939, 1950, 1965, 1979, 1984, 1986, 2006 and 2008), including a run of four annual consecutive promotions/ relegations from the 2005–6 season to the 2008–9 season.

Sir Stanley Matthews is the oldest ever soccer international. He was over 42 when he played for England against Denmark in 1957. He was fifty when he played his final game for Stoke City in 1965 making him, by far, not only the oldest man to play in top flight football (Stoke were then in the First Division – the equivalent of today's Premier League) but also the oldest man to appear in a professional football match in Britain.

Leslie Compton became the oldest player to make his debut for the England football team when he played against Wales in 1950 at the age of 38 years and 2 months.

James Gordon of Rangers was selected to play for the club in all eleven positions, including goalkeeper, during his career at Ibrox Park from 1910 to 1930.

In a 1964 international football match, 350 fans died in a riot after an equalizer by Peru was disallowed. Afterwards, the referee said, 'Anyone can make a mistake'.

The first League match to be played under floodlights was between Portsmouth and Newcastle on 22 February 1956. The game was held up for 30 minutes when the fuses failed.

In 2003, Sunderland, at home to Charlton Athletic, scored three own-goals in just over half-an-hour. Stephen Wright put through his own goal after 24 minutes, Mark Proctor after 29 minutes, and Proctor did so again in the 31st minute. Statistics showed that Charlton were leading 3–0 without having had a single shot on target.

One of the most unusual injuries in the history of the World Cup occurred in the very first tournament in 1930. In the semi-final between the US and Argentina, the American trainer ran onto the pitch to attend an injured player and dropped his medicine box, breaking a bottle of chloroform. He inhaled the fumes and fell straight to the ground and had to be stretchered off the field. The injured player recovered without any treatment.

The first game in each of the football World Cups of 1966, 1970, 1974 and 1978 finished in a goalless draw. In other words, there were no goals scored in 360 minutes of football.

The Czech team that reached the 1934 World Cup final contained players from just two clubs.

In 1922–23, Southampton finished mid-table in Division Two (what would now be the Championship); their record read won 14, drawn 14, lost 14, goals for 40, goals against 40, 42 points from 42 matches. During the season Southampton were awarded four penalties and conceded four penalties.

During a 1936 match between Chesterfield and Burnley, the Chesterfield striker Walter Ponting fired a shot which beat the opposition goalkeeper only for the ball to burst and fail to cross the goal-line.

In 1973, three Notts County players missed the same penalty in a game against Portsmouth. The original penalty was missed but was ordered to be retaken because the goalkeeper had moved (an offence then as the goalkeeper was obliged to stand absolutely still). The second attempt, by a different player, was also missed but the referee ordered it to be retaken because he adjudged that a Portsmouth player had encroached into the penalty area. The third attempt, by a third Notts County player, was placed wide of the goal.

In the 1950 World Cup, the USA beat England 1–0. Many British newspapers couldn't believe the scoreline and so printed the result as 10–1 to England.

In the 1974 Spurs vs Burnley match, both Mike England and John Pratt scored goals against their team in the first half (i.e. own goals) and goals *for* their team in the second half.

The goalkeeper of Turkish team Orduspor was given a £50 bonus in 1980 after his team lost 4–0. Normally he let in twice as many goals.

The quickest booking in a Football League/Premiership match was after just *five* seconds. The culprit? Vinnie Jones playing for Sheffield United against Manchester City. He was booked again later in the match and was therefore sent off.

ALL THE CLUBS TO HAVE FINISHED RUNNERS-UP WITHOUT EVER WINNING THE PREMIER LEAGUE (OR THE OLD FIRST DIVISION) TITLE

Bristol City (1906/7)

Oldham Athletic (1914/15)

Cardiff City (1923/24)

Leicester City (1928/29)

Charlton Athletic (1936/37)

Blackpool (1955/56)

QPR (1975/76)

Watford (1982/83)

Southampton (1983/84)

PEOPLE WHO CHANGED THEIR NAMES

Frank Skinner (Chris Collins)

Shane Richie (Shane Roche)

Simon Pegg (Simon Beckingham)

Graham Norton (Graham Walker)

Whoopi Goldberg (Caryn Johnson)

Billy Idol (William Broad)

Cheryl Baker (Rita Crudgington)

Michael Crawford (Michael Dumble-Smith)

Elaine Paige (Elaine Bickerstaff)

Elle Macpherson (Eleanor Gow)

Sir Tom Jones (Thomas Woodward)

Demi Moore (Demetria Guynes)

Georgie Fame (Clive Powell)

Siouxsie Sioux (Susan Ballion)

Sir Cliff Richard (Harry Webb)

Winona Ryder (Winona Horowitz)

Jane Seymour (Joyce Frankenberg)

Christian Slater (Christian Hawkins)

Sir Michael Caine (Maurice Micklewhite)

Manfred Mann (Michael Lubowitz)

Sigourney Weaver (Susan Weaver – took the name from her favourite book: *The Great Gatsby*)

Elvis Costello (Declan McManus)

Dame Julie Andrews (Julia Wells)

Bobby Davro (Robert Nankeville)

Mel Brooks (Melvin Kaminsky)

Charles Aznavour (Shahnour Aznourian)

Iggy Pop (James Osterburg)

Diane Keaton (Diane Hall)

Gary Numan (Gary Webb)

Les Dennis (Leslie Heseltine)

Jennifer Jason Leigh (Jennifer Morrow)

Paul Jones (Paul Pond)

Nicolas Cage (Nicholas Coppola)

Adam Ant (Stewart Goddard)

Helen Mirren (Helen Mironoff)

Mica Paris (Michelle Wallen)

Janis Ian (Janis Fink)

Chris de Burgh (Christopher Davidson)

Lou Reed (Louis Firbank)

Donna Summer (Donna Gaines)

David Essex (David Cook)

Axl Rose (William Bailey)

Seal (Sealhenry Samuel – his first name comes from his Brazilian father's custom of having the grandparents choose the name (they wanted Seal) coupled with his parents' fascination with British royalty (they selected Henry)

SNAILS

The average garden snail has a top speed of 0.03 miles per hour.

When a snail hatches from an egg, it is a miniature adult, complete with shell. The shell grows as the snail does.

Snails can live for up to ten years.

A snail breathes through its foot.

A snail has two pairs of tentacles on its head. One pair is longer than the other and houses the eyes. The shorter pair is used for smelling and feeling its way around.

Most snails are hermaphrodites, meaning they have both female and male reproductive organs.

A snail will sometimes eat another snail. It does so by drilling a hole in the shell of the snail.

The giant African snail grows to 30 centimetres long and can weigh more than 500 grams – which is heavier than the world's smallest dog.

A snail has about 25,000 teeth.

A snail's reproductive organs are in its head.

The average French person eats 500 snails a year.

GENUINE PRODUCTS

I'm So Sorry Please Forgive Me (Swiss chocolate bar)

Atum Bom (Portuguese tinned tuna)

Bimbo (Mexican biscuits)

Kevin (French aftershave)

Polio (Czech detergent)

Vaccine (Dutch aftershave)

Flirt (Austrian cigarettes)

Meltykiss (Japanese chocolate)

Naked (New Zealand fruit and nut bar)

Noisy (French butter)

Happy (Swedish chocolate)

Prison (Ugandan body spray)

Barf (Iranian detergent powder)

Pee (Ghanaian cola)

SOME EXPLANATIONS OF BRAND NAMES

Harpic: from the first three letters of the first name and surname of the man who developed it – Harry Pickup.

Ryvita: from the word 'rye' and the Latin for life, 'vita'.

Findus: from the words 'fruit industries' (i.e. F and Indus).

7-Up: named by the inventor who had already rejected six names for his product.

Mazda: named after the Persian god of light.

Hovis: derives its name from the Latin words 'hominis vis' meaning 'man's strength'.

Lego: from the Danish words *leg godt* meaning 'play well'.

CROCODILES

Crocodiles carry their young in their mouths.

From crocodile farms, Australia exports about 5,000 crocodile skins a year. Most go to Paris, where a crocodile purse can sell for more than $10,000.

The Nile crocodile lives for about 45 years in the wild, and up to 80 years in captivity.

A baby crocodile is three times as long as the egg it has hatched from.

The saltwater crocodile – kills people because it is fast in and out of water. It can outrun a galloping horse and it kills in seconds.

A crocodile can run at speeds of 11 miles per hour.

A crocodile cannot move its jaws from side to side and so cannot chew. It bites off a lump of food with a snap of its jaws and then swallows it whole.

A crocodile can't stick out its tongue. This is a means of self-protection. With its sharp teeth and powerful jaws it would bite off its own tongue.

The saltwater crocodile is the biggest crocodile.

Thailand is home to the biggest crocodile farm in the world.

The ancient Egyptians bought jewellery for their pet crocodiles.

Crocodiles can't chew. They swallow and digest their food whole.

More people are killed in Africa by crocodiles than by lions.

Large crocodiles feed on smaller crocs, not just for the food but also to keep down the crocodile population and so, by limiting the number of crocodiles challenging them for the same prey, preserve their food supply.

NOT SO!

Leaves **don't** change colour in autumn. They look green because they contain chlorophyll. When the leaf dies, the chlorophyll disappears and the other colours, which were there all along, emerge.

Nero **didn't** fiddle while Rome burned.

Handling frogs **doesn't** cause warts.

The Vikings **never** wore horned helmets.

There are **no** igloos in Alaska.

Bats are **not** blind, do **not** become entangled in human hair, and **seldom** transmit disease to other animals or humans.

Dinosaur droppings **aren't** rare – in fact, they're actually fairly common.

A man uses **more** energy shaving with a hand razor at a sink (because of the water power, the water pump and so on) than he would by using an electric razor.

Caligula **didn't** make his horse a consul.

LOST IN TRANSLATION

According to a poll of a thousand translators, the most untranslatable word in the world is ILUNGA, from the Bantu language of Tshiluba, and means a person ready to forgive an abuse the first time, tolerate it the second time, but neither the third time. The runners-up were:

SHLIMAZL
Yiddish for a chronically unlucky person.

RADIOUKACZ
Polish for a person who worked as a telegrapher for the resistance movements on the Soviet side of the Iron Curtain.

NAA
A Japanese word used only in the Kansai area of Japan for emphasis or to agree with someone.

ALTAHMAM
Arabic for a kind of deep sadness.

GEZELLIG
Dutch for an atmosphere or feeling that is cosy.

SAUDADE
Portuguese for a certain type of longing.

SELATHIRUPAVAR
Tamil for a certain type of truancy.

POCHEMUCHKA
Russian for a particular kind of person who asks a lot of questions.

KLLOSHAR
Albanian, for something like 'loser'.

FASCINATING FACTS (1)

The modern city of Budapest was once two separate cities: Buda and Pest.

In 1657, a Japanese priest decided to burn a kimono because he thought it carried bad luck. A fire resulted that led to the destruction of over ten thousand buildings and the death of a hundred thousand people. Guess the priest was right: the kimono was unlucky.

At the turn of the nineteenth century, Azerbaijan was producing half of all the world's oil.

Ethiopia celebrated the dawn of the new millennium in September 2007.

In a book entitled *Civilisation and its Discontents*, Sigmund Freud wrote that civilisation only became possible when men resisted the urge to put out their camp fires by peeing on them. In other words, they had to be able to look into the future and realize that they would want a fire the next day rather than only satisfying the short-term urge to pee on a fire.

Old-fashioned Chinese typewriters have 5,700 characters.

A five and a half year old girl who wasn't able to sweat, weighed 113 kilos. She was put on display at an exhibition in Vienna in 1894.

The largest lake in the world is the Caspian Sea. (The largest lake-that-isn't-really-a-sea is Lake Superior.)

In 1967, there was a case of a man with 12,568 boils on his body. No part of his skin was left uncovered by boils. The largest boil measured was 9 cm in diameter. That's 3cm short of being the same size as a CD.

In 1848, a railroad worker named Phineas P. Gage was working with some dynamite that exploded unexpectedly. A metre-long iron bar weighing six kgs went straight through his brain. He remained conscious, but couldn't see out of his left eye. After a while his sight returned and he fully recovered, although many people who knew him said his personality changed and that he became lazy and irritable. Mind you, he was entitled to, wasn't he?

There's a monastery in Ethiopia that can only be entered by climbing up a rope dropped over the side of a cliff.

In 1981, a man named Mr Bedlow consumed 5.8kg of earwax. His target was 6kg but he puked it all up before he could succeed.

Fiji is right on top of the International Date Line which has been bent round to accommodate Fiji's understandable desire to have its whole country living in the same day.

A Russian scientist tried to cross-breed humans with apes to create the Humanzee. This was, fortunately for both species, unsuccessful. However, another Russian scientist did succeed in creating a two-headed dog.

A map of South America sold in Peru differs from one sold in Ecuador. There's a dispute between the countries as to who owns the area around the Amazon headwater.

Graca Machel, born in Mozambique, married the presidents of two different countries. She was married to Samora Machel, the President of Mozambique, until his death in 1986. Then in 1998, she married Nelson Mandela, the President of South Africa.

People who make world maps hate Montenegro because it's so hard to fit the whole name of the country on to such a small space on the map.

There are places in Egypt where it's free to use the toilet, but you have to bring or buy your own toilet paper.

Montezuma, Aztec Emperor of Mexico, drank up to 50 glasses of chocolate a day.

There was once an undersea post office in the Bahamas.

Since the eighteenth century it has been illegal for the bull to be killed in Portuguese bullfighting – while in Costa Rican bullfights, the bull often wins.

There was a Zambian President who threatened to resign unless the people stopped drinking so much alcohol.

There was a person in Yemen who had four kidneys.

Dubai is home to the world's most advanced artificial ski centre. It's just under three thousand square metres and they use real snow. It even snows inside.

In Bolivia, the voting age is 18 for married citizens but 21 for single people.

In 1969, there was a week-long war between El Salvador and Honduras. It was called the Soccer War because it started at a football match (which El Salvador won). Of course, the football riot was just the trigger for tension that had built up between the two countries for a couple of years. But a lot of people thought that the war was just over a football match. Incidentally it was a World Cup qualifying match which El Salvador won. It wasn't worth a war though because they both ended up getting knocked out in the first round of the 1970 World Cup.

The Tonle Sap river in Cambodia flows north for one half of the year and then south for the other half.

From 1990–2000, Alberto Fujimori was President of Peru – even though he had dual nationality (Peruvian and Japanese – both his parents were Japanese). After his presidency, he was sent to jail for six years for 'abuse of power'.

The three wealthiest families in the world have more assets than the combined wealth of the 48 poorest nations.

Because he felt matches should be public property, English chemist John Walker never patented his invention.

More than 25 per cent of the world's forests are in Siberia.

The largest swimming pool in the world is in the Chilean resort of San Alfonso del Mar. It's a kilometre long and 35 metres deep.

The Cairo Opera House was destroyed by fire in 1970. Unfortunately, the Cairo fire station was located inside the same building.

St George, the patron saint of England, never actually visited England.

The world record for skimming stones across the water is 51 skips.

In 1924, the French Boxing Federation banned boxers from kissing each other at the end of a contest.

In 1977, a 13-year-old child found a tooth growing out of his left foot.

The capital of San Marino, the city of San Marino, isn't the largest city in San Marino. Dogana is.

The most pushups ever performed in one day was 46,001.

There are so many vehicles in Hong Kong that if they were all on the road at the same time they wouldn't fit on the roads.

Just over a hundred people in Scotland own almost a third of the country's land.

In medieval Japan, when men wished to seal an agreement, they urinated together, crisscrossing their streams of urine.

The men who served as guards along the Great Wall of China in the Middle ages were often born on the wall, grew up there, married there, died there and were buried within it. Many of these guards never left the wall in their entire lives.

At the height of its popularity in Japan, the arcade game Space Invaders caused a nationwide coin shortage.

In Taiwan, drunk-drivers are given the option of playing Mah Jong with the elderly instead of paying a fine.

PATRON SAINTS

Animals and Birds: **Francis of Assisi**

Archaeologists and Librarians: **Jerome**

Architects and Miners: **Barbara**

Artists: **Luke**

Astronauts: **Joseph of Cupertino**

Astronomers: **Dominic**

Athletes: **Sebastian**

Authors and Journalists: **Francis de Sales**

Bankers: **Matthew**

Basket-makers: **Antony of Egypt**

Beekeepers: **Bernard**

Blacksmiths: **Dunstan**

Booksellers: **John of God**

Boyscouts: **George**

Children: **Nicholas**

Comedians and Dancers: **Vitus**

Cooks: **Lawrence**

Dentists: **Apollonia**

Engineers: **Ferdinand**

Firefighters: **Agatha**

Fishermen: **Andrew**

Florists: **Rose of Lima**

Gravediggers: **Antony**

Hairdressers (women): **Mary Magdalen**

Hairdressers (men): **Martin de Porres**

Messengers and Television workers: **Gabriel**

Mountaineers: **Bernard of Montjoux**

Policemen: **Michael**

Scientists: **Albert the Great**

Secretaries: **Genesius**

Singers: **Cecilia**

Students: **Thomas Aquinas**

Taxi drivers: **Fiacre**

PIGS

Pigs are the cleanest farm animals. They will even take a shower if one is available.

If a pig is sick it stops curling its tail.

Although the Jewish religion forbids the eating of pork, there are 30 pig farms in Israel.

In France, it used to be forbidden to call a pig Napoleon.

By the age of six months, a baby pig will have increased its weight 7,000 times.

Besides humans, the only animal that can suffer sunburn is the pig.

The oldest pig in the world lived to the age of 68.

The largest pig on record was a Poland-China hog named Big Bill, which weighed 1160 kgs.

The trial and punishment of animals was especially common in France. The reason why pigs were so often on trial is because in the Middle Ages, they were allowed to wander freely around French villages – sometimes with disastrous consequences.

Here are some examples:

1266: In Fontenay-Aux Roses, near Paris, a pig convicted of having eaten a child was publicly burned.

1386: In Falaise, a sow was accused of killing a baby in its crib. Awaiting trial, the sow was placed in a (human) prison cell. The court heard evidence that the sow had torn the baby's face and arms and decided to apply the Biblical law of "an eye for an eye". So they ordered the sow to be mangled and maimed in the head and forelegs (the equivalent to its arms) and then to be hanged. To make the execution as realistic as possible, the sow was dressed in a man's clothes and hanged in the public square as a human being would have been.

1457: In Savigny, France, a sow killed a five-year-old boy and ate him, with her six piglets joining in. The sow was put on trial, found guilty and was condemned to be hanged by her hind legs until dead. But what about the piglets? The court decided that there was a lack of proof that they had helped to kill the child (i.e. that they were their mother's 'accomplices') and, taking into account that they were young and only following their mother, they were acquitted.

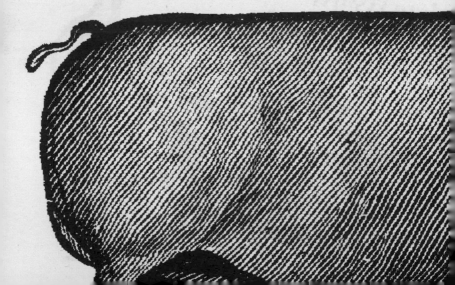

1463: In Amiens, France, two pigs were sentenced to be buried alive because they had "torn and eaten with their teeth a little child...who for this cause passed from life to death".

1497: In Charonne, France, a sow ate the chin of a child. The court condemned the sow to death – by a blow on the head. So far, so fair but they didn't stop there. They ordered that the sow's flesh be cut into pieces and fed to dogs, and that the sow's owner and his wife go "on a pilgrimage to Notre-Dame of Pontoise on the day of Pentecost".

1557: In the Commune of Saint-Quentin, a pig was condemned to be "buried all alive ... for having devoured a little child".

1799: In Woodbridge, England, a judge found two pigs guilty of digging up and eating a corpse. The pigs were sentenced to death by drowning.

IMMORTALIZED IN SONG TITLES

Jennifer Lopez (Xiu Xiu)

Ray Liotta (Linoleum)

Tom Courtenay (Yo La Tengo)

Clark Gable (The Postal Service)

Lulu – *It's Lulu* (The Boo Radleys)

Levi Stubbs – Levi Stubbs' Tears (Billy Bragg)

Pablo Picasso (Jonathan Richman)

Brian Wilson (Barenaked Ladies)

Clint Eastwood (Gorillaz)

Joan Crawford (Blue Oyster Cult)

Donovan (The Happy Mondays)

Joan of Arc (Leonard Cohen)

Louis Walsh (The Revs)

Mischa Barton (Rozino Smith)

David Duchovny (Bree Sharp)

Natalie Portman (Team Sleep and Ozma)

John Kettley – *John Kettley Is A Weatherman* (Tribe of Toffs)

Kevin Carter (The Manic Street Preachers)

VEGETARIANS

Willem Dafoe, Russell Brand, Leona Lewis, Fearne Cotton, Joss Stone, Clint Eastwood, Jack Johnson, Dave Gorman, Kate Winslet, Cillian Murphy, Orlando Bloom, Brian May, Chris Martin, Kelly Osbourne, Anne Hathaway, Jared Leto, Robert Redford, Christian Bale, Leonard Cohen, Jamie Lee Curtis, Bryce Dallas Howard, Oliver Stone, Brad Pitt, Claudia Schiffer, Morrissey, Andy Serkis, Samuel L. Jackson, Jason Orange, Joan Armatrading, Sean Hughes, Martin Kemp, Paul McGann, Sandie Shaw, Jenny Seagrove, Siouxsie Sioux, Kirsty Wade, Tony Benn, Howard Goodall, Tracy Ward, Baroness Ruth Rendell, Clare Francis, Smokey Robinson, Alan Davies, Amanda Holden, Anna Paquin, Forest Whitaker, Janeane Garofalo, Joanna Lumley, John Cleese, Josh Hartnett, Juliet Stevenson, Mena Suvari, Naomi Watts, Natalie Imbruglia, Ricky Martin, Sadie Frost, Shannon Elizabeth.

UNUSUAL DEATHS

Chrysippus (philosopher): In 207AD, he is believed to have died of laughter after watching his drunken donkey try to eat figs.

Attila the Hun (warrior): In 453, he bled to death from a nosebleed on his wedding night.

The Duke of Clarence (royal): In 1478, he died after (reportedly) falling into a barrel of wine.

Pope Adrian VI: In 1523, the only Dutchman ever to be Pope, choked to death after a fly got stuck in his throat as he was taking a drink from a fountain.

Sir Francis Bacon (philosopher and statesman): In 1626, he died from pneumonia caught from experimenting with freezing a chicken by stuffing it with snow.

William Huskisson (politician): In 1830, he became the first person to be killed by a train. The accident happened when he was attending the opening of the Liverpool–Manchester Railway. As he stepped on the track to meet the Duke of Wellington, Stephenson's Rocket hit him.

Allan Pinkerton (detective): In 1884, he died of gangrene as a result of biting his tongue after stumbling on the pavement.

King Alexander I of Greece: In 1920, he died from blood poisoning after being bitten by his gardener's pet monkey.

Frank Hayes (jockey): In 1923, he died from a heart attack during a race. His horse went on to finish first – making him the only dead jockey to win a race.

Isadora Duncan (dancer): In 1927, she was strangled when her scarf was caught in the spokes of a car's wheel.

Jerome Napoleon Bonaparte (the last member of the famous Bonaparte family): In 1945, he died of the injuries he got after tripping over his dog's lead.

Alex Mitchell (bricklayer): In 1975, he died laughing at a sketch on the TV show *The Goodies*.

Tennessee Williams (playwright): In 1983, he choked to death on a nose-spray bottle cap that dropped into his mouth while he was using the spray.

Garry Hoy (lawyer): In 1993, he died after throwing himself through the glass wall on the 24th floor of the Toronto-Dominion Centre in order to prove the glass was 'unbreakable'. It wasn't.

PEOPLE WHO GAVE THEIR NAMES TO THINGS

Laszlo Bíro – Biro

Count Stroganoff – Beef Stroganoff

Louis Antoine de Bougainville – Bougainvillea

Charles Boycott – Boycott

Louis Braille – Braille

Robert Bunsen – Bunsen Burner

Edmund Clerihew Bentley – Clerihew

Rudolf Diesel – Diesel

Commodore Benedict – Eggs Benedict

George Ferris – Ferris Wheel

Sir William Gage – Greengage

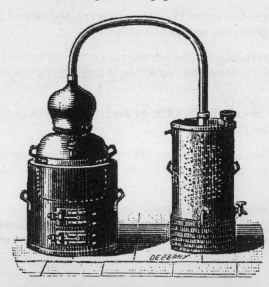

DEBERNY

Jules Léotard – Leotard

Ned Ludd – Luddite

John Macadam – Macadamia nut

Colonel Jean Martinet – Martinet

Samuel Maverick – Maverick

Franz Mesmer – Mesmerize

Jean Nicot – Nicotine

Anna Pavlova – Pavlova

Adolphe Sax – Saxophone

Earl Silas Tupper – Tupperware

CREATURES AND THE NAMES WE GIVE TO THEIR OFFSPRING

Ant – antling

Alligator – hatchling

Badger – cub

Barn owl – owlet

Beaver – kit, kitten or pup

Bird – chick

Cat – kitten

Chicken – chick

Cow – calf

Deer – fawn

Dog – puppy

Dolphin – calf

Duck – duckling

Eel – elver

Elephant – calf

Ferret – kit

Fish – fry

Frog – tadpole or froglet

Goat – kid

Goose – gosling

Guinea pig – pup

Hare – leveret

Hippopotamus – calf

Hedgehog – hoglet

Horse – foal

Kangaroo – joey

Koala – joey

Otter – cub

Pig – piglet

Pigeon – squab

Rabbit – kitten

Rat – pup

Seal – pup

Sheep – lamb

Spider – spiderling

Swan – cygnet

Toad – tadpole

Tortoise – hatchling

Wolf – cub

Zebra – foal

SALAMANDERS

Bullfrogs pretend to be dead if captured, but then quickly hop away if the captor releases its grip.

Amphibians see only in black and white. Their eyes come in a variety of shapes and sizes, and some have square or heart-shaped pupils.

A single toad can eat 10,000 insects in the course of a summer.

Toads have dry 'warty' skin, dull-coloured fat bodies and poison glands behind the eyes. They walk or waddle, while frogs hop.

Alpine salamanders always give birth to twins.

Lungless salamanders – the largest group of salamanders – breathe through their skin, which must be kept damp to allow oxygen in. If they dry out, they suffocate and die.

The ozark blind salamander begins life with eyes. As the animal matures, its eyelids fuse together.

The Argentinian horned toad can swallow a mouse in one gulp.

The poison-arrow frog has enough poison to kill about 2,200 people but loses its poison when it's kept in captivity because the source of its poison is a chemical found in small beetles which only exist in the wild.

Twenty tons of toads are killed on Britain's roads every year.

All known amphibians and reptiles that live in the earth below the surface are carnivores, eating creatures such as worms and ants.

Frogs have teeth but toads don't.

Toads only eat prey that moves.

Frog-eating bats find and identify edible frogs by listening to the mating calls. Frogs counter this by hiding and using short calls that are hard to locate.

The Asian giant salamander is the largest amphibian. It lives in the cold streams of China and Japan and can reach lengths of 1.5 metres and weights of 40 kilograms.

The eggs of the marsupial frog are laid in a pouch on the mother's back and the young hatch out in a zip-like fashion from the pouch.

Several salamanders make squeaking noises when disturbed. The Pacific giant sends out a scream and a rattle to ward off enemies. Some salamander species arch their back and raise their head to imitate a poisonous snake and deter an attacker that way.

About 10,000 Albanians make their livelihood hunting frogs. Albania exports 400 tons of live and frozen frogs every year, mostly to France and Italy, where frogs legs are considered a delicacy.

Frogs have eardrums on the outside of their bodies – behind their eyes.

Flying frogs change colour at different times of the day and night. During the day, they're greenish-blue then, as twilight falls, they turn green, but when it gets dark, they turn black.

The more lush the vegetation, the more poisonous the toads that live in it.

The glass frog has a transparent stomach and so you can see its intestines and all its innards.

Some frogs can be frozen solid then thawed and still be alive.

There's a frog in South America that has a fabulous survival tool. Whenever a predator comes along the frog turns its back and 'moons' at it. The frog's bottom has (what looks like) two enormous eyes that make it seem as if it's much much bigger than it really is – causing the would-be attacker to go away. If that doesn't work, the frog can also let rip with a foul-smelling liquid from its bottom.

THINGS YOU CAN ORDER IN AN AMERICAN DINER ... AND WHAT YOU'LL GET

Belch water (a glass of seltzer or soda water).

Adam and Eve on a raft (two poached eggs on toast).

Bowl of red (a serving of chilli).

Cowboy with spurs (an omelette with chips).

Eve with the lid on (apple pie).

Murphy carrying a wreath (ham and potatoes with cabbage).

Nervous pudding (jelly).

Put out the lights and cry (liver with onions).

Brown cow (chocolate milk).

Wreck a pair (two scrambled eggs).

SOME OF HOMER SIMPSON'S 'LIFELONG DREAMS'

Seeing a car shaped like a bowling pin.

Managing a beautiful country & western singer.

Living in the wilderness.

Becoming a monorail conductor.

Running out on to the baseball field during a game.

Becoming a blackjack dealer.

Being a contestant on *The Gong Show*.

Living under the sea.

Working in a bowling alley.

Working from home.

Owning the Dallas Cowboys.

Being the next Thomas Edison.

Becoming a hippy.

Ending crime and injustice.

Bowling a perfect game.

Getting rid of Bart.

Being a rock star.

Seeing Stevie Nicks naked.

SNAKES

Rattlesnakes are born without rattles.

Laying claim to being the most poisonous snake in the world are the inland taipan and the gaboon viper.

A snake can digest bones and teeth – but not fur or hair.

Most snakes lay eggs. However, the anaconda, one of the world's largest snakes, gives birth to live young, which can hunt, swim and look after themselves within a few hours of being born.

The flying snake of Java and Malaysia can flatten its body like a glider and sail from one tree to another.

When a snake sticks out its tongue, it is 'smelling': detecting chemicals on the air.

Some female rattlesnakes eat their young as a way of recovering lost energy; it's quicker and safer than having to hunt for food.

When tree snakes fight, they try to swallow one another.

Snakes do not have eyelids. Instead, they have a layer of clear scales, called brille, protecting their eyes.

Rattlesnakes gather in groups to sleep through the winter. As many as 1,000 might coil up together to keep warm.

Snakes 'hear' through their jaws.

The heads of a freak two-headed snake will fight over food – despite sharing the same stomach.

Breathing for most snakes is done with one lung. The left lung is either reduced in size or missing completely.

The poisonous copperhead snake smells like freshly cut cucumbers.

Sidewinders move by looping their bodies up in the air and pushing against the ground when they land. Their tracks look like a series of straight lines angling in the direction the snake was travelling.

Snakes do not urinate. They excrete uric acid, which is a solid, chalky, usually white substance.

The rock star Alice Cooper liked to wear a pet boa constrictor round his neck while on stage. One day, while Cooper was rehearsing in his hotel room, the snake started to constrict his neck. A bodyguard couldn't get the snake to release its grip, so he took out a penknife and cut off the snake's head.

It takes about 50 hours for a snake to digest a frog.

Snakes shed their skin three or four times a year. It normally comes off in a single layer, taking with it any parasites that have attached themselves to it.

Some snakes can survive for up to a year without eating.

For most snakes, breathing is accomplished with just one lung.

The gastric juices of a snake can digest bones and teeth – but not fur or hair.

A snake can eat a whole goat per day.

Snakes don't bite in rivers or swamps – they would drown if they did.

Milk snakes lay about 13 eggs – in piles of animal manure.

Tiger snakes can survive perfectly well when their eyes are pecked out by seagulls.

None of the snakes in Madagascar are poisonous.

When it comes to hunting, snakes have nothing to fear as they're immune to their own poison.

An anaconda can swallow a pig.

The West Indian wood snake pretends to be dead when confronted by a predator. It lies very still and allows its eyes to fill up with blood and turn red; the blood then drips out of its mouth. This works because its main predators will only eat food that they themselves have killed.

SOCCER TRIALISTS/PLAYERS

Mike Yarwood (Stockport County and Oldham Athletic).

Mike Gatting (Arsenal).

James Major (Aston Villa).

Terry Alderton (played in goal for Southend before being dismissed for letting in a goal after moonwalking during a game).

Ray Stubbs (played for Tranmere Rovers).

Chris Hollins (Charlton, Queens Park Rangers and Aldershot Town).

Michael Sheen was offered a trial at Arsenal FC after being spotted by the father of Tony Adams during a family holiday at Pontin's on the Isle of Wight.

Matt Smith aspired to be a professional footballer, and played for the youth teams of Northampton Town, Nottingham Forest and Leicester City but a back injury forced him out of the sport.

FLAGS

The Swiss flag is square.

The Isle of Man's flag is three legs joined together.

The colours of Jamaica's flag are symbolic. Black signifies the strength and creativity of the people; gold, the natural wealth and beauty of sunlight; and green, hope and agricultural resources.

The cedar tree on Lebanon's flag symbolizes strength, holiness and eternity. The white background stands for peace, and the red bands represent sacrifice.

Libya has the only flag that's just one colour with nothing else on it. The one colour is green and it represents Islam.

Zambia has a bird on its flag.

Mozambique and Guatemala are the only two countries with flags that have guns or rifles on them.

The Nepalese flag is the only flag that's not four-sided. It takes the form of two overlapping triangles on top of each other.

The Ukrainian flag of blue and yellow symbolizes a field of yellow grain with a blue sky overhead.

SHAKESPEARE'S LONGEST ROLES

Falstaff (1,614 lines in *Henry IV, Parts 1 & 2* and *The Merry Wives of Windsor*).

Hamlet (1,422 lines in *Hamlet* – making Hamlet the longest role in any *single* Shakespeare play).

Richard III (1,124 lines in *Richard III*).

Iago (1,097 lines in *Othello*).

Henry V (1,025 lines in *Henry V*).

Othello (860 lines in *Othello*).

Vincentio (820 lines in *Measure For Measure*).

Coriolanus (809 lines in *Coriolanus*).

Timon (795 lines in *Timon of Athens*).

Marc Antony (766 lines in *Antony And Cleopatra*).

TWELVE CLASSIC ENGLISH ICONS

In 2006, the Department for Culture launched a new project – Icons: a portrait of England. Its aim was to create an evolving list of symbols that reflect the character of England and the English. For the launch of the project a panel of art experts and academics proposed the following twelve icons:

Alice in Wonderland

The Angel of the North

A cup of tea

SS Empire Windrush

The FA cup

Henry VIII by Holbein

The *King James Bible*

Punch and Judy

The Routemaster bus

Stonehenge

The Spitfire

Blake's *Jerusalem*

THE TEN DISTINCT TYPES OF LAUGHTER

Amused laugh

Joy laugh

Sympathetic laugh

Polite laugh

Relief laugh

Disappointment laugh

Embarrassed laugh

Stressed laugh

Comment laugh

Ironical laugh

REPTILES

Many reptiles can replace limbs or tails if they're lost or damaged but only the aquatic newt has the ability to regenerate the lens of its eye.

Most lizards will replace their tail within a month of losing it.

The gecko lizard can run on the ceiling because its toes have flaps of skin that provide suction.

Tortoises are the longest-living animals – living in excess of 175 years.

The female green turtle sheds tears as she lays her eggs on the beach. This washes sand particles out of her eyes and rids her body of excess salt.

It can take the Galapagos turtle up to three weeks to digest a meal.

Galapagos turtles were named after a type of Spanish saddle because of the shape of their shells.

Marine iguanas, saltwater crocodiles, sea snakes and sea turtles are the only surviving seawater-adapted reptiles.

Some alligators can survive the winter by allowing their heads to be completely frozen – just leaving their nose out to breathe.

Reptiles are never slimy. Their scales have few glands, and are usually silky to the touch.

Basilisks are also called Jesus Christ lizards because of their ability to run on water.

Tortoises drink water through their noses.

The tuatara's metabolism is so slow it only has to breathe once an hour.

The mountain devil, a lizard-like creature native to Australia, never drinks: it absorbs tiny drops of dew through its skin.

In 1999, a three-headed turtle was discovered in Taiwan.

The distance between an alligator's eyes, in inches, is directly proportional to the length of the alligator in feet.

The chameleon releases its tongue at 26 body lengths per second – faster than the human eye can see. It hits its prey in about 0.03 seconds.

An iguana can end its own life.

A threatened horned lizard can shoot blood from its eyes for over a metre. It's a useful survival trick that serves to surprise would-be predators and enables the lizard to escape.

A komodo dragon tears large chunks of flesh off its prey while holding the carcass down with its forelegs. It can eat a smaller animal, such as a goat, whole by using its loosely articulated jaws, flexible skull and expandable stomach. It will sometimes ram the carcass against a tree to help force it down its throat. Large dragons can survive on as few as twelve meals a year.

An alligator can go through 2,000 to 3,000 teeth in a lifetime.

Female alligators protect their young for up to two years after they have hatched (which is more mothering than most reptiles get).

The biggest lizards in the world are the varanus (or monitor lizards) of New Guinea, which can reach a maximum length of up to 5 metres.

Whether a sea turtle is male or female depends on the temperature of the sand in which it incubated as an egg. Warm temperatures (greater than 29°C) produce more females; cooler temperatures (less than 29°C) produce more males.

NATIONAL ANTHEMS

La Marseillaise, France's national anthem, was composed in Strasbourg (in 1792) and not in Marseilles.

The Vanuatu national anthem is called *Yumi, Yumi, Yumi*.

Five per cent of Canadians don't know the first seven words of the Canadian national anthem, but do know the first nine of the American anthem.

The Estonian national anthem has the same tune as Finland's but different words.

The Ethiopian national anthem is based on Jean Sibelius's *Finlandia*.

The Dutch national anthem doesn't mention the name of the country.

SOME OF THE MORE EXTRAORDINARY EXPRESSIONS TRADITIONALLY ASSOCIATED WITH BINGO NUMBERS

1 Kelly's eye

2 One little duck

5 Man alive

9 Doctor's orders

11 Legs eleven

16 Never been kissed

22 Two little ducks

25 Duck and dive

26 Bed and breakfast

27 Little duck with a crutch

30 Burlington Bertie

39 Those famous steps

44 Droopy drawers

55 Snakes alive

56 Was she worth it?

57 Heinz varieties

59 Brighton line

66 Clickety click

88 Two fat ladies

90 Top of the shop

ALL THE BRITISH OR IRISH WRITERS TO BE AWARDED THE NOBEL PRIZE FOR LITERATURE

Rudyard Kipling (1907)

W.B. Yeats (1923)

George Bernard Shaw (1925)

John Galsworthy (1932)

T.S. Eliot (1948)*

Bertrand Russell (1950)

Sir Winston Churchill (1953)

Samuel Beckett (1969)

Sir William Golding (1983)

Seamus Heaney (1995)

Sir V.S. Naipaul (2001)**

Harold Pinter (2005)

Doris Lessing (2007)

*Born in the US but became a British subject
**Born in Trinidad but resident in the UK

GENUINE DISHES FROM AROUND THE WORLD

Wasp Pupae (Japan)

Sheep's Feet With Yoghurt (Turkey)

Sea Urchin Gonad Sauce (France)

Stuffed Pig's Stomach (Hungary)

Grilled Snakemeat (Japan)

Weasels (Japan)

Turkey Testicles (US)

Lamb's Organs With Artichokes (Italy)

Monkey's Heads (Japan)

Barbecued Cow Heart (Peru)

Fried Mole Cricket (Vietnam)

Pork Lights (Lungs) And Liver Stew (US)

Pig's Feet With Bananas (Philippines)

Lambs' Brains Tacos (Mexico)

Banana Worm Bread (Iowa State University, US)

Stuffed Frogs (Philippines)

Dandelion Salad (Slovenia)

Ox Palates In Browned Sauce (France)

Hare Giblets (Germany)

Earthworm Broth (China)

Giant Bullfrog And Pineapple Salad (US)

Stuffed Calf's Eyes (France)

Brain Dumplings (Norway)

Broiled Beetle Grubs (Japan)

Fried Cactus Caterpillars (Mexico)

Starlings In Crust (France)

Broiled Sparrows (Japan)

Fried Grasshopper (China)

Locust Dumplings (North Africa)

Roasted Caterpillars (Laos)

Fried Calf's Head (Hungary)

Stir-fried Dog (China)

Golden Calf Testicles (France)

Rabbit Excrement (Red Indians of Lake Superior used this as a flavouring in red wine)

Minced Giant Bullfrog Savoury Sandwich Spread (US)

Deep-Fried Horsemeat (Switzerland)

Mixed Organ Beef Stew (Austria)

Caterpillar Larvae Of The Large Pandora Moth (Pai-utes Indians of Oregon)

Roast Wallaby (Australia)

Calf's Head With Brain Fritters (nineteenth century US)

Steamed Cat And Chicken (China)

Burgoo (squirrel, rabbit, pigeon, wild duck and/or chicken, vegetables stew) (US Appalachian)

Bandicoote Stewed In Milk (Australia – early twentieth century)

Pork Testicles In Cream (France)

Pork Intestines With Fish Cake And Liver (China)

Tripe Soup (Czech Republic)

White Ant Pie (Zanzibar)

Pea Soup With Pigs' Ears (Germany)

Pigs' Tails (France)

Smoked Dog (Philippines)

Crisp Roasted Termites (Swaziland)

Dragon, Phoenix And Tiger Soup (consists of snake, chicken and cat) (China)

Roasted Palmworms With Orange Juice (French West Indies)

Baked Opossum (US)

Calf's Foot Stew (Philippines)

Stewed Veal Shins (Italy)

Pot-Roasted Cow's Udder (France)

Bear's Paws Dalmatian Style (Croatia and Dalmatia)

Dog Ham (China)

Pigs' Ears (Germany)

Baked Elephant Paws (Africa – nineteenth century)

Broiled Puppy (Hawaii)

Boiled Locusts (Vietnam)

ANIMAL ADJECTIVES

Alligator – eusuchian

Ant – formicine

Anteater – myrmecophagine

Ape – simian

Armadillo – tolypeutine

Ass – asinine

Badger – musteline

Barracuda – percesocine

Bat – pteropine

Bear – ursine

Bee – apiarian

Bird – avian

Bison – bisontine

Buffalo – bubaline

Bull – taurine

Calf – vituline

Camel – cameline

Chicken – galline

Civet – viverrine

Cobra – elapine

Cow – bovine

Crab – cancrine

Crocodile – crocodilian

Deer – cervine

Dodo – didine

Dolphin – delphine

Dormouse – myoxine

Dragon – draconine

Earthworm – lumbricine

Elephant – elephantine

Elk – cervine

Ferret –musteline

Fish – piscine

Flea – pulicine

Flying fox – pteropine

Fox – vulpine

Frog – ranine

Gerbil – cricetine

Gibbon – hylobatine

Giraffe – giraffine

Goat – caprine

Hamster – cricetine

Hare – leporine

Hippopotamus – hippopotamine

Hornet – vespine

Horse – equine

Human – hominine

Hyena – hyenine

Kangaroo – **macropodine**

Lemming – microtine

Lemur – lemurine

Leopard – pardine

Limpet – patelline

Lion – leonine

Lobster – homarine

Louse – pediculine

Mink – musteline

Mole – talpine

Moose – cervine

Moth – arctian

Mouse – murine

Octopus – octopine

Opossum – didelphine

Otter – lutrine

Ox – bovine

Oyster – ostracine

Panther – pantherine

Pig – porcine

Porcupine – hystricine

Porpoise – phocaenine

Rabbit – lapine

Rat – murine

Reindeer – rangiferine

Rhinoceros – ceratorhine

Rodent – glirine

Seahorse – hippocampine

Sheep – ovine

Shrew – soricine

Skunk – musteline

Slug – limacine

Snake – ophidian

Squirrel – sciurine

Stag – cervine

Tiger – tigrine

Toad – batrachian

Tortoise – chelonian

Turtle – chelonian

Vole – microtine

Wasp – vespine

Wolf – lupine

Wombat – phascolomian

Worm – vermian

Zebra – zebrine

BRITAIN'S FAVOURITE PAINTINGS – AS VOTED FOR IN A BBC RADIO 4 POLL

The Fighting Temeraire Tugged to Her Last Berth to Be Broken up by J.M.W. Turner.

The Hay Wain by John Constable.

A Bar at the Folies-Bergère by Edouard Manet.

The Arnolfini Portrait by Jan Van Eyck.

Mr And Mrs Clark And Percy by David Hockney.

Sunflowers by Vincent Van Gogh.

The Reverend Dr Robert Walker Skating on Duddingston Lock by Sir Henry Raeburn.

The Last of England by Ford Madox Brown.

The Baptism of Christ by Piero della Francesca.

A Rake's Progress III: 'The Orgy' by William Hogarth.

WORDS OF YIDDISH OR JEWISH ORIGIN

bagel: a ring-shaped bread roll (ideal with 'lox' – see below)

chutzpah: cheek, audacity, effrontery

glitch: a minor malfunction

klutz: clumsy person

kvetch: complain, gripe

lox: smoked salmon

mensch: decent human being

nosh: snack

schlep: to drag or carry (something); make a tedious journey

schmaltz: excessive sentimentality

schmendrik: fool

schmooze: chat, butter up

schmutter: (cheap) clothing

shtick: comic theme, defining habit

spiel: sales pitch

ST GEORGE IS THE PATRON SAINT OF ENGLAND. HE'S ALSO THE PATRON SAINT OF ...

Canada	**Portugal**
Germany	Russia
Greece	**Serbia**
Lithuania	Montenegro
Malta	**Ethiopia**
Moldova	

THINGS SAID ABOUT THE WORLD

'Don't go around saying the world owes you a living. The world owes you nothing: it was here first.' (Mark Twain)

'Don't worry about the world coming to an end today. It's already tomorrow in Australia.' (Charles M. Schulz)

'Remember that the most beautiful things in the world are the most useless; peacocks and lilies, for instance.' (John Ruskin)

'People try to change the world – instead of themselves.' (John Cleese)

'The whole problem with the world is that fools and fanatics are always so certain of themselves, but wiser people are so full of doubts.' (Bertrand Russell)

'Even if I knew that tomorrow the world would go to pieces, I would still plant my apple tree.' (Martin Luther)

'The world is a looking glass and gives back to every man the reflection of his own face.' (William Makepeace Thackeray)

'The most incomprehensible thing about the world is that it is at all comprehensible.' (Albert Einstein)

'There are more fools in the world than there are people.' (Heinrich Heine)

'Although the world is full of suffering, it is full also of the overcoming of it.' (Helen Keller)

'The world remains ever the same.' (Johann Von Goethe)

GENUINE HAIRSTYLES FROM THE PAST

Flat-Top

Argentine Ducktail

Crewcut

Quiff

Elephant's Trunk

Conk

Beehive

Spike-Top

Suedehead

Flop

BOOK FIRSTS

The first book published is thought to be *The Epic of Gilgamesh*, written in about 3000 BC in cuneiform, an alphabet based on symbols.

The first history book, *The Great Universal History,* was published by Rashid-Eddin of Persia in 1311.

***Uncle Tom's Cabin* by Harriet Beecher Stowe was the first American novel to sell a million copies.**

The first novel, *The Tale of Genji*, was written in 1007 by the Japanese noblewoman, Murasaki Shikibu.

The first illustrated book for children was published in Germany in 1658.

The term 'autobiography' was first used by Robert Southey in 1809 in the English periodical *Quarterly Review* in which he predicted an 'epidemical rage for autobiography'.

COUNTRIES FOUND IN ENGLAND

America, Cambridgeshire

Canada, Hampshire

Egypt, Buckinghamshire

Gibraltar, Buckinghamshire

Greenland, South Yorkshire

Holland, Surrey

Ireland, Bedfordshire

New Zealand, Buckinghamshire

Scotland, Lincolnshire

FOREIGN PLACES IN THE UK

California, Buckinghamshire

Dresden, Staffordshire

Jerusalem, Lincolnshire

Maryland, Gwent

Moscow, Scotland

New York, Tyne and Wear

Normandy, Surrey

Pennsylvania, Gloucestershire

Quebec, County Durham

Toronto, County Durham

MUSIC

The earliest example of musical notation is from 200 BC Sumeria. It was written in harmonies of thirds, and used the diatonic scale.

The world's most extraordinary musical instrument was made in France in the fifteenth century. A long row of spikes was connected to a keyboard. Under each spike was a pig, arranged according to the pitch of its oink.

The Nutcracker was one of Tchaikovsky's most successful compositions but he didn't rate it at all.

Summertime by George Gershwin is the most recorded song of all time with over thirteen thousand versions.

Three Gershwin songs, _I Got Rhythm_, _Nice Work if You Can Get It_ and _I'm About to Become a Mother_, all contain the phrase 'Who could ask for anything more?'

The piano covers the full spectrum of all orchestra instruments, from below the lowest note of the double bassoon to above the top note of the piccolo.

There is a name for a 64th note – a hemidemisemiquaver.

After Beethoven went deaf, he could still 'hear' his music by resting one end of a stick on the piano and holding the other end in his teeth.

Some 10 per cent of all the recorded music sold worldwide is bought and sold in Britain.

Mozart wrote a piano piece that required the player to use both hands and his nose.

Violins weigh less than 448 grams yet resist string tension of 29 kilograms.

Some bands for the Rara festival in Haiti have a thousand or more members.

In Zambia, the vingwengwe is a local instrument played by four women. Four overturned metal pots are placed in a row. Each woman places a stool on top of the pot and then turns it to make the pots resonate. As they turn the stools, they create a quartet of 'voices'.

The harmonica is the world's most popular musical instrument to play.

The song *Chopsticks* was written in 1877 by Euphemia Allen, aged 16. She said that the correct way to play it was to chop the keys with the hands turned sideways.

Kate Moss was namechecked by Lily Allen in the song *Everything's Just Wonderful*, by Jewel in the song *Intuition* and by Kanye West in the song *Stronger*.

Irving Berlin, the man who wrote *White Christmas*, never learned to read music or to write it. He hummed or sang his songs to a secretary, who wrote them down in musical notation.

In 2006, Katie Melua entered the *Guinness Book of Records* for playing the deepest underwater concert (303 metres below sea level on Statoil's Troll A platform in the North Sea).

The term 'rhythm & blues' – later shortened to R&B – was coined in 1948 by Jerry Wexler, to replace the negative term 'race records'.

Aerosmith went berserk on their first Japanese tour. On the opening night, they destroyed the backstage area when they found turkey roll on the buffet table. Lead singer Steven Tyler commented, 'I explicitly said, 'No turkey roll.''

THE MOST VISITED COUNTRIES IN THE WORLD

France

Spain

China (inc. Hong Kong)

US

Italy

UK

Austria

Mexico

Germany

Canada

Hungary

Greece

Poland

Turkey

Portugal

Malaysia

Thailand

Netherlands

Russia

Sweden

COUNTRIES AT RISK FROM FLOODING

Bangladesh is one of the countries most at risk from sea levels rising. Much of the country would be underwater if sea levels rose.

The Iles Eparses (literally 'scattered islands) are in the Indian Ocean situated off the coast of Madagascar and have no permanent population – which is just as well as they're only two metres above sea level. Administered by the French, the islands are mainly used for meteorological purposes (e.g. cyclone warnings).

Eighty per cent of the 1,200 islands that make up the Maldives are no more than a metre above sea level. Within a hundred years, the Maldives could become uninhabitable.

There is nowhere in Tuvalu that's more than five metres above sea level. So, if sea levels rise, the islands of Tuvalu will disappear.

Half of the Netherlands is less than a metre above sea level. A lot of it is lower than sea level. Disastrous flooding in 1953 killed 1,800 people and destroyed more than 70,000 homes. This led to a huge flood-control project. Flooding struck again in 1995. Rising rivers forced 240,000 people to move out of their homes until the water receded.

Tokelau, a territory of New Zealand, is just five metres above sea level.

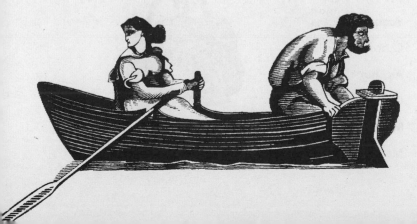

THE COUNTRIES WHICH CONSUME THE MOST ...

(*per person)

Rice: China (32 per cent of the world's rice)

Cigarettes: China (a third of the world's cigarettes)

Cigarettes*: Greece (an average 2,800 per person per year)

Fresh pork: China

Turkey-based products*: Israel

Bread*: Poland

Coca-Cola*: Mexico

Eggs*: Japan

Toilet paper: US (In just one day, Americans use enough toilet paper to wrap around the world nine times. If all the toilet paper they used were on one giant roll, they would be unrolling it at the rate of 7,600 miles per hour)

Olive Oil*: Greece

Honey*: Greece

Yogurt*: Bulgaria

Chocolate*: Belgium

Alcohol*: Luxembourg

Olives*: Syria

Meat: US

Meat*: US (an average 120kg per person per year)

Pasta*: Italy (an average 27kg per person per year)

Sugar*: Singapore

Tomato Ketchup: US

Tomato Ketchup*: Sweden

Beer*: The Czech Republic (an average 160 litres per person per year)

Sweets*: The Netherlands

Wine*: France (an average 60 litres per person per year)

Bottled Water*: France

Tea*: Ireland (an average 3.2kg per person per year)

Baked Beans*: UK

Crisps*: UK

Coffee*: Finland (an average 4.5 cups of coffee per person a day)

Butter*: France (an average 8.5kg per person per year)

Cheese*: France (an average 23kg per person per year)

Potatoes*: Ireland (an average 170kg per person per year)

Milk*: Ireland (an average 165 litres per person per year)

THE COUNTRIES WHICH PRODUCE THE MOST ...

Apples: China

Apricots: Turkey

Artichokes: Italy

Asparagus: Spain

Attar Of Roses: Bulgaria (about 70 per cent of the world's attar of roses)

Avocados: Mexico

Bananas: Ecuador

Barley: Russia

Bauxite: Australia

Beans: India

Beer: US

Butter: India

Cabbages: China

Camels: Somalia

Carrots: China

Cars: Japan

Cashew nuts: Vietnam

Cauliflowers: India

Cereals: China

Chestnuts: South Korea

Cheese: US

Cherries: Italy

Chick peas: India

Coal: China

Cocoa: The Ivory Coast (almost half the world's cocoa)

Coffee: Brazil

Commercial vehicles: US

Consumer electronics: China

Copper: Chile

Cork: Portugal (half the cork in the world)

Corn: US

Cotton: China

Currants: Russia

Dates: Iran

Diamonds: Australia

Eggs: China

Figs: Turkey

Flowers: The Netherlands

Fluorine: Mongolia

Gas: Russia

Goats: China

Gold: South Africa (two-thirds of the world's gold)

Grapefruits: US

Green peas: India

Gum arabic: Sudan (it's used in inks, adhesives, certain types of sweets and soft drinks)

Hazelnuts: Turkey

Honey: China

Ice hockey pucks: Slovakia

Iron: China

Jute: Bangladesh

Lead: Australia

Lemons: Mexico

Lentils: India

Linseed: Egypt

Mangoes: India

Manioc: Nigeria

Maple syrup: Canada (more than 75 per cent of the world's supply)

Mercury: Spain

Milk: US

Millet: India

Mustard seeds: Canada

Oil: Saudi Arabia (the discovery of oil in Saudi Arabia in the 1930s improved the country's economy tremendously: today, Saudi Arabia's oil reserves are estimated at 260 billion barrels)

Olives: Spain

Oranges: Brazil

Oxen: India

Palm oil: Malaysia

Papayas: Brazil

Phosphates: US

Pigs: China

Pineapples: Thailand

Pistachio nuts: Iran

Potash: Australia

Potatoes: China

Raspberries: Russia

Rice: China

Salmon (farmed): Norway

Salt: US

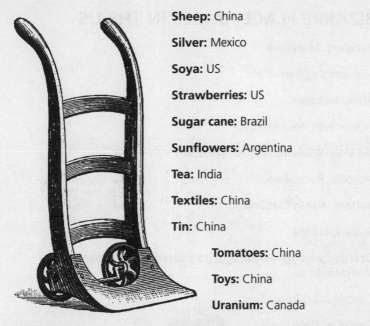

Sheep: China

Silver: Mexico

Soya: US

Strawberries: US

Sugar cane: Brazil

Sunflowers: Argentina

Tea: India

Textiles: China

Tin: China

Tomatoes: China

Toys: China

Uranium: Canada

Vanilla: Madagascar (supplies over half the world's vanilla. Over three-quarters of the vanilla beans used to make vanilla ice cream are grown in Madagascar. The Madagascan economy suffered briefly in the 1980s when Coca-Cola stopped using as much vanilla in their drinks)

Wheat: China

Wine: France

Wood: US

Wool: Australia

Yams: Nigeria

Zinc: China

BIZARRE PLACE NAMES IN THE US

Accident, Maryland

Alphabet City, New York

Arab, Alabama

Arsenic Tubs, New Mexico

Big Ugly Wilderness Area, West Virginia

Blueballs, Pennsylvania

Bottom, North Carolina

Buddha, Indiana

Chargoggagoggmanchauggagoggchaubunagungamaugg, Massachusetts

Cheesequake, New Jersey

Coolville, Ohio

Cut 'n' Shoot, Texas

Cut Off, Louisiana

Dismal, Tennessee

Double Trouble, New Jersey

Dry Prong, Louisiana

Duel, Michigan

Earth, Texas

Economy, Pennsylvania

Elephant Butte, New Mexico

Fertile, Minnesota

Foggy Bottom, Washington, DC

Forks of Salmon, California

Friendly, Maryland

Garden, Michigan

Gas, Kansas, USA

Gnaw Bone, Indiana

Grandmother Gap, North Carolina

Gross, Nebraska

Gun Barrel City, Texas

Half.com, Oregon

Held For Certain, Kentucky

Helper, Colorado

Hoard, Wisconsin

Honor, Michigan

Hot Coffee, Mississippi

Index, Washington

Jackpot, Nevada

Jobsville, New Jersey

Jupiter, Florida

Manunka Chunk, New Jersey

Monkey's Eyebrow, Kentucky

Neck City, Missouri

No Name, Colorado

North, South Carolina

Paradise, Michigan

Pie Town, New Mexico

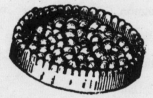

Plain Dealing, Louisiana

Rabbit Hash, Kentucky

Rule, Texas

Welcome, South Carolina

Why, Arizona

Winter, Wisconsin

Wynot, Nebraska

Zap, North Dakota

Zzyzx, California

BIZARRE PLACE NAMES IN THE UK

Beer, Devon

Bunny, Nottinghamshire

Catbrain Hill, Gloucestershire

Christmaspie, Surrey

Cold Christmas, Hertfordshire

Foul Mile, West Sussex

Foulness, Essex

Frisby on the Wreake, Leicestershire

Great Fryup, North Yorkshire

Heart's Delight, Kent

Lickey End, Worcestershire

Mumbles, Swansea

New Delight, West Yorkshire

No Place, County Durham

Nose's Point, Durham

Pease Pottage, West Sussex

Puddletown, Dorset

Queen Camel, Somerset

Rest And Be Thankful, Argyll and Bute

Sandwich, Kent

Twenty, Lincolnshire

Ugley, Essex

Westward Ho!, Devon (The punctuation mark is part of the name)

Woon Gumpus Common, Cornwall

BIZARRE PLACE NAMES IN THE REST OF THE WORLD

Apples, Switzerland

Bad Kissingen, Germany

Bastardo, Italy

Bitey Bitey, Pitcairn Island

Bong Bong, Australia

Bulls, New Zealand

Burrumbuttock, Australia

Chinaman's Knob, Australia

Coca Cola, Panama

Condom, France

Egg, Austria

Frenchman's Butte, Canada

Halfway House, Canada

Hells Gate Roadhouse, Australia

Hotazel, South Africa (pronounced 'hot-as-hell')

Howlong, Australia

John Catch a Cow, Pitcairn Island

Kissing, Germany

Maidslain, Canada

Middelfart, Denmark

Moose Jaw, Canada

Mutters, Austria

No Guts Captain, Pitcairn Island

Ogre, Latvia

Police, Poland

Punkeydoodles Corners, Canada

Rum, Austria

Saint-Louis-du-Ha! Ha!, Canada

Salmon Arm, British Columbia, Canada

Terry Hie Hie, Australia

Tubbercurry, Ireland

U, Panama

Wagga Wagga, Australia

Where Freddy Fall, Pitcairn Island

Where Reynolds Cut The Firewood, Pitcairn Island

Worms, Germany

BIZARRELY NAMED LAKES, RIVERS, HILLS & MOUNTAINS etc.

Awe, a loch in Scotland

Bang Bang Jump Up, a rock formation in Australia

Blow Me Down, a provincial park in Canada

Cadibarrawirracanna, a lake in Australia

Darling, a river in Australia

Grandfather, a mountain in the US

Great Slave, a lake in Canada

Hungry Law, a peak on the border of England and Scotland

Hopeless, a mountain in Australia

Piddle, a river in Dorset

Pis Pis, a river in Nicaragua

Possum Kingdom, a lake in the US

THE WORLD'S FIRST FEMALE LEADERS

In 1881, the Isle of Man was the first territory to give women (property-owning unmarried women and widows) the right to vote. In 1893, New Zealand became the first country to do likewise – followed by Australia in 1902. Finland – in 1906 – was the first European country to give women the vote. In the UK, women over 30 got the vote in 1918 but it wasn't till 1928 that they had equality with men (when the minimum voting age was 21)

Sirimavo Bandaranaike was the world's first female Prime Minister (Ceylon – now Sri Lanka – in 1960)

Isabel Perón was the world's first female President (Argentina in 1974)

Margaret Thatcher was Europe's first female Prime Minister (UK in 1979. She was just ahead of Maria de Lourdes Pintasilgo who, later the same year, became Portugal's first female Prime Minister)

Simone Veil of France was the first female President of the European Parliament (in 1979)

Ellen Johnson Sirleaf was Africa's first female president (Liberia in 2006)

Eugenia Charles was the Caribbean's first female Prime Minister (in Dominica in 1980)

Benazir Bhutto was the first female to be elected as Prime Minister of a Muslim country (Pakistan in 1988)

Sylvie Kinigi was Africa's first female Prime Minister (Burundi in 1993. She was just ahead of Agathe Uwilingiyimana who became Prime Minister of Rwanda just eight days later)

Vigdís Finnbogadóttir was the world's first female President to be elected* (Iceland in 1980)
*Isabel Perón wasn't actually elected President but served out the rest of her husband's term of office when he died

NB In 2008, New Zealand was the only country in the world in which all the highest offices in the land were occupied by women – The Sovereign Queen Elizabeth II of New Zealand, Governor-General Dame Silvia Cartwright, Prime Minister Helen Clark, Speaker of the New Zealand House of Representatives Margaret Wilson and Chief Justice Dame Sian Elias. That ended in November 2008 when Helen Clark lost the general election and was replaced as Prime Minister by a man.

ONLYs (1)

The donkey is the **only** domestic animal to have originated from Africa.

Giraffes are the **only** animals born with horns. Both males and females are born with bony knobs on the forehead.

The **only** Shakespeare play in which tennis balls appear is *Henry V*.

The **only** Nobel prizewinner to win an Oscar was George Bernard Shaw (for *Pygmalion*).

Lichfield is the **only** British city with letters all in the first half of the alphabet.

The bullfrog is the **only** animal that never sleeps.

In 1958, Zsa Zsa Gabor became the first – and **only** – recipient of a Golden Globe Award for 'Most Glamorous Actress' (the award was never given again).

Humans, ants and, to a lesser degree, chimpanzees are the **only** beings that wage organized warfare.

The bloodhound is the **only** animal whose evidence is admissible in an American court.

Monday is the **only** day of the week that has an anagram: dynamo.

Libra (the scales) is the **only** inanimate symbol in the zodiac.

The **only** rock that floats in water is pumice.

'Forty' is the **only** number with its letters in alphabetical order.

Only male turkeys gobble; females make a clicking noise.

The Iolani Palace of Oahu in Hawaii is the **only** royal palace in the United States.

The **only** purple animal is the South African blesbok.

The **only** time the world's population declined was in the fourteenth century – in the years following the 'Black Death'

The **only** fruit that has its seeds on the outside is the strawberry.

Former Prime Minister William E. Gladstone and Dr Barnado were the **only** people ever to have their coffins transported by Tube.

The Chihuahua is the **only** breed of dog that's born with an incomplete skull (it has a little hole that closes as it matures)

The Parisian McDonald's has the **only** white 'golden arches' in the world (it was thought that yellow was too tacky)

Sir Isaac Newton's **only** recorded utterance while he was a member of Parliament was a request to open the window.

The sea otter is the **only** non-primate that can use tools to break open hard shells to access food.

The **only** bone in the human body not connected to another is the hyoid, a V-shaped bone located at the base of the tongue between the mandible and the voice box. Its function is to support the tongue and its muscles.

Albania was the **only** European country occupied by the Axis powers (that's Germany and Italy) that ended World War 2 with a larger Jewish population than before the start of the War. Only one Jewish family was deported and killed during the Nazi occupation of Albania. Not only did the Albanians protect their own Jews, but they provided refuge for Jews from neighbouring countries.

Tonga is the **only** country ever to have issued a banana-shaped stamp.

Thimphu in Bhutan is the **only** capital city in Asia that doesn't have traffic lights. They use traffic policemen instead.

Colombia is the **only** country in South America that has a coast on both the Pacific and Atlantic Oceans.

Qatar is the **only** country that starts with a Q; Iraq is the only country that ends with a Q.

Saudi Arabia is the **only** country where women aren't allowed to drive.

Tonga's **only** golf course has just 15 holes. And there's no penalty if a monkey steals your ball.

Brazil is the **only** country which is crossed by both the Equator and the Tropic of Capricorn.

Australia boasts the **only** bird – the Australian mound-builder bird – that can fly the moment it hatches.

Belize is the **only** country in the world with a jaguar reserve. Belize is also the only Central American country where English is the official language.

SPORTING ONLYs

There are **only** four clubs in the Football League with names starting and ending with the same letter: Liverpool, Charlton Athletic, Northampton Town and Aston Villa.

Great Britain is the **only** team to have won at least one gold medal at every Summer Olympic Games.

The **only** Olympian ever to be awarded the Nobel Peace Prize was Philip (later Lord) Noel-Baker (Great Britain), who won the 1500 metres silver medal in 1920.

Greece and Australia are the **only** two countries to have participated in every single one of the Modern Olympic Games.

There are **only** two Olympic sports where men and women compete against each other: sailing and equestrianism.

The 1900 Olympics featured pigeon shooting. It was the first – and **only** – time animals were killed on purpose in an Olympic event.

In Rome, 1960, Ethiopian Abebe Bikila became the **only** man to win the marathon running barefoot (becoming, in the process, the first black African to win a gold medal). He successfully defended his title four years later in Tokyo, but this time he wore shoes.

American Eddie Eagan, who was a boxing champion in the 1920 Games, became the **only** person to win gold medals in both the Summer and Winter Games, when he won gold at the 1932 Winter Olympics in the team bobsled event.

Ralph Craig is the **only** man to have competed in two Olympic Games 36 years apart. In 1912, he ran the 100 metres. He next competed in the 1948 Olympics at the age of 59, as an alternative in the US yachting team.

Princess Anne (now the Princess Royal) was the **only** female competitor not to have to submit to a sex test at the 1976 Olympics.

In 1908, Wyndham Halswelle, a British veteran of the Boer War, became the **only** Olympian to win a gold medal (400 metres) without any opponents. In the first, void race, Halswelle was obstructed by Carpenter, an American who crossed the line first but was disqualified. Carpenter's American team-mates refused to take part in the rerun and so Halswelle ran a solo race.

1900 was the first – and **only** time – that the Olympic swimming events were held in a river. (In the Seine, Paris.)

Only two players – Pele (Brazil) and Uwe Seeler (West Germany) – have scored in four consecutive World Cup finals – and, interestingly, both players scored during the same four World Cups (1958–1970).

Robert Prosinecki is the **only** player to have scored for two different countries at the World Cup Finals. He scored for Yugoslavia in 1990 and for Croatia in 1998.

Peter Judge is the **only** cricketer to have been dismissed off consecutive deliveries in the same first-class match. This happened in 1946 when Glamorgan were playing the touring Indians. Judge was bowled by the last bowl of the Glamorgan innings and the Indians invited the county to follow-on. At this point, the Glamorgan captain, Wilf Wooller, decided to waive the 10-minute interval between innings and instructed the last pair to remain in the middle and open the innings: in other words, he was reversing the entire batting order.

The first ball of Glamorgan's second innings saw Judge bowled again (by the very same bowler) – thus becoming the **only** cricketer to be bowled by consecutive balls in the same match.

Neil Paterson is the **only** British footballer to win an Oscar. He played for Dundee United in the 1940s while also working as a freelance writer. In 1959, he won the Oscar for his screenplay for *Room at the Top*.

The **only** European countries where football isn't the most popular spectator sport are Ireland (Gaelic football), Finland (ice hockey) and Latvia and Estonia (both basketball).

On **only** one occasion have (a part of) all four innings of a Test match been played on the same day. It was on the second day of the Lord's Test match between England and West Indies in 2000.

The American Bobby Riggs **only** played Wimbledon once – in 1939 – but left with the perfect record, winning the Singles, the Doubles and the Mixed Doubles. Always a hustler, he played deliberately badly in a pre-Wimbledon tournament and then backed himself with bookmakers at high odds to win Wimbledon. Nowadays, he's probably best remembered for challenging the then-women's champion Billie-Jean King in a famous 'Battle of the Sexes' which he lost.

Dundee is the **only** British professional club with a name that doesn't contain any letters that appear in the word 'football'.

Hemulal Yadav is the **only** first-class cricketer to have been given out 'timed out'.

R.E. 'Tip' Foster is the **only** man to captain England at both football and cricket. He also still holds the world record for the highest score on Test debut – having scored 287 for England against Australia in 1903/04.

In 1982, Duleep Mendis of Sri Lanka scored 105 in both innings of a Test match against India – making him the **only** batsman to hit identical hundreds in both innings of a Test.

Sam Wynne is the **only** footballer to have scored two goals for *each* side in a single first-class game. It happened in a match between his team Oldham Athletic and Manchester United in the 1923/24 season. He scored two goals for Oldham and two own-goals. His team ended up winning 5–2.

The **only** person to have played both World Cup Football and World Cup Cricket is Sir Viv Richards – Antigua at football and West Indies at cricket.

Lala Amarnath and Surinder Amarnath are the **only** father and son to both score Test centuries on debut. Incredibly, neither scored another Test century.

The **only** track and field event in which a men's world record has never been set during the Olympic Games.

ONLY IN BRITAIN

Only in Britain ... do chemists make ill people walk all the way to the back of the store to get their prescriptions while healthy people can buy chocolate bars at the front.

Only in Britain ... do people order double cheeseburgers, large fries and a Diet Coke.

Only in Britain ... do banks leave both doors open and chain the pens to the counters.

Only in Britain ... were 142 men injured in a single year because they didn't remove all the pins from new shirts.

Only in Britain ... are 58 people injured every year by using sharp knives instead of screwdrivers.

Only in Britain ... are more than 200 people a year admitted to A&E after opening bottles of beer with their teeth.

CARIBBEAN COUNTRIES AND THEIR ORIGINAL NAMES (AND MEANINGS)

COUNTRY	ORIGINAL NAME	MEANING
St Martin	Soualiga	Land of Salt
St Kitts	Liamuiga	Fertile Land
Nevis	Oualie	Land of Beautiful Water
Anguilla	Malliouhana	Arrow-Shaped Sea Serpent
Montserrat	Alliouagana	Land of Prickly Bush
Antigua	Wadadli	Land of Fish Oil
Guadeloupe	Karukera	Island of Beautiful Waters
Dominica	Wai'tukubuli	Tall is Her Body
Martinique	Madinina	Land of Flowers
St Lucia	Hiwanarau	Land of the Iguana
St Vincent	Hairoun	Land of the Blessed
Trinidad	Kairi	Land of the Hummingbird

COUNTRIES AND THEIR MOST POPULAR SURNAMES

Argentina: Fernandez

Austria: Grüber

Belgium: Peeters.

Canada: Johnson.

China: Li.

Costa Rica: Jiminez

Czech Republic: Novak

Denmark: Jensen.

Estonia: Oak (many popular Estonian surnames have something to do with nature)

Finland: Virtanen

France: Martin

Georgia: Beridze

Germany: Müller

Greece: Papadopolous

Hungary: Nagy

Ireland: Murphy

Italy: Rossi

Japan: Sato

Latvia: Berzins

Lithuania: Kazlauskas (men); Kazlauskien (women)

Malta: Borg

Mexico: Hernandez

The Netherlands: De Jong

Norway: Hansen

The Philippines: Santos

Poland: Nowak

Russia: Smirnov

Singapore: Tan

Slovakia: Horvath

Slovenia: Novak

Spain: Garcia

Sweden: Johansson

Taiwan: Chen

Turkey: Yilmaz

UK: Smith

Vietnam: Nguyen

OSTRICHES

The ostrich, the world's largest living bird, is the only bird that provides us with leather.

The ostrich egg is 2,000 times bigger than the smallest egg, which is the hummingbird's. An ostrich egg weighs 1.2 kilograms. A hummingbird egg weighs half a gram.

An ostrich egg is equal to 24 chicken eggs.

An adult male bird can weigh 150 kilograms.

It takes 42 days for an ostrich egg to hatch.

In Africa, ostriches are used to herd sheep.

The ostrich has four eyelids. The inner lids are for blinking and keeping the eyeballs moist, the outer lids for attracting potential mates.

An ostrich's intestinal tract is over 13 metres long.

An ostrich has only two toes, unlike most birds, which have three or four.

Ostriches use their powerful legs as a means of defence. They can kick a lion to death.

SONGS WITH FALSE ENDINGS

Light My Fire (The Doors)

Good Vibrations (The Beach Boys)

I Got You Babe (Sonny and Cher)

Monday Monday (The Mamas And The Papas)

Strawberry Fields Forever (The Beatles)

In The Mood (Glenn Miller)

The Twist (Chubby Checker)

Visions (Stevie Wonder)

All By Myself (Eric Carmen)

The Best Part of Breaking Up (The Ronettes)

PEOPLE WHO WERE APPOINTED AS SHERIFF OR LIEUTENANT OF COUNTIES

Penelope Keith (High Sheriff of Surrey)

Richard Stilgoe (High Sheriff of Surrey)

Richard Whiteley (Deputy Lieutenant of West Yorkshire)

Noel Edmonds (Deputy Lieutenant of Devon)

Jools Holland (Deputy Lieutenant of Kent)

Alan Titchmarsh (High Sheriff of the Isle of Wight)

Sir Terry Wogan (Deputy Lieutenant of Buckinghamshire)

PEOPLE WHO WERE THANKED ON THE BONZO DOG BAND'S *THE INTRO AND THE OUTRO*

John Wayne – Xylophone

Robert Morley – Guitar

Billy Butlin – Spoons

Princess Anne – Sousaphone

Liberace – Clarinet

Harold Wilson – Violin

Eric Clapton – Ukelele ('Hi, Eric')

Sir Kenneth Clark – Bass Saxophone ('A great honour, sir')

Peter Scott – Duck Call

Casanova – Horn

General De Gaulle – Accordion ('Really wild, General. Thank you, sir')

Max Jaffa – Bell Ringing and Pealing

Val Doonican – Himself

J. Arthur Rank – Gong

PAIRS OF PEOPLE WHO ATTENDED THE SAME SCHOOL

Vanessa Feltz & Natasha Kaplinsky (Haberdashers Aske's School For Girls)

Robert Redford & Paula Abdul (Van Nuys High, California)

Will Young & Catherine Zeta-Jones (Arts Educational)

Snoop Dogg & Cameron Diaz (Long Beach Polytechnic, California)

Lewis Moody & Matthew Macfadyen (Oakham)

Trinny Woodall & Camilla, Duchess of Cornwall (Queen's Gate)

Toby Flood & Sir Ridley Scott (The King's School, Tynemouth)

Emma Thompson & Geri Halliwell (Camden School For Girls)

Al Murray & Andy Gomarsall (Bedford)

Rachel Weisz & The Princess Royal (Benenden)

Professor Stephen Hawking & Sir Tim Rice (St Albans School)

Dale Winton & Anthony Horowitz (Orly Farm)

Oliver Cromwell & Samuel Pepys (Huntingdon Grammar School)

Lily Allen & Sophie Dahl (Millfield)

Jemima Khan & Vanessa-Mae (Francis Holland School)

David Hockney & Charlie Hodgson (Bradford GS)

Andy Kershaw & John Stapleton (Hulme Grammar)

Edward Fox & James Blunt (Harrow)

Chris Martin & Chris Chataway (Sherborne)

Natasha Richardson & Rachel Weisz (St Paul's Girls)

Daniel Day-Lewis & Minnie Driver (Bedales)

Princess Eugenie & James Mates (Marlborough)

Penny Junor & The Princess Royal (Benenden)

Dido & Helena Bonham Carter (Westminster)

Kevin Spacey and Val Kilmer (Chatsworth High School, California)

Alicia Silverstone & Nicolas Cage (Beverly Hills High, California)

Sacha Baron Cohen & David Baddiel (Haberdashers Aske's)

Sting & Dec (St Cuthbert's Catholic High School in Benwell, Newcastle)

Nicole Richie & Paris Hilton (Buckley Kindergarten School in Sherman Oaks, California)

Jimmy Carr & Matt Dawson (Royal Grammar School, High Wycombe)

Jimmy Carr & Ulrika Jonsson (Burnham Grammar School)

Rebecca Adlington & Jim McGrath (The Brunts, Mansfield)

Angela Griffin & Mel B (Leeds West Academy)

Lewis Hamilton & Ashley Young (The John Henry Newman School)

Ashton Kutcher & Chris Farley (Washington High School (Cedar Rapids, Iowa))

Harry Enfield & Holly Willoughby (The College of Richard Collyer)

Ben Elton & Simon Pegg (Stratford-upon-Avon College)

Sir Bruce Forsyth & Johnny Haynes (The Latymer, Edmonton)

Emily Blunt & Ben Chaplin (Hurtwood House School)

Derren Brown & Danny Cipriani (Whitgift School)

Daniel Craig & Chris Boardman (Hilbre High)

Matt Smith & Courtney Lawes (Northampton School For Boys)

Russell Howard & Alexa Chung (Perins)

COUNTRIES AND THEIR SYMBOLS

Some countries have many symbols but here's a selection

Argentina – **Puma**

Austria – **Edelweiss**

Australia – **Kangaroo**

Bangladesh – **Water lily**

Belgium – **Red poppy**

Bolivia – **Llama**

Bulgaria – **Lion**

Canada – **Maple leaf**

Colombia – **Condor**

China – **Dragon**

Denmark – **Beech tree**

Ecuador – **The Galapagos tortoise**

England – **Rose, Bulldog**

Eritrea – **Camel** (during Eritrea's war of independence from Ethiopia, the camel was the main means of transportation for moving food supplies, arms, ammunition and people across the country)

France – **Rooster**

Germany – **Black eagle**

Greece – **Olive branch**

Guatemala – **The quetzal** (a bird that signifies freedom because it dies in captivity: it's also the currency)

India – **Lotus**

Ireland – **Shamrock**

Iceland – **Falcon**

Mexico – **Dahlia**

Monaco – **Carnation**

Nepal – **Cow**

Netherlands – **Tulip**

New Zealand – **Kiwi bird**

Pakistan – **Jasmine**

Portugal – **Cockerel**

Russia – **Bear**

Scotland – **Thistle**

Singapore – **Orchid**

Slovakia – **Gothic shield** (with a silver double cross mounted on the central peak of three blue mountains, which represent the three ranges of the Carpathian mountains)

South Africa – **Springbok**

Switzerland – **Edelweiss**

Thailand – **Elephant** (the country's shaped like an elephant's head)

United Arab Emirates – **Arabian horse**

US – **Bald eagle**

Vietnam – **Water buffalo**

Wales – **Daffodil, leek, dragon**

DISNEY AROUND THE WORLD

Walt Disney wanted to build a park near his Burbank studio for his employees and their families but, over time, his dream grew and his plans grew bigger. He bought over 160 acres of orange groves around Anaheim and, in 1954, set about building his 'Magic Kingdom'.

Originally he planned a 9-million-dollar 45-acre park, but by the grand opening day, 17 July 1955, the park covered the full 160 acres. After the success of Disneyland California, Walt Disney and his brother Roy began buying land near Orlando, Florida – eventually ending up with 27,000 acres. Disneyworld, the Magic Kingdom was much bigger than Disneyland. It was the first of Disney's many theme parks in Florida.

There are currently five Disney resorts:

Disneyland Los Angeles 1955

Disneyworld Florida 1971

Euro Disney Paris 1992*

Disneyland Tokyo 1983

Disney Hong Kong 2005

There's also a community in Florida named Celebration: a town where people actually live all year round.. World Drive connects Celebration directly to the Walt Disney World parks and resorts; the north end of World Drive begins near the Magic Kingdom and its south end connects to Celebration Boulevard, allowing Celebration residents and guests to drive to Disney attractions without having to use any busy roads.

There are other Disney properties that don't have theme parks – like Disney's Hilton Head Island Resort in South Carolina. In October 2007, Disney announced plans to build a resort at in Kapolei, Hawaii, featuring both a hotel and Disney Vacation Club timeshare units, scheduled to open in 2011.

The Disney Cruise Line was formed in 1995 with two ships, the *Disney Magic* and *Disney Wonder*, which began operation in 1998 and 1999, respectively. Both offer Caribbean cruises, and a stop at Castaway Cay, Disney's private island in the Bahamas. A post office issues special postmarks which are exclusive to the Disney Cruise Line, and a 'Castaway Cay' postmark.

*Not all French people wanted Euro Disney to be opened, to the extent that some outraged citizens took their anger out on the park's characters and started beating up Mickey and Goofy.

HELPLINE CONVERSATIONS

Customer: 'I've been ringing your call centre on 0700 2300 for two days and can't get through to Enquiries, can you help?'

Operator: 'Where did you get that number from, sir?'

Customer: 'It was on the door to the travel centre.'

Operator: 'Sir, they are our opening hours.'

• •

Tech: 'Ridge Hall computer assistant; may I help you?'

Customer: 'Yes, well, I'm having trouble with WordPerfect.'

Tech: 'What sort of trouble?'

Customer: 'Well, I was just typing along, and all of a sudden the words went away.'

Tech: 'Went away?'

Customer: 'They disappeared.'

Tech: 'Hmm. So what does your screen look like now?'

Customer: 'Nothing.'

Tech: 'Nothing?'

Customer: 'It's blank; it won't accept anything when I type.'

Tech: 'Are you still in WordPerfect, or did you get out?'

Customer: 'How do I tell?'

Tech: 'Can you see the 'C' prompt on the screen?'

Customer: 'What's a sea-prompt?'

Tech: 'Never mind. Can you move the cursor around on the screen?'

Customer: 'There isn't any cursor: I told you, it won't accept anything I type.'

Tech: 'Does your monitor have a power indicator?'

Customer: 'What's a monitor?'

Tech: 'It's the thing with the screen on it that looks like a TV. Does it have a little light that tells you when it's on?'

Customer: 'I don't know.'

Tech: 'Well, then look on the back of the monitor and find where the power cord goes into it. Can you see that?'

Customer: '...Yes, I think so.'

Tech: 'Great. Follow the cord to the plug, and tell me if it's plugged into the wall.'

Customer: '...Yes, it is.'

Tech: 'When you were behind the monitor, did you notice that there were two cables plugged into the back of it, not just one?'

Customer: 'No.'

Tech: 'Well, there are. I need you to look back there again and find the other cable.'

Customer: '...Okay, here it is.'

Tech: 'Follow it for me, and tell me if it's plugged securely into the back of your computer.'

Customer: 'I can't reach.'

Tech: 'Uh huh. Well, can you see if it is?'

Customer: 'No.'

Tech: 'Even if you maybe put your knee on something and lean way over?'

Customer: 'Oh, it's not because I don't have the right angle – it's because it's dark.'

Tech: 'Dark?'

Customer: 'Yes – the office light is off, and the only light I have is coming in from the window.'

Tech: 'Well, turn on the office light then.'

Customer: 'I can't.'

Tech: 'No? Why not?'

Customer: 'Because there's a power outage.'

Tech: 'A power... a power outage? Aha. Okay, we've got it licked now. Do you still have the boxes and manuals and packing stuff your computer came in?'

Customer: 'Well, yes, I keep them in the closet.'

Tech: 'Good. Go get them, and unplug your system and pack it up just like it was when you got it. Then take it back to the store you bought it from.'

Customer: 'Really? Is it that bad?'

Tech: 'Yes, I'm afraid it is.'

Customer: 'Well, all right then, I suppose. What do I tell them?'

Tech: 'Tell them you're too stupid to own a computer.'

• •

Tech Support: 'Customer Support, this is David, may I help you?'

Customer: 'Hello, yes, it's me.'

Tech Support: 'Oh, it's me too.' [chuckle]

Customer: 'No, Esmie. E, s, m, i, e.'

Tech Support: 'Oh, sorry.'

• •

Caller: 'Does your European Breakdown Policy cover me when I am travelling in Australia?'

Operator: 'Doesn't the product give you a clue?'

• •

Customer: 'How much does it cost to Bath on the train?'

Operator: 'If you can get your feet in the sink, then it's free.'

• •

Caller: 'I'd like the number of the Argoed Fish Bar in Cardiff, please.'

Operator: 'I'm sorry, there's no listing. Is the spelling correct?'

Caller: 'Well, it used to be called the Bargoed Fish Bar but the 'B' fell off.'

PEOPLE WHO HAD WEAPONS NAMED AFTER THEM

Mikhail Kalashnikov: Kalashnikov Rifle

Sir William Mills: Mills Bomb

Wilhelm & Peter Mauser: Mauser Magazine Rifle

Jim Bowie: Bowie Knife

Samuel Colt: Colt Revolver

Sir William Congreve: Congreve Rocket

Oliver Winchester: Winchester Rifle

Vyacheslav Molotov: Molotov Cocktail

Bertha Krupp: Big Bertha Mortar

Henry Shrapnel: Shrapnel Shell

Uziel Gal: Uzi Sub-machine Gun

BIRDS (2)

Parrots have much better hearing than humans. During World War I, the French kept parrots on the top of the Eiffel Tower to warn of the approach of German planes.

A parrot can shut its beak with a force of up to 60 kilograms per square centimetre.

Birds don't sleep in their nests, although they may rest in them from time to time.

Emperor penguins will sometimes kidnap baby penguins.

Birds have the ability to change the level of their birdsong if they have to overcome the sound of traffic or other urban noise.

In Japan, the carrion crow has discovered a brilliant way to get walnuts out of their shells. They wait until cars stop at traffic lights, then they fly down and place walnuts in front of the tyres. When the lights change, the cars run over the nuts and crack them.

In Singapore, many people enjoy bird-singing competitions. The owners of the birds spend a lot of time training them and a bird that sings well can bring in thousands of dollars in prize money. A National Songbird Competition has been held annually since 1982.

The Puerto Rican parrot that makes its home in hollowed-out tree trunks in the mountains is one of the most endangered birds in the world.

Peru is home to more than 1,800 bird species, 120 of which are found nowhere else in the world.

Perhaps the most deadly bird in the world is the Hooded Pitohui of Papua New Guinea, a songbird with black and white plumage. Poison in its feathers and skin causes numbness and tingling in anyone who touches it. Beetles in the diet supply the raw material for the poison.

Over 10,000 birds a year die from smashing into windows.

There are about 40 different muscles in a bird's wing.

Hummingbirds are the smallest birds in the world. They're so tiny that one of their enemies is actually an insect (the praying mantis).

Some birds use ants to clean them. The birds puff up their feathers and allow the ants to crawl over their skin. The ants kill other insects living on the birds by squirting them with acid, then eat them.

To survive, many birds must eat half their own weight in food each day.

The frigate bird chases other birds until they throw up and then eats their vomit.

At 3.6 metres, the wandering albatross has the largest wingspan of any bird in the world.

The Australian butcherbird impales insects alive on thorns (in bushes) to eat them later.

The harpy eagle of South America feeds on monkeys.

Green herons catch fish by dropping bits of bread and debris on the surface of the water as bait.

Owls swallow mice, rats, birds and insects whole. Then they throw up bits of these creatures and use the vomit to feed their young in the nest.

Most wild birds have a lifespan of just six months.

ENGLISH (WELL, ALMOST) AS IT IS WRITTEN AROUND THE WORLD (1)

In an East African newspaper: 'A new swimming pool is rapidly taking shape since the contractors have thrown in the bulk of their workers.'

Notice outside an American factory: 'Closing down, thanks to all our customers.'

Sign in a bargain basement store: 'Don't go into another shop to be cheated – come in here.'

Sign in an American chemist's: 'We dispense with accuracy.'

Found on the instruction sheet of an American hairdryer: 'Warning: Do not use in shower. Never use while sleeping.'

On the label of a Taiwanese shampoo: 'Use repeatedly for severe damage.'

Found on the handle of an American hammer: 'Caution: Do not use this hammer to strike any solid object.'

In a Tokyo hotel: 'Is forbidden to steal hotel towels please. If you are not a person to do such thing is please not to read notis.'

On the box of a clockwork toy made in Hong Kong: 'Guaranteed to work throughout its useful life.'

DON'T GO INTO ANOTHER SHOP TO BE CHEATED – COME IN HERE.

Found on a Batman costume box in the US: 'Parent: Please exercise caution, mask and chest plate are not protective; cape does not enable wearer to fly.'

In a Bangkok bar: 'It is forbidden to enter a woman even a foreigner if dressed as a man.'

From Singapore: 'Sir Loin steak with potato cheeps.'

From Macao: 'Utmost of chicken fried in bother.'

In the lobby of a Moscow hotel across from a Russian Orthodox monastery: 'You are welcome to visit the cemetery where famous Russian and Soviet composers, artists, and writers are buried daily except Thursday.'

Sign in a Paris restaurant: 'We serve five o'clock tea at all hours.'

In a Paris hotel elevator: 'Please leave your values at the front desk.'

On the menu of a French restaurant: 'Egg – an extract of fowl, peached or sunside up.'

Two signs from a Majorcan shop entrance: 'English well talking.' 'Here speeching American.'

Sign in a British school: 'If you think you've got a problem, you should see the head.'

WE SERVE
FIVE
O'CLOCK
TEA
AT ALL
HOURS.

Specialist in women and other diseases.

Sign outside a British nightclub: 'Closed tonight for special opening.'

Advert in a British shop window: 'Home wanted for friendly labrador. Will eat anything – loves children.'

Sign in a hotel in Madrid: 'If you wish disinfection enacted in your presense, cry out for the chambermaid.'

In a Budapest zoo: 'Please do not feed the animals. If you have any suitable food, give it to the guard on duty.'

In the office of a Roman doctor: 'Specialist in women and other diseases.'

In a Swiss mountain inn: 'Special today – no ice cream.'

In an Austrian hotel catering to skiers: 'Not to perambulate the corridors in the hours of repose in the boots of ascension.'

On the menu of a Polish hotel: 'Salad a firm's own make; limpid red beet soup with cheesy dumplings in the form of a finger; roasted duck let loose; beef rashers beaten up in the country people's fashion.'

In a Leipzig lift: 'Do not enter the lift backwards, and only when lit up.'

In a hotel in Athens: 'Visitors are expected to complain at the office between the hours of 9 and 11 a.m. daily.'

In a Czechoslovakian tourist agency: 'Take one of our horse-driven city tours – we guarantee no miscarriages.'

In a Vienna hotel: 'In case of fire, do your utmost to alarm the hotel porter.'

From the *Soviet Weekly*: 'There will be a Moscow Exhibition of Arts by 150,000 Soviet Republic painters and sculptors. These were executed over the past two years.'

From a Yugoslavian elevator: 'Let us know about an unficiency as well as leaking on the service. Our utmost will improve it.'

In a Rhodes tailor shop: 'Order your summers suit. Because is big rush we will execute customers in strict rotation.'

Portuguese patent agent: 'It will not be necessary to state the name and address of the inventor if the applicant is not himself.'

On a Soviet ship in the Black Sea: 'Helpsavering apparata in emergings behold many whistles. Associate the stringing apparata about the bosoms and meet behind. Flee then to the indifferent lifesaving shippen obediencing the instructs of the vessel chef.'

Sign in a hotel lift: 'Please do not use the lift when it is not working.'

Sign in a dry-cleaners: 'If you feel we have failed you in any way, we shall be only too pleased to do it again at no extra charge.'

Sign in a jewellery shop: 'Our gifts will not last long at these prices.'

Sign in a beauty parlour: 'Ears pierced while you wait. Pay for two and get another one pierced free.'

Order your summers suit. Because is big rush we will execute customers in strict rotation.

UNUSUAL COLLECTIVE NAMES

A sounder of boar

An obstinacy of buffalo

A caravan of camels

An intrusion of cockroaches

A quiver of cobras

A float of crocodiles

A murder of crows

A dule of doves

A paddling of duck

A parade of elephants

A gang of elk

A cast of falcons

A business of ferrets

A charm of finches

A skulk of flamingoes

A tower of giraffes

An implausibilty of gnus

A troubling of goldfish

A leash of greyhounds

A husk of hares

A kettle of hawks

An array of hegehogs

A bloat of hippopotamuses

A parcel of hogs

A smack of jellyfish

A mob of kangaroo

An exultation of larks	A clamour of rooks
A leap of leopards	**A host of sparrows**
A gulp of magpies	A murmuration of starlings
A mischief of mice	**A mustering of storks**
A labour of moles	A lamentation of swans
A troop of monkeys	**An ambush of tigers**
A romp of otters	A knot of toads
A parliament of owls	**A gang of turkeys**
A company of parrots	A carpet of vultures
A parcel of penguins	**A huddle of walruses**
A bouquet of pheasants	A descent of woodpeckers
A crash of rhinos	**A zeal of zebra**

HOW SCRABBLE COMPARES AROUND THE WORLD

British and English-language editions of Scrabble have 100 letter tiles:

2 blank tiles (worth 0 points)

1 point: E ×12, A ×9, I ×9, O ×8, N ×6, R ×6, T ×6, L ×4, S ×4, U ×4

2 points: D ×4, G ×3

3 points: B ×2, C ×2, M ×2, P ×2

4 points: F ×2, H ×2, V ×2, W ×2, Y ×2

5 points: K ×1

8 points: J ×1, X ×1

10 points: Q ×1, Z ×1

This distribution of letters hasn't changed since Alfred Butts invented the game in 1938.

French-language editions of Scrabble have 102 letter tiles:

2 blank tiles (scoring 0 points)

1 point: E ×15, A ×9, I ×8, N ×6, O ×6, R ×6, S ×6, T ×6, U ×6, L ×5

2 points: D ×3, G ×2, M ×3

3 points: B ×2, C ×2, P ×2

4 points: F ×2, H ×2, V ×2

8 points: J ×1, Q ×1

10 points: K ×1, W ×1, X ×1, Y ×1, Z ×1

Accents are ignored.

German-language editions of Scrabble have 102 letter tiles:

2 blank tiles (scoring 0 points)

1 point: E ×15, N ×9, S ×7, I ×6, R ×6, T ×6, U ×6, A ×5, D ×4

2 points: H ×4, G ×3, L ×3, O ×3

3 points: M ×4, B ×2, W ×1, Z ×1

4 points: C ×2, F ×2, K ×2, P ×1

6 points: Ä ×1, J ×1, Ü ×1, V ×1

8 points: Ö ×1, X ×1

10 points: Q ×1, Y ×1

Italian-language editions of Scrabble have 120 letter tiles:

2 blank tiles (scoring 0 points)

1 point: O ×15, A ×14, I ×12, E ×11

2 points: C ×6, R ×6, S ×6, T ×6

3 points: L ×5, M ×5, N ×5, U ×5

5 points: B ×3, D ×3, F ×3, P ×3, V ×3

8 points: G ×2, H ×2, Z ×2

10 points: Q ×1

The letters J, K, W, X, and Y are absent since these letters aren't used in Italian (except in words they've borrowed from other languages)

Spanish-language editions of Scrabble have 100 letter tiles:

2 blank tiles (scoring 0 points)

1 point: A ×12, E ×12, O ×9, I ×6, S ×6, N ×5, L ×4, R ×5, U ×5, T ×4

2 points: D ×5, G ×2

3 points: C ×4, B ×2, M ×2, P ×2

4 points: H ×2, F ×1, V ×1, Y ×1

5 points: CH ×1, Q ×1

8 points: J ×1, LL ×1, Ñ ×1, RR ×1, X ×1

10 points: Z ×1

Apart from the Ñ, accents are ignored. The letters K and W are absent since these two letters are rarely used in Spanish words.

SAME WORDS –
DIFFERENT PRONOUNCIATION.

The bandage was wound around the wound.

The farm was used to produce produce.

The dump was so full that it had to refuse more refuse.

We must polish the Polish Furniture.

He could lead if he would get the lead out.

The soldier decided to desert his dessert in the desert.

Since there is no time like the present, he thought it was time to present the present.

To help with planting, the farmer taught his sow to sow.

When shot at, the dove dove into the bushes.

I did not object to the object.

The insurance was invalid for the invalid.

There was a row among the oarsmen about how to row.

They were too close to the door to close it.

The buck does funny things when the does are present.

A seamstress and a sewer fell down into a sewer line.

A bass was painted on the head of the bass drum.

The wind was too strong to wind the sail.

Upon seeing the tear in the painting I shed a tear.

I had to subject the subject to a series of tests.

How can I intimate this to my most intimate friend?

SEA LIFE

Coral and jellyfish are closely related.

The sponge is an animal without a nervous system.

Jellyfish sometimes evaporate if stranded on a beach.

The giant squid is the largest creature without a backbone.

Giant squids have tentacles as long as telephone poles and eyes bigger than footballs. They (probably) have the largest eyes in the world. But scientists still know very little about the giant squid, other than what can be gleaned from a hundred or so beached carcasses, dating back to 1639. Despite centuries of myths and tales of sightings, more is known about dinosaurs.

The noise made by a pistol shrimp is so loud that it can shatter glass.

A sea urchin walks on its teeth.

The quahog, a marine clam, can live for up to 200 years, making it the longest living ocean creature in the world. Second place goes to the killer whale at 90 years, third is the blue whale at 80 years, fourth is the sea turtle at 50 years and fifth is the tiger shark at 40 years.

Pea crabs (the size of a pea) are the smallest crabs in the world.

Schools of South American (Pacific) Humboldt squid have been known to strip 225-kilo marlins to the bone.

Plankton produce nearly three-quarters of the Earth's oxygen.

At the end of a lobster's second year, it will have grown to only about 5 centimetres long – still smaller than a jumbo shrimp.

Mussels can thrive in polluted water because of their ability to purify bacteria, fungi and viruses.

Only 1 in 1,000 creatures born in the sea survives to maturity.

Average number of eggs laid by the female American oyster per year: 500 million. About one oyster will reach maturity.

Squid have three hearts.

One in 5,000 north Atlantic lobsters are born bright blue.

More than 20 million seahorses are harvested each year for folk medicinal purposes.

Sea sponges are used in drugs for treating asthma and cancer.

The national fish of Hawaii is the Humuhumunukunukuapua'a (or the reef triggerfish as it is also known).

The sea cucumber, a relative of the starfish, has the ability to change from solid to fluid in order to escape predators.

A starfish can regrow an arm if one is torn off.

There's a lake in Palau called Jellyfish Lake. It's famous because the jellyfish in this lake don't sting (they don't need to because they have no predators).

The lethal lion's mane jellyfish is the world's biggest jellyfish. The largest specimen ever found had a bell (body) with a diameter of 2.3 metres and its tentacles reached 36.5 metres, making it longer than a blue whale, which is commonly considered to be the largest animal in the world.

PHRASES FIRST COINED BY SHAKESPEARE

A fool's paradise – *Romeo and Juliet*

Bated breath – *The Merchant of Venice*

Cold comfort – *King John*

Come full circle – *King Lear*

Good riddance – *Troilus and Cressida*

In my heart of hearts – *Hamlet*

Let slip the dogs of war – *Julius Caesar*

Milk of human kindness – *Macbeth*

More sinned against than sinning – *King Lear*

My own flesh and blood – *The Merchant of Venice*

Neither a borrower nor a lender be – *Hamlet*

Once more unto the breach – *Henry V*

One fell swoop – *Macbeth*

Sorry sight – *Macbeth*

Spotless reputation – *Richard III*

Stood on ceremonies – *Julius Caesar*

Strange bedfellows – *The Tempest*

The course of true love never did run smooth – *A Midsummer Night's Dream*

The naked truth – *Love's Labour's Lost*

The world's mine oyster – *The Merry Wives of Windsor*

'Tis neither here nor there – *Othello*

To make a virtue of necessity – *The Two Gentlemen of Verona*

To the manner born – *Hamlet*

Too much of a good thing – *As You Like It*

Unkindest cut of all – *Julius Caesar*

We are such stuff as dreams are made on – T*he Tempest*

Wear my heart on my sleeve – *Othello*

What's in a name? – *Romeo and Juliet*

THE NAMES OF COUNTRIES AND THEIR ORIGINS

Albania: 'Tribe that lived on the hill'

Australia: Latin for 'southern (land)'

Austria: Latin for 'eastern (land)'

Belgium: Celtic for 'brave, warlike'

Brazil: 'Heat'

Cameroon: Portuguese for 'prawns' which were seen in the river Cameroon

Chad: Named after Lake Chad

China: Named after the Ch'in dynasty

Cyprus: Named after copper, of which it had loads

El Salvador: 'The saviour'

England: Named after the 'Angles', who came from Germany

Estonia: Named after the Ests people who lived there 2,000 years ago

France: Named after the Franks, a Germanic tribe that invaded the country more than a thousand years ago

Haiti: 'Mountainous'

Hong Kong: 'Fragrant harbour'

Iran: 'Worthy'

Iraq: 'Lowland'

Italy: Named after the Vitali tribe

Japan: The Chinese for 'the land of the rising sun'

Kenya: Named after its highest mountain peak

Lebanon: 'White mountain'

Mexico: 'Moon water'

Mongolia: 'Brave ones'

Morocco: 'The western Kingdom'

Netherlands: 'Low lands'

New Zealand: Named after Zeeland, a Dutch province

Norway: 'Northern seaway'

Panama: 'Place of many fish'

Philippines: Named after King Philip II of Spain

Portugal: Latin for 'warm harbour'

San Marino: Named after Saint Marinus

Saudi Arabia: Named after King Ibn-Saud

Singapore: Sanskrit for 'lion town' (curious, as there are no lions in Singapore)

Switzerland: Named after 'Schwyz', one of its cantons

Tanzania: Combination of Zanzibar and Tanganyika which united to form it in 1964

Tobago: 'Tobacco (pipe)'

Trinidad: 'Trinity' (as in the Holy Trinity)

Turkey: 'Strong owner'

Venezuela: 'Little Venice' (the houses built on stilts over the water made it look like Venice)

Vietnam: 'Land of the south'

Wales: 'Foreigners'

Yemen: Named after the Arabic for 'right' – i.e. it's on one's right, when facing Mecca

COUNTRIES WITH UNORIGINALLY NAMED CAPITAL CITIES

Algeria – Capital: Algiers

Andorra – Capital: Andorra La Vella

Brazil – Capital: Brasilia

Djibouti – Capital: Djibouti

El Salvador – Capital: San Salvador

Gibraltar – Capital: Gibraltar

Guatemala – Capital: Guatemala City

Guinea-Bissau – Capital: Bissau

Kuwait – Capital: Kuwait City

Luxembourg – Capital: Luxembourg

Mexico – Capital: Mexico City

Panama – Capital: Panama City

Sãn Marino – Capital: City of Sãn Marino

São Tomé and Principé – Capital: São Tomé

Singapore – Capital: Singapore City

Tunisia – Capital: Tunis

Vatican City – Capital: Vatican City

THE COUNTRIES WITH THE MOST CARS PER CAPITA

1st United States 765 cars per thousand people

2nd Luxembourg 686

3rd Malaysia 641

4th Australia 619

5th Malta 607

6th Italy 566

7th Canada 563

8th New Zealand 560

9th Austria 558

10th Germany 546

The UK comes 21st with 426 cars per thousand people

GROUND CREW GET THEIR REVENGE

Here are some maintenance complaints/problems made by pilots from the Australian airline QANTAS...and the response of the engineers and ground crew.

(P – The problem, as logged by the pilot.)
(S – The solution, as logged by the engineers.)

P – Left inside main tyre almost needs replacement.
S – Almost replaced left inside main tyre.

P – Test flight OK, except autoland very rough.
S – Autoland not installed on this aircraft.

P – Something loose in cockpit.
S – Something tightened in cockpit.

P – Evidence of leak on right main landing gear.
S – Evidence removed.

P – DME volume unbelievably loud.
S – Volume set to more believable level.

P – Friction locks cause throttle levers to stick.
S – That's what they are there for.

P – IFF inoperative.
S – IFF always inoperative in OFF mode.

P – Suspected crack in windscreen.
S – Suspect you're right.

P – Number 3 engine missing.
S – Engine found on right wing after brief search.

P – Aircraft handles funny.
S – Aircraft warned to 'Straighten up, Fly Right, and Be Serious.'

P – Target radar hums.
S – Reprogrammed target radar with words.

P – Mouse in cockpit.
S – Cat installed,

WORDS

There are only two sequences of four consecutive letters that can be found in the English language: 'rstu' and 'mnop.' Examples of each are 'understudy' and 'gymnophobia.'

Faulconbridge a town in the Blue Mountains of Australia, uses half of the alphabet, including all five vowels, and doesn't use any individual letter twice.

The ten-letter word 'soupspoons' consists entirely of letters from the second half of alphabet, as does the hyphenated topsy-turvy.

'Queue' is the only word in the English language to be pronounced the same way even if the last four letters are removed.

The word 'bigwig', meaning someone important, comes from King Louis IV of France, who wore big wigs.

Only two words in the English language end in '-gry': hungry and angry.

'Accommodate' is the most misspelt word in English.

The longest words with vertical symmetry (the left half is a mirror image of the right half) are 'otto', 'maam' and 'toot'.

The words polysyllabic, fifteen-lettered and unhyphenated are all autological in that they truly describe themselves. So 'polysyllabic' – meaning having many syllables – has many syllables. Similarly, the word 'fifteen-lettered' has fifteen letters and 'unhyphenated' is indeed unhyphenated.

'COUSCOUS' is the longest word in the English language that can look the same whether written all in lower case or all in capitals.

'Strengthlessnesses' is the longest word in the English language with just one (repeated) vowel.

The longest English word that uses only the letters in the last half of the alphabet is 'non-supports'.

The longest word with horizontal symmetry (the top half is a mirror image of the bottom half) is 'COOKBOOK'. It is only horizontally symmetrical when written in capitals. The longest English words that are composed only of letters that each have 180° rotational symmetry independently are 'SOONISH' and 'ONIONS'.

'Spoonfeed', nine letters long, is the longest word with its letters in reverse alphabetical order.

The word 'ushers' contains five personal pronouns spelled consecutively: he, her, hers, she and us.

'Rugged' and 'ague' are two-syllable words that can be turned into one-syllable words by the addition of two letters ('sh' to make shrugged; 'pl' to make plague).

'Are' and 'came' are one-syllable words that can be turned into three-syllable words by the addition of just one letter at the end ('a' to make area; 'o' to make cameo).

There is no single word for the back of the knee.

Thirteen per cent of the letters in a given book are 'e'.

A six-word sequence in which letters are added to the beginning of the words is: hes (plural of he, used as a noun to mean a male), shes (plural of she), ashes, lashes, plashes (plural of plash, a splashing sound), splashes.

'Widow' is the only female word in the English language that is shorter than its corresponding male term ('widower').

There are only two words in English that end in the letters 'shion' (though many words end in this sound): cushion and fashion.

A kangaroo word is a word that contains all letters of another word, in order, with the same meaning. Examples include 'masculine' (male), 'observe' (see) and 'inflammable' (flammable).

The three-syllable word 'hideous' with the change of a single consonant, becomes a two-syllable word with no vowel sounds in common: 'hideout'.

Only three English words end in the letters 'cion'. These are 'coercion', 'scion' and 'suspicion'.

'Zzyzx', a place in California, and 'zyzzyx', a type of wasp, consist of only the last three letters of the alphabet.

The word 'iouea', (meaning a genus of sea sponges), is the only word to contain all five vowels and no other letters.

'Subbookkeeper' is the only word found in an English dictionary with four pairs of double letters in a row.

The word 'shampoo' comes from the Hindu word champ, meaning 'to massage'.

The longest English word that uses only the letters in the last half of the alphabet is 'non-supports'.

Words that came to English via the Czech language include 'robot', 'pistol' and 'dollar'.

'Asthma' and 'isthmi' are the only six-letter words that begin and end with a vowel and have no other vowels between.

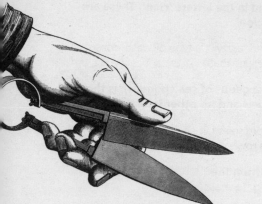

CONTRANYMS

A contranym is a single word that has opposite meanings, for example:

Sanction can mean (to) approve or (a) punishment

Clip can mean to cut or to fasten (together)

Cleave can mean to split apart or to join together

Screen can mean to shield or to present

Bound can mean to be going (to be bound for London) or to be tied up, unable to move

Left can mean remaining or to have gone

THE BIBLE

Salt is mentioned more than thirty times in the Bible.

The three most mentioned animals in the Bible are sheep, lamb and lion in that order.

Pigs are mentioned just twice. There is no mention of rats or cats.

The longest verse is Esther 8:9.

There are more than 1,700 references to gems and precious stones in the Bible.

There are 929 chapters in the Old Testament containing 592,439 words.

There are 260 chapters in the New Testament containing 181,253 words.

It is believed that Shakespeare was 46 around the time the King James version of the Bible was written. In Psalms 46, the 46th word from the first word is 'shake' and the 46th word from the last word is 'spear'.

A bible published in 1631 contained the unfortunate commandment: 'Thou shalt commit adultery.' The printers were fined the then huge sum of £300 and went out of business – just for missing out the word 'not'. Understandably, that Bible became known as The Wicked Bible.

The Bible has been translated into 2,200 languages and dialects – including Klingon.

Fifty years ago, 90 per cent of British adults owned a Bible; today less than two-thirds do.

Defenestration is the act of throwing someone out of a window and it gets its name from the Latin words meaning 'out of' and 'window'. The first recorded defenestration was several years before the word was even invented. In the Bible, Jezebel was defenestrated by her own servants.

Thou shalt commit adultery.

Nowhere in the Bible does it say or suggest that angels have wings.

Gabriel, Michael and Lucifer are the three angels mentioned by name in the Bible.

In Christian theology there are nine choirs of angels. From highest to lowest, they are: seraphim, cherubim, thrones, dominions, virtues, powers, principalities, archangels and angels.

The seven archangels are Michael, Gabriel, Raphael, Uriel, Chamuel, Jophiel and Zadkiel.

GENUINE COMMENTS MADE BY DOCTORS IN THEIR PATIENTS' NOTES

Patient has chest pain if she lies on her left side for over a year.

On the 2nd day the knee was better and on the 3rd day it disappeared completely.

Discharge status: alive but without permission.

The patient refused an autopsy.

The patient has no past history of suicides.

Patient has left his white blood cells at another hospital.

Patient's past medical history has been remarkably insignificant with only a 40-pound weight gain in the past three days.

She is numb from her toes down.

The skin was moist and dry.

Occasional, constant, infrequent headaches.

Patient was alert and unresponsive.

She stated that she had been constipated for most of her life, until she got a divorce.

I saw your patient today, who is still under our car for physical therapy.

Patient has two teenage children but no other abnormalities.

Skin: Somewhat pale but present.

Patient was seen in consultation by Dr—, who felt we should sit on the abdomen, and I agree.

By the time he was admitted, his rapid heart stopped, and he was feeling better.

The patient was in his usual state of good health until his airplane ran out of gas and crashed.

When she fainted, her eyes rolled around the room.

Patient was released to outpatient department without dressing.

The patient expired on the floor uneventfully.

She slipped on the ice and apparently her legs went in separate directions in early December.

The patient left the hospital feeling much better except for her original complaints.

She was divorced last April. No other serious illness.

Apparently the mother resented the fact that she was born in her forties.

PEOPLE WHO GAVE THEIR NAMES TO THINGS OR PLACES

Achilles: Achilles heel

Adam: Adam's apple

André-Marie Ampère: Ampere (unit of electric current)

Francis Beaufort: Beaufort scale (measuring wind speeds)

Louis de Béchamel: Béchamel sauce

Simón Bolívar: Bolivia

General Ambrose Burnside: Sideburns

Anders Celsius: Celsius (unit of temperature)

Gustave Eiffel: Eiffel Tower

Bartolomeo Eustachi: Eustachian tube (in the ear)

Sir George Everest: Mount Everest

Gabriel Fahrenheit: Fahrenheit scale

Leonhart Fuchs: Fuchsia (flower)

Giuseppe Garibaldi: Garibaldi biscuit

Dr. Joseph Ignace Guillotin: Guillotine (even though he didn't invent it)

Heinrich Rudolf Hertz: Hertz (a unit of frequency)

James Prescott Joule: Joule (unit of energy or heat)

John Loudon McAdam: Tarmac (tar+macadam) road surface

Samuel Morse: Morse code

Georg Ohm: Ohm (unit of electrical resistance)

Louis Pasteur: Pasteurisation

William Penn: Pennsylvania

Joseph Pilates: Pilates (exercise method)

Joel Roberts Poinsett: Poinsettia (plant)

Charles Ponzi: Ponzi scheme (a type of fraud)

Vidkun Quisling: Quisling (traitor)

Charles Richter: Richter scale (for measuring earthquakes)

Romulus: Rome

John Montagu, 4th Earl of Sandwich: the Sandwich

Henry S. Shrapnel: Shrapnel

Etienne de Silhouette: Silhouette

Alessandro Volta: Volt (a unit of electromotive force)

James Watt: Watt (a unit of power)

Duke of Wellington: Wellington boot

WHAT IS A GRANDPARENT?

HERE'S WHAT A CLASS OF EIGHT-YEAR OLDS WROTE WHEN ASKED TO ANSWER THE QUESTION

'Grandparents are a lady and a man who have no little children of her own. They like other people's'.

'When they read to us, they don't skip. They don't mind if we ask for the same story over again.'

'Grandparents don't have to do anything except be there when we come to see them. They are so old they shouldn't play hard or run. It is good if they drive us to the shops and give us money'.

'When they take us for walks, they slow down past things like pretty leaves and caterpillars'.

'Usually grandmothers are fat but not too fat to tie your shoes'.

'They wear glasses and funny underwear'.

'Everybody should try to have a grandmother, especially if you don't have television because they are the only grown ups who like to spend time with us'.

FRENCH WORDS OR PHRASES COMMONLY USED IN ENGLISH

à la carte (food ordered off the menu – as opposed to the set menu)

à propos (regarding/concerning)

adieu (farewell – as opposed to au revoir which means 'see you later')

adroit (dexterous, clever. This comes from the French word 'droit' meaning 'right'. Compare this to gauche – or left – which has come to mean 'clumsy')

aperçu (insight)

apéritif (drink before a meal)

attaché (person attached to an embassy)

au courant (up-to-date)

au fait (knowing something)

au pair (young foreigner who does domestic chores in exchange for room and board)

avant-garde (cutting-edge art, music and literature)

blasé (jaded)

bon mot (witty remark)

bon vivant (someone who enjoys the good life)

bon voyage (have a good journey)

bric-à-brac (small ornamental objects)

brunette (brown-haired girl)

bureau de change (place to change currency)

café (a coffee shop)

canard (unfounded rumour or story)

carte blanche (unlimited authority)

cause célèbre (topical issue)

c'est la vie (such is life)

chaise longue (a long chair for lying down on)

chanteuse (female singer)

chauffeur (driver)

chef d'œuvre (masterpiece)

chic (stylish)

chignon (woman's hairstyle worn in a roll
at the nape of the neck)

cliché (stereotype)

clique (small exclusive group of friends)

communiqué (official communication)

concierge (receptionist, janitor)

confrère (colleague)

contretemps (disagreement, clash)

cortège (funeral procession)

coup d'état (revolution)

**coup de grâce (the final blow that results in
victory or defeat)**

couture (high fashion)

crèche (place where parents leave young children)

crème de la crème (best of the best)

crêpe (pancake)

critique (critical analysis or evaluation of a work)

cul-de-sac (dead-end street)

de rigueur (expected)

de trop (too much)

déjà vu ('already seen': an impression of having seen or experienced something before)

dénouement (the end result)

dossier (a file containing detailed information)

élan (flair or style)

éminence grise (person with little formal power but great influence over those in power)

en famille (with one's family)

en masse (all together)

en route (on the way)

enfant terrible (a disruptively unconventional person)

ennui (boredom)

entente (diplomatic agreement)

entre nous (between us)

esprit de corps (feeling of solidarity among members of a group)

fait accompli (something that has already happened and so can't be undone)

faux (false, fake)

faux pas (mistake)

force majeure (an event outside of anyone's control)

froideur (coldness in someone's attitude)

grand prix (first prize – e.g. in motor racing)

haute cuisine (fine cooking)

hauteur (arrogance)

hors de combat (out of action)

hors d'œuvre (starter, appetizer)

idée fixe (obsession)

joie de vivre (joy of living)

laissez-faire (letting people get on with things)

métier (area of expertise)

nom de plume (author's pseudonym)

objet d'art (work of art)

papier-mâché (craft using paper and paste)

parvenu (social upstart**)**

pied-à-terre (small place to stay in a city)

sang-froid (coolness and composure under pressure)

savoir-faire (knowing how to do things)

soigné (fashionable, elegant)

soirée (an evening party)

sommelier (wine waiter)

soupçon (very small amount)

tête-à-tête (private conversation between two people)

volte-face (complete reversal of opinion)

GERMAN WORDS OR PHRASES COMMONLY USED IN ENGLISH

abseil (drop to the ground using a rope)

angst (general feeling of fear or worry)

blitz (lightning-fast)

bratwurst (type of sausage)

doppelgänger (double or lookalike)

ersatz (replacement)

fest (festival)

flak (criticism)

frankfurter (type of sausage – usually served as a hot dog)

hinterland (other interests apart from your main occupation)

kaput (broken)

kindergarten (preschool)

kitsch (cheap, sentimental, gaudy)

lager (type of beer)

poltergeist (alleged paranormal phenomenon where objects appear to move)

pumpernickel (type of rye bread)

putsch (overthrow of those in power; coup d'état)

Realpolitik (the way politics really works)

rucksack (backpack)

sauerkraut (fermented cabbage)

schadenfreude (delight at the misfortune of others)

spritzer (white wine and soda water)

strudel (pastry)

wanderlust (the yearning to travel)

weltschmerz (world-weariness)

wunderkind (child prodigy)

zeitgeist (spirit of the age)

ANIMALS THAT ARE NOW EXTINCT IN THE BRITISH ISLES

Arctic fox (became extinct in the British Isles around 10,000 BC)

Arctic lemming (*c.* 8000 BC)

Brown bear (*c.* 1000 AD)

Cave lion (*c.* 10,000 BC)

Eurasian wolf (1740)

Irish elk (*c.* 6000 BC)

Eurasian lynx (*c.* 400 AD)

Narrow-headed vole (*c.* 8000 BC)

Root vole (*c.* 1500 BC)

Saiga antelope (*c.* 10,000 BC)

Wolverine (*c.* 6000 BC)

Woolly mammoth (*c.* 10,000 BC)

Woolly rhinoceros (*c.* 10,000 BC)

CUSTOMS AND TRADITIONS AROUND THE WORLD

In Burundi, the importance of cattle is demonstrated in the traditional greeting, 'May you have herds of cattle.' Wishing people 'herds of cattle' is a way to wish them good health and prosperity.

Scarification, the ritual application of scars to the faces of tribal members, is practised by many groups in Chad. Lines and other symbols are made on the faces of young men to mark them permanently as members of a particular tribe.

Korean women cover their mouths while laughing.

The Onge of the Andaman Islands don't ask 'How are you?' but 'How is your nose?' The correct response is to say you are 'heavy with odour'.

Very young Burmese children wear holy thread around their necks or wrists to protect them from bad spirits or spells.

In the marriage ceremony of the ancient Inca Indians of Peru, the couple was only considered properly wed when they took off their sandals and handed them to each other.

After a marriage, Somalis hold dances for three to seven days in a row.

Although Thais like to give and get presents, it's considered rude to open a gift in the presence of the giver. So they put the gift aside and only open it when they're alone.

In Malaysia, they celebrate a child's birth when the child is one month old by shaving the child's head.

When people in Mauritius are given a gift, they always accept it with their right hand.

In Korea, it's considered good manners to give and receive objects with both hands. If one Korean wants to receive an object from another, they'll put out their right hand to accept the object and their left hand under the right wrist.

If a Congolese offers to share a meal with a guest, that guest is expected to show reluctance to join the host's table. But the guest should ultimately accept the offer. Not to do so would be considered rude.

It is customary for Rwandan children to avoid eye contact when talking to an elder.

A wedding feast in Yemen lasts for up to 21 days.

Filipino children will often take the hand of an elder and place it on their forehead as a sign of respect.

In Rwanda, rich women often wore heavy copper bracelets and anklets. Because of the weight of the jewellery, the women were unable to do much work. So the very wearing of jewellery served to distinguish rich women from the women who worked in the fields.

Every year there's a Great Tomato Fight in Buñol, Spain. Tens of thousands of people come from all over the world to participate in a great battle during which more than a hundred tons of over-ripe tomatoes are thrown in the streets. For the week leading up to the battle, the town of Buñol is filled with parades, fireworks, food and street parties.

On New Year's Eve in Spain, people eat grapes as the clock strikes midnight. Twelve grapes symbolize good luck for each month of the New Year.

Eritreans will commonly scoop up food and put it in the mouth of a loved one or guest. The act is a sign of affection.

Some Bolivians bring their new cars to the shrine of the Virgin of Candelaria to have them blessed. A local priest blesses the car, and then the owner showers it with champagne.

Men from the Dassanetch tribe of Ethiopia daub their bodies with cow dung.

In Bosnia and Herzegovina, it's considered impolite to beckon with the index finger or to shout in public.

In Thailand, when two strangers meet, they begin by establishing who has the higher status. Questions such as 'How old are you?' and 'How much do you earn?' are not considered rude.

In Japan, it is customary to wash before getting into the bath. The bath is for soaking and relaxing, not for washing. The water stays clean so that another family member can soak in the same water later.

In Denmark, when it's a child's birthday, they fly a flag out of a window so that everyone knows.

Cloth is highly valued in Bhutan. Traditional gifts at funerals and other occasions are pieces of cloth, given in uneven numbers (for superstitious reasons). The more cloth given, the higher the status of the giver. Money put in an envelope may be used as a substitute, along with the obligatory white scarf. The symbolic value of the scarf is of vital importance when visiting monasteries or taking part in official ceremonies. The act of giving a white scarf is a must for every Bhutanese at any important event. These scarves are recycled until they show signs of wear and tear. Generally speaking, Bhutanese exchange presents as a form of etiquette. Those receiving a gift don't open it until they are alone. To do otherwise would be bad manners and would imply that the recipient wants another gift. Gifts between equals are always reciprocated. However, when a gift is of significant value and comes from a person of high status, it is reciprocated with loyalty and service rather than with a gift.

Young Croatians celebrate the arrival of the summer solstice by jumping over bonfires.

At Czech weddings they throw peas instead of rice.

Argentinians celebrate a Day of Friendship every year at the end of June.

In Ancient Egypt, the High Priest was the only person who could wear cotton.

Traditionally, an Albanian bride gave her mother-in-law a carpet woven either by her mother or herself.

The Berbers of Algeria pride themselves on their hospitality. They have a saying: 'When you come to our house, it is we who are your guests, for this is your house.'

In Algeria using your fingers to point at objects or people is considered impolite. Care is also taken not to let the sole of the foot point towards another person.

In the Andes, before people drink chicha, a maize-based drink, they sprinkle a few drops on to the ground for Pachamama (the goddess known as 'Mother Universe') to 'guarantee' a good harvest.

In Singapore, 40 days after its birth, a baby is dressed in the lucky colour red and shown off to relatives.

In Swaziland, girls and boys have their ears pierced and they keep bits of straw in the holes because they don't have earrings.

WORDS AND NAMES THAT ARE ACTUALLY ACRONYMS

BAFTA (as in the annual TV and film awards) – British Academy of Film and Television Arts

DAB (Radio) – Digital Audio Broadcasting

DEFCON – Defence readiness condition

DIY – Do It Yourself (home improvements)

Laser – Light Amplification by Stimulated Emission of Radiation

NAAFI (military canteen) – Navy, Army and Air Force Institute

NATO – North Atlantic Treaty Organization

Pakistan – Punjab, Afghan states, Kashmir, sIndh, baluchiSTAN

PAYE – Pay As You Earn

PIN – Personal Identification Number

Qantas – Queensland And Northern Territory Aerial Services

Quango – QUasi Autonomous Non-Governmental Organisation

Scuba – Self Contained Underwater Breathing Apparatus

SWAT (team) – Special Weapons And Tactics

TARDIS (*Doctor Who*) – Time And Relative Dimensions In Space

TASER – Thomas A. Swift's Electric Rifle

MARINE MAMMALS

Seals sleep in snatches of one and a half minutes.

Sea otters have the densest fur of any creature – 100,000 hairs per square centimetre. That's about the same in a square centimetre as a human has on his or her entire head.

Seals hold their breath while they sleep on the surface of the water.

Walruses use their long downward tusks to help them get about and their zoological name actually means 'toothwalk'.

Walruses have an astonishing sucking power and can suck the brains of seal pups out through their nostrils.

There once were more sea lions on Earth than people.

THE CHANCE OF ...

... being struck by lightning is one in 10 million.

... being hit by a meteorite is one in 200 million.

... a girl being colour blind is one in 1,000.

... a boy being colour blind is one in 100.

... winning first prize on the National Lottery: one in 14 million.

... being killed by a bee sting is one in 6 million.

... hitting two holes-in-one during the same round of golf is one in 8 million.

... being hijacked on a plane by terrorists twice in the same year is one in 150 million.

... every match in a full Premier League programme finishing in a 0–0 draw is one in 60 million.

SECRET SERVICE CODENAMES

POTUS – President of the United States

FLOTUS – First Lady of the United States

VPOTUS – Vice President of the United States

Eagle – Bill Clinton

Evergreen – Hillary Clinton

Renegade – Barack Obama

Renaissance – Michelle Obama

Celtic – Joe Biden

Denali – Sarah Palin

Kittyhawk – Queen Elizabeth II

Unicorn – Prince Charles

CARTOONS AND ANIMATION

In 1938, Joe Shuster and Jerry Siegel sold all rights to the comic-strip character Superman to their publishers for $130.

Clark Kent, the name of Superman's alter ego, was derived from the names of the Hollywood stars Clark Gable and Kent Taylor.

Walt Disney named Mickey Mouse after the child star Mickey Rooney, whose mother he dated.

Mickey Mouse's birthday is 18th November.

Mickey Mouse is known as Topolino in Italy.

Scooby-Doo's first name is Scoobert.

The animator who created the cartoon dog Scooby-Doo got the inspiration for his name from the ending of Frank Sinatra's *Strangers In The Night*.

Dr William Moulton Marston, the man who created the comic book character Wonder Woman, also invented the lie detector test.

The most common set of initials for Superman's friends and enemies is LL.

Bart Simpson's hair has precisely nine spikes.

Homer Simpson's pin number is 7431.

The comic strip 'Peanuts' is known as 'Radishes' in Denmark.

Captain Euro was a superhero commissioned by the European Union to promote itself. His arch-enemy is Dr D. Vider.

MAMMALS, BIRDS AND INSECTS AND THE SOUNDS THEY MAKE

Alligators – bellow, hiss

Apes – gibber

Badgers – growl

Bats – screech

Bears – growl

Bees – hum and buzz

Beetles – drone

Bulls – bellow

Camels – grunt

Cats – purr, miaow and hiss

Chickens – cluck

Cocks – crow

Cows – moo

Coyotes – yelp, cry

Crickets – chirp

Cuckoos – coo, cuckoo

Dogs – bark, woof

Dolphins – click

Donkeys – bray, hee-haw

Doves – coo

Ducks – quack

Eagles – scream, cry

Elephants – trumpet

Frogs – croak

Goats – bleat

Geese – cackle, honk, quack

Hamsters – squeak

Hippopotamuses – bellow, rumble, roar, growl

Hogs – grunt

Horses – neigh, snort, whinny

Hyenas – laugh

Jackals – howl

Lambs – bleat

Lions – roar

Llamas – growl

Magpies – chatter

Mice – squeak

Monkeys – chatter, gibber

Nightingales – sing, warble

Owls – hoot

Parrots – talk, screech, squawk

Penguins – honk

Pigs – oink, snort, grunt, squeal

Pigeons – coo

Rabbits – squeak, drum

Rats – squeak

Rhinos – bellow

Seagulls – scream

Sheep – bleat, baa

Snakes – hiss

Stags – bellow

Tigers – growl, roar

Tortoises – grunt

Turkeys – gobble

Vultures – scream

Walruses – groan

Whales – sing

Wolves – howl

Zebras – neigh, whinny

Cheetahs make a chirping sound – a bit like a bird's chirp or a dog's yelp – but the sound is so intense, it can be heard a mile away.

The dwarf mongoose has a range of different sounds. When a predator is spotted by a mongoose acting as a sentry, it lets out a scream meaning that danger is close by. When the threat is further away, the sentry uses a churring sound. When the mongoose finds food, it lets out a shrill twittering to alert its friends.

The roar of a male lion, used to intimidate rivals and communicate with other lions, is audible five miles away.

The two best-known cat noises are roaring and purring. But only four kinds of cat can roar – lions, leopards, tigers and jaguars – and none of them can purr.

Elephants and chimps have around 30 different sorts of sounds to communicate different things to one another (by comparison, horses have just six).

The orangutan's warning signal to would-be aggressors is a loud belch.

Lions cannot roar until they reach the age of two.

But the noisiest (in terms of the distance from which it can still be heard) land animal is the howler monkey of central and South America. The sound that it makes has been measured at 88 decibels from five metres away and can be heard up to ten miles away.

Wolves howl to avoid territorial fights with other packs of wolves.

Meerkats looking for food keep in touch with each other by making a soft murmuring sound. But when they spot a predator, they cluck and bark to warn the others to rush back to the burrow.

Each species of grasshopper has its own song. This is to stop the different species from breeding with each other. The female needs to know that she's listening to a male from her own species.

Gibbons communicate through high-pitched songs that can be heard over a distance of miles.

CRICKET

In a 1958 cricket Test against New Zealand, England's innings was opened by an international rugby union player and an international soccer player. Arthur Milton also represented England at soccer while his opening partner, Mike Smith, won a rugby union cap for England.

The world's oldest Test cricketer was England's Wilfred Rhodes who was 52 years and 165 days old at the end of his final Test against the West Indies in 1930. Having begun his Test career at the age of just 21, Rhodes could also boast the world's longest Test career: 30 years and 315 days.

In the 1979/80 India vs Pakistan Test match at Bangalore, an invasion of bees halted play, prompting the players and umpires to lie face down and cover their ears.

The game of cricket has been traced back to shepherds in seventeenth century England. The shepherds would bat in front of a tree stump – hence the term 'stumps'. Sometimes, a game was played in front of a wicket-gate – hence the term 'wickets'.

Jack MacBryan is the only Test cricketer never to have batted, bowled or taken a catch in his entire Test career. He played his only Test for England in 1924 but very few (just 66.5) overs were possible because of the rain and he never got a look in.

Thirteen cricketers have scored double hundreds in Test matches but finished on the losing side. Twelve of the thirteen batsmen suffered this fate once but it happened to the West Indian cricketer Brian Lara on three separate occasions.

Plenty of men have played Test cricket for two countries but John Traicos is the only man to be born in one country and then play Test cricket for two other countries. He was born in Egypt, played Test cricket for South Africa in 1970 and then for Zimbabwe more than 22 years later when they were awarded Test status in 1992.

Only two Test matches have ever been tied – the first between West Indies and Australia at Brisbane in 1960/61 and the second between Australia and India in Madras in 1986/87.

In 1979, England were playing Australia in Perth when the Australian Dennis Lillee was caught by Peter Willey off the bowling of Graham Dilley. So it was Lillee caught Willey bowled Dilley.

In a 1997/98 Test match between Pakistan and South Africa, Mushtaq Ahmed was bowling to Pat Symcox when he knocked back Symcox's middle stump. However, the immense heat had fused together the bails and so they didn't fall. In fact, the middle stump bounced back into place and Symcox continued on his way to his second highest Test score.

There are only two families to play Test cricket in three consecutive generations. George Headley and his son Ron both played Test cricket for the West Indies and Ron's son Dean played for England. Jahangir Khan played Test cricket for India while his son, Majid, and grandson, Bazid, both played for Pakistan.

Only thirteen bowlers have taken a wicket with their very first ball in Test cricket. However, over a hundred bowlers have taken a wicket with their very last ball in Test cricket. No bowler appears on both lists.

In the nineteenth century, grazing sheep helped keep the grass down at Lords cricket ground.

No bowler can bowl two consecutive overs but in the 1951 Test against England, Alex Moir of New Zealand did just that. He bowled the last over before the tea break and the first over afterwards.

Five batsmen have been left stranded on 99 not out in a Test match. Four of them had either already made Test centuries or would go on to do so. However, 99 turned out to be the England cricketer Alex Tudor's highest test score.

The MCC (Marylebone Cricket Club) used to represent England in overseas cricket matches. It was due to play its first overseas fixture in 1789 against France but the French Revolution got in the way. Two hundred years later in 1989, they played the game and the French won by seven wickets.

DUCKS

A batsman who is dismissed without scoring is said to have scored a duck. This is supposedly because a duck's egg looks like a zero. There are a few variations on this theme.

A Golden Duck is when a player is dismissed on the very first ball he faces.

If he doesn't even face a ball – probably because he was run out coming from the non-striker's end – it's called a Diamond Duck.

If a player is out on the very first ball of the season, it's called a Platinum Duck.

If a player is dismissed for nought in both innings of the same two-innings match, it's called a Pair.

If a player is dismissed *first ball* in both innings, it's called a King Pair.

HOW LONG INSECTS LIVE FOR

This is a rough guide: different species will live longer or shorter lives. This is especially true of beetles: those species that live on easily accessible and nutritionally rich foods will live longer than those that don't. Note also that many of these creatures will be alive for longer in their larval stages.

Moth: Less than one day (this applies to some moths and only in their final adult stages).

Mayfly: One day (or less).

Daddy Longlegs (or Crane Fly): Two weeks.

Housefly: One month.

Dragonfly: Four months.

Worker Bee: One month.

Mosquito: Three months (though the male mosquito won't live that long).

Spider: Two years (again, the female lives longer than the male).

Pine Weevil: Three years.

Dung Beetle: Four years.

Black Widow Spider: Five years (only the female: as we've seen, the male doesn't survive mating.)

Queen Bee: Five years.

Worker Ant: Five years.

Stag Beetle: Seven years.

Female Ant: Fifteen years (her male partner will die at a much younger age – after mating).

Tarantula: Twenty years (the tarantula can take ten years just to become an adult).

African Termite: Up to fifty years.

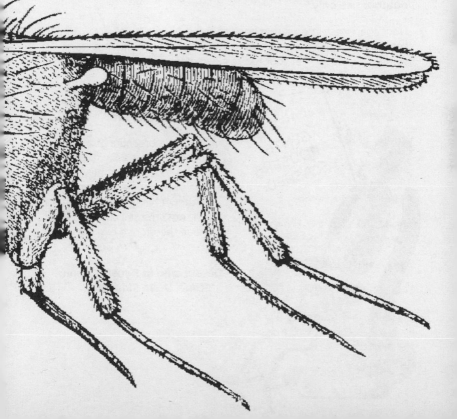

ENGLISH (WELL, ALMOST) AS IT IS WRITTEN AROUND THE WORLD (2)

In an Acapulco hotel: 'The manager has personally passed all the water served here.'

Sign in an American hospital: 'Guard dogs operating.'

Sign outside a Mexican disco: 'Members and non-members only'

Sign in an American drapery shop: 'Gents' trousers slashed.'

On a string of Chinese-made Christmas lights: 'For indoor or outdoor use only.'

From a Japanese information booklet about using a hotel air conditioner: 'Cooles and Heates: If you want just condition of warm in your room, please control yourself.'

Found on an American butane lighter: 'Warning: Flame may cause fire.'

GENTS' TROUSERS SLASHED.

From a brochure of a car rental firm in Tokyo: 'When passenger of foot heave in sight, tootle the horn. Trumpet him melodiously at first, but if he still obstacles your passage then tootle him with vigor.'

Detour sign in Kyushi, Japan: 'Stop – Drive Sideways.'

Advertisement for donkey rides in Thailand: 'Would you like to ride on your own ass?'

On a Korean kitchen knife: 'Warning keep out of children.'

Sign outside a Bangkok bar: 'The shadiest cocktail bar in town.'

Sign in a Sri Lankan swimming pool: 'Do not use the diving board when the swimming pool is empty.'

Outside a Hong Kong tailor shop: 'Ladies may have a fit upstairs.'

DO NOT USE THE DIVING BOARD WHEN THE SWIMMING POOL IS EMPTY.

German-English text book: 'After a certain time cheques are stale and cannot be cashed.'

Sign in a travel agents in Barcelona: 'Go away.'

Sign in a French swimming pool: 'Swimming forbidden in the absence of a saviour.'

From a restaurant in France: 'A sports jacket may be worn to dinner, but no trousers.'

Sign in a hotel in Ankara: 'Please hang your order before retiring on your doorknob.'

In a Copenhagen airline ticket office: 'We take your bags and send them in all directions.'

Sign in a British hospital: 'Dangerous drugs must be locked up with the matron.'

In a British community centre: 'Visitors with reading difficulties should proceed to front desk for information.'

On the door of a Moscow hotel room: 'If this is your first visit to the USSR, you are welcome to it.'

VISITORS WITH READING DIFFICULTIES SHOULD PROCEED TO FRONT DESK FOR INFORMATION.

In a Norwegian cocktail lounge: 'Ladies are requested not to have children in the bar.'

From Budapest: 'All rooms not denounced by twelve o'clock will be paid for twicely.'

On the menu of a Swiss restaurant: 'Our wines leave you nothing to hope for.'

In a Bucharest hotel lobby: 'The lift is being fixed for the next day. During that time we regret that you will be unbearable.'

In a Belgrade hotel lift: 'To move the cabin, push button for wishing floor. If the cabin should enter more persons, each one should press a number of wishing floor. Driving is then going alphabetically by national order.'

In a Rome laundry: 'Ladies, leave your clothes here and spend the afternoon having a good time.'

In a Balkan hotel: 'The flattening of underwear with pleasure is the job of the chambermaid.'

From a restaurant in Vienna: 'Fried milk, children sandwiches, roast cattle and boiled sheep.'

Sign in an Istanbul hotel: 'To call room service, please oen the door and call room service.'

Rhodes tailor's shop: 'Order your summer suit. Because is big rush, we will execute customers in strict rotation.'

In the window of a Swedish furrier: 'Fur coats made for ladies from their own skin.'

Sign in a greengrocers: 'Please don't handle the fruit. Ask for Debbie.'

Instructions with a hair dryer: 'Warning: never use while sleeping.'

Sign on a building site: 'Night watchman patrols this area 24 hours a day.'

Directions for mosquito repellent: 'Replacing battery – Replace the old battery with a new one.'

Sign in a hotel: 'All fire extinguishers must be examined at least ten days before any fire.'

Sign on lion cage at a Czech zoo: 'No smoothen the lion.'

PLEASE DON'T HANDLE THE FRUIT. ASK FOR DEBBIE.

ENGLAND CRICKET CAPTAINS NOT BORN IN ENGLAND

Andrew Strauss (South Africa)

Tony Greig (South Africa)

Ted Dexter (Italy)

Colin Cowdrey (India)

Mike Denness (Scotland)

Douglas Jardine (India)

Lord Harris (Trinidad)

Sir Timothy O'Brien (Ireland)

Freddie Brown (Peru)

Tony Lewis (Wales)

Pelham 'Plum' Warner (Trinidad)

Freddie Fane (Ireland)

Gubby Allen (Australia)

Nasser Hussain (India)

Kevin Pietersen (South Africa)

Allan Lamb (South Africa)

BABIES

When Eskimo babies have colds, their mothers suck the snot out of their noses.

A newborn baby's head accounts for one-quarter of its weight.

The world's biggest baby – Samuel Timmerman – was born in Belgium in 2006. He weighed 5.4kgs.

A baby knows its mother's voice and is able to distinguish it from others while still in the womb.

Within the first hour of birth, a baby is able to recognize its mother's smell.

A newborn baby sees the world upside down because it takes some time for the baby's brain to learn to turn the picture the right way up.

Cradle cap is caused by leftover chemicals from the mother's body. They make oil glands in the baby's head become active after birth.

A baby balances on two feet and an arm when it crawls.

The average baby uses a total of 5,800 nappies.

In Costa Rica, babies are allowed to drink coffee.

ANNUAL AMERICAN EVENTS

St Stupid's Day Parade (celebrating the patron saint of the
First Church of the Last Laugh).

Xtreme Rat Challenge.

Frozen Dead Guy Days.

Spamarama.

Chitlin' Strut (a festival based around chitterlings – boiled and
fried hog intestines).

Big Mountain Furniture Race.

International Whistlers' Convention.

Billy The Kid Tombstone Race.

IFOCE Hot Dog Eating Tournament.

**The Great Arkansas Pig-Out (which features a contest
called Running of the Fat Guys
in which contestants weighing
between 110 and 135 kgs run
through three checkpoints,
where they have to guzzle
pizzas, cola and bars of
chocolate).**

EXTRAORDINARY EVENTS

TURTALLY UNBELIEVABLE. In 1976, builders in Texas were breaking up concrete they had laid a year before. To their amazement, they found a green turtle within the concrete, still alive because it had found an air pocket. Obviously it had got in when the concrete was poured a year earlier but there were no signs of holes or cracks in the concrete through which the turtle could have entered.

Even more amazing, perhaps, is that many creatures have also been found in natural formations such as rocks and trees. There are several authenticated cases where frogs, toads and other small animals have been found entombed, but still alive, within solid stone. There are other examples where workers have cut down trees and found frogs living deep inside them.

KILL ME IF YOU CAN. Wenseslao Moguel was captured while fighting in the Mexican revolution in 1915. Without any trial, he was sentenced to be executed by firing squad. Moguel was duly shot by no fewer than nine soldiers with rifles. An officer then put a final bullet through his head at close range to ensure death.

Incredibly, Moguel survived all the bullets and also managed to escape. He went on to live a full life after his 'execution'.

FALLING DOWN: During World War I, a German soldier was riding in the back seat of a plane when the engine suddenly stalled and he fell out of his seat. Parachutes weren't used in military aircraft and, being two miles above the ground, he would almost certainly have died. However, as he was falling, the plane started falling too and he was blown back into his own seat. The pilot, who'd managed to remain in the plane all along, was able to land the plane safely.

POSTCARD PLEASE: When Jim Wilson's father died in Natal, South Africa, in April 1967, he informed his sister Muriel, who was living in Holland.

Muriel's husband was working in Portugal, and on hearing the news, flew to South Africa. He had to change planes at Las Palmas airport in the Canary Islands, and while he waited for the connecting flight, he bought a postcard showing Margate Beach, Natal, and sent it to Muriel.

To her astonishment, she realised that the photograph on the postcard featured her own father walking along the beach with other holidaymakers.

BOULDERS ON HIGH: The mystery of how enormous boulders ended up high in the trees is completely unexplained. In 1997, a hunter in Yellowwood State Forest, Indiana, discovered a huge sandstone boulder that had wedged itself between three branches of an oak tree some 12 metres above the ground. The arrow shaped rock was estimated to weigh about 220 kilos.

Another four equally massive boulders were found wedged high up in trees in the same remote forest. The strange thing is that none of the trees had been damaged. There was no record of there having been any tornadoes that might have lifted and dumped them nor any evidence that heavy equipment had been used and nobody could think there had been any mishaps involving dynamite in the area.

GONE WITH THE WIND. A nine-year-old Chinese girl was playing in Songjian near Shanghai, in July 1992 when she was picked up off the ground and carried off by a whirlwind. She was deposited uninjured, in treetops some two miles away. Six years earlier, a freak wind lifted up 13 children in Hami in Western China and deposited them all – unharmed – in sand dunes and scrub an incredible 12 miles away.

A HEAD FOR LEAD. In 2001, William Adrian Milton, from New York, discovered that – without knowing it – he had had a bullet lodged in his skull for 25 years. He only found out when

he had a brain scan for a non-related head problem. Mr Milton then remembered an incident in 1976 when blood started spurting from his head, apparently spontaneously. He assumed that he had been hit by falling debris from a building site but, in fact, he had been shot in the head. As the bullet hadn't given him any problems – and as an operation might have been dangerous, he and his doctors decided to let the bullet remain in his head.

BUSY BEES: Margaret Bell, who kept bees in her garden in a village home near Ludlow, Shropshire, died in June 1994. Soon after her funeral, mourners were amazed to see hundreds of bees swarming on the corner of the street opposite her home where she had lived for 26 years. The bees stayed for an hour before buzzing off and never coming back.

BALLOON BUDDIES: A Staffordshire girl named Laura Buxton released a helium filled balloon during celebrations for her grandparents' gold wedding anniversary in June 2001. As is usual, attached to the balloon was a tag with her her name and address and a note requesting any eventual finder to write back. Ten days later she received a reply – from none other than another Laura Buxton who had found the balloon stuck in the garden hedge of her home in Pewsey, Wiltshire, some 140 miles away. The coincidence didn't stop there. It turned out that both Lauras were aged 10 and both had three-year-old black Labradors, a guinea pig, and a rabbit.

CRIME AND PUNISHMENT AROUND THE WORLD

In the seventeenth century, people who were deemed to be enemies of the British crown were sent to Barbados as indentured servants. This practice was so widespread that the punishment was sometimes described as 'being Barbadoed.'

During the 1920s there was a law in Russia that all private automobiles (i.e. those not used by the Communist government) had to have a yellow stripe painted around them.

It is illegal in Arizona to hunt camels.

In Switzerland, every citizen is legally required to have access to a bomb shelter.

In Qatar, pedestrians have to pay a fine if they don't walk properly on the pavement.

In Helsinki, Finland, police don't always give parking tickets: sometimes they deflate a car's tyres instead.

The Vatican City has a higher crime rate than Italy.

In China, 98 per cent of software is pirated.

Hundreds of years ago in Japan, anyone attempting to leave the country was executed.

In theory, a Chilean can be imprisoned for not voting in an election.

In 1976, microwave ovens were banned in Russia.

In Antwerp, Belgium, it used to be illegal to walk down the main street if you were wearing a red hat.

In Malta, it is illegal to drive a car if you're not wearing a top.

Strikes and trade unions are illegal in the United Arab Emirates.

At one time it was against the law to slam car doors in Switzerland.

Chewing gum is illegal in Singapore.

In 1954, the French town of Chateauneuf-du-Pape enacted a law prohibiting flying saucers from landing within its borders. (It worked.)

These laws still technically apply in Germany: every office must have a view of the sky; it is illegal to wear a mask; a pillow counts as a weapon.

In Saudi Arabia, people who steal can be punished by having their hands cut off.

Internet sites such as Myspace and Facebook are banned in the United Arab Emirates.

Technically, it's illegal to die in the British Houses of Parliament.

Mexico considers all pre-Colombian objects to be the property of the nation; the unauthorized export of such objects is theft.

Hand-gliding is illegal in most Ethiopian national parks because it scares antelopes, and when they get scared they cause a lot of damage.

In Taiwan, drunk-drivers are given the option of playing mah jong with the elderly instead of paying a fine.

In Thailand, it's illegal to leave the house without wearing underwear.

In Singapore, a fine is given to people who use public toilets without flushing. Spitting and feeding pigeons are also offences in Singapore.

Switzerland has the highest number of reported car thefts, while Holland has the most reported burglaries.

St Kitts & Nevis are two islands but a single country. It is illegal to swear on Nevis – but it isn't on St Kitts.

OCTOPUSES*

Octopus (and squid) can change their skin colour. Normally brown, their skin becomes green or blue when they are under threat or trying to attract a mate.

Despite its great strength, the octopus tires easily. The oxygen-carrying component of its blood, hemocyanin, is copper-based and is less efficient than the iron-based haemoglobin of humans. A struggling octopus quickly suffers oxygen deprivation.

To us, one giant octopus looks the same as another. This might explain why divers claim to have seen the same octopus occupy a den for ten or more years even though the creature seldom lives longer than four.

The pupil of an octopus's eye is rectangular.

Because it has no backbone, a 35-kilo octopus can squeeze through a hole the size of a large coin.

An octopus's arm typically has about two hundred suckers. When threatened, an octopus can detach an arm to confuse an enemy. A detached arm will regrow in a few months.

Unlike humans, the octopus doesn't have a blind spot.

The Pacific giant octopus, the largest octopus in the world, grows from the size of a pea to a 70-kilogram monster measuring nearly 10 metres across in just two years (which also happens to be its entire lifespan).

According to Maori legend, New Zealand was first discovered when fishermen were chasing a massive octopus.

Lobsters are scared of octopuses. The sight of one makes a lobster freeze.

Using its web – the skin between its arms – an octopus can carry up to a dozen crabs back to its den to eat.

If they get very upset, octopuses can eat themselves.

An octopus can undo the lid of a screw-top jar.

*The strictly correct plural of 'octopus' is 'octopodes', but 'octopuses' is much more commonly used.

SPORTING SUPERSTITIONS

Sportsmen and sportswomen train so hard and prepare so well for their sports that it's little surprise that many are also highly superstitious. The reason for this is that if you've done all that you can possibly do before a big game or event (i.e. all the 'proper' preparation) and you're still not convinced that you're going to win, then you'll probably be tempted to turn to less rational things like luck and superstition.

Sports psychologists reckon that successful sportsmen and sportswomen tend, by nature, to be at least slightly obsessive. The same compulsive nature that gives them the drive to keep on practising until they are the very best they can possibly be can also lead them to adopt rituals that often seem rather strange to observers.

According to a university lecturer in sport and psychology, 'Superstition is absolutely rife in sport. It goes back to one of the oldest theories in the psychology, which is that if you execute a certain behaviour and get a pleasurable outcome then that strengthens the link between the behaviour and the result.

'You get into the habit of doing something because it is associated with winning, and once you get the momentum going it becomes part of what I would call the 'pre-performance routine'. That then becomes very hard to break.'

SPORTS AND THEIR SPECIFIC SUPERSTITIONS

ANGLING

Spitting on your bait before casting your rod to make fish bite.

Not changing rods while fishing.

Throwing back your first catch for good luck.

Not telling anyone how many fish you've caught until you're finished (or, supposedly, you won't catch another)

BASEBALL

Spitting into the hand before picking up the bat.

Not stepping on the baselines while running off and on to the field between innings.

Not lending a bat to another player

Sticking some chewing-gum on a player's hat

Making sure that a dog doesn't walk across the diamond before the first pitch (it's supposedly bad luck).

BASKETBALL

Bouncing the ball before taking a foul shot.

The last person to shoot a basket during the warm-up will have a good game.

Wiping the soles of your sneakers for good luck.

CRICKET

Putting on kit in a certain order

Hopping on one leg when the score is 111 (222, 333 etc.) if you're British

FOOTBALL

Putting on the left boot before the right

Not shaving during a winning run

Not talking before a match

GOLF

Starting with only odd-numbered clubs.

Not using a ball with a number higher than four (supposedly bad luck)

Carrying coins in your pockets.

ICE HOCKEY

Not shouting 'shutout' in the locker room before the game.

Not allowing hockey sticks to be crossed.

Tapping the goalkeeper on his shin pads before a game.

TENNIS

Not holding more than two balls at a time when serving.

Avoiding wearing the colour yellow.

Walking around the outside of the court when switching sides.

TEN-PIN BOWLING

Wearing the same clothes to continue a winning streak.

Putting the number 300, the sport's perfect score, on your number plate

Carrying charms

THE NAMES OF THINGS YOU DIDN'T KNOW HAD NAMES

Adelaster: meaning 'unknown star' in Greek, this is the name given to newly discovered plants awaiting classification by botanists

Aglet: the metal or plastic covering on the end of a shoelace

Armsate: the hole in a shirt or a jumper through which you put your hand and arm

Brannock device: the metal instrument used in shoe shops to measure feet

Brassard: a band worn around the arm

Buccula: a person's double chin

Chanking: food that's spat out

Drupelets: the bumps on raspberries

Epizootic: an animal epidemic

Ferrule: the metal band on the top of a pencil that holds the rubber in place

F-hole: the S-shaped opening in a violin

Fillip: the technical term for snapping your fingers

Griffonage: scribbled handwriting

Harp: the metal part of a lamp that surrounds the bulb and supports the shade

Jiffy: one-hundredth of a second

Keeper: the loop on a belt that holds the end in place after it has passed through the buckle

Mucophagy: the medical term for 'snot-eating', the consumption of the nasal mucus obtained from nose-picking

Obdormition: when an arm or a leg goes to 'sleep' as a result of numbness caused by pressure on a nerve

Octothorpe: the # symbol on a computer keyboard

Ophyron: the space between your eyebrows

Pandiculation: the act of stretching and yawning

Peen: on a hammer, the end opposite the striking face

Pips: the little bumps on the surface of a table tennis bat

Purlicue: the space between the extended thumb and index finger

Rasceta: the creases on the inside of your wrist

Rowel: the revolving star on the back of a cowboy's spurs

Tines: the prongs on forks

Toque: a chef's tall hat

Tragus: the little lump of flesh just in front of the ear

Truck: the ball on top of a flagpole

Ullage: the empty space in a bottle between the surface of the liquid and the bottle top

Vamp: the upper front top of a shoe

Vibrissae: a cat's whiskers

Walla: a sound engineer's term for the murmur of a crowd in the background

Zarf: a holder for a hot cup or mug

(GENUINE) JOB PERFORMANCE REVIEWS

'Since my last report, this employee has reached rock bottom – and has started to dig.'

'His men would follow him anywhere – but only out of morbid curiosity.'

'I would not allow this employee to breed.'

'This employee is really not so much of a "has-been", but more of a definite "won't be".'

'Works well when under constant supervision and cornered like a rat in a trap.'

'When she opens her mouth, it seems that it is only to change feet.'

'He would be out of his depth in a parking lot puddle.'

'This young lady has delusions of adequacy.'

'He sets low personal standards and then consistently fails to achieve them.'

'This employee is depriving a village somewhere of an idiot.'

'This employee should go far ... and the sooner he starts, the better.'

'A gross ignoramus – 144 times worse than an ordinary ignoramus.'

'I would like to go hunting with him sometime.'

'He would argue with a signpost.'

'He has a knack for making strangers immediately.'

'He brings a lot of joy whenever he leaves the room.'

'When his IQ reaches 50, he should sell.'

'If you see two people talking and one looks bored – he's the other one.'

'A photographic memory but with the lens cover glued on.'

'Donated his brain to science before he was done using it.'

'Gates are down, the lights are flashing, but the train isn't coming.'

'Has two brains: one is lost and the other is out looking for it.'

'If he were any more stupid, he'd have to be watered twice a week.'

'If you give him a penny for his thoughts, you'd get change.'

'The wheel is turning, but the hamster is dead.'

FOOTBALL CLUBS AND THEIR ORIGINAL NAMES

Arsenal: Dial Square
Barnsley: Barnsley St Peters
Birmingham City: Small Heath Alliance
Blackburn Rovers: Blackburn Grammar School Old Boys
Blackpool: Blackpool St Johns
Bolton Wanderers: Christ Church
Bournemouth: Boscombe
Bristol City: Bristol South End
Bristol Rovers: Black Arabs
Cambridge United: Abbey United
Cardiff City: Riverside
Coventry City: Singers FC
Everton: St Domingo's FC
Fulham: Fulham St Andrew's Church Sunday School
Gillingham: New Brompton
Leyton Orient: Glyn Cricket & FC
Manchester City: Ardwick
Manchester United: Newton Heath
Newcastle United: Newcastle East End
Oldham: Pine Villa
Oxford United: Headington United
Port Vale: Burslem Port Vale
Queens Park Rangers: St Jude's
Rotherham County: Thornhill
Southampton: St Marys YMA
Stockport County: Heaton Norris Rovers
Sunderland: Sunderland & District Teachers
Tranmere Rovers: Belmont FC
West Bromwich Albion: West Bromwich Strollers
West Ham United: Thames Ironworks
Wolverhampton Wanderers: St Luke's

WORDS RARELY USED IN THE SINGULAR

trivia (trivium), paparazzi (paparazzo), assizes (assize), auspices (auspice), timpani (timpano), minutiae (minutia), grafitti (grafitto), scampi (scampo), scruples (scruple), measles (measle).

WORDS RARELY USED IN THE POSITIVE

inadvertent (advertent), immaculate (maculate), inclement (clement), disconsolate (consolate), indelible (delible), feckless (feckful), unfurl (furl), insipid (sipid), unspeakable (speakable), unkempt (kempt), incorrigible (corrigible), implacable (placable), ineffable (effable), innocuous (nocuous), impervious (pervious), expurgated (purgated), impeccable (peccable), inevitable (evitable).

WORDS DERIVED FROM ARABIC

satin, cotton, tariff, cheques, saffron, caraway, algebra, alcohol, chemistry, alkali, zenith, sherbet, carafe, coffee, syrup, mattress.

THE GREATEST COMEBACK OF ALL TIME?

When England won the 1966 World Cup – yes, my friends, there was a time – they played Portugal in the semi-finals. With Eusebio in their team, the Portuguese were formidable opponents, but they only got to the semi-finals after an extraordinary comeback against North Korea. The Koreans were 3–0 up after just 24 minutes and it looked like an extraordinary giant-killing feat was going to take place. But Eusebio scored four goals to help his team to recover from 3–0 down to win 5–3.

Pretty incredible, huh? But not as amazing as this comeback. In April 2010, Arsenal were away to Wigan in the Premiership. With just ten minutes to go, Arsenal were cruising to victory with a 2–0 lead. Surely nothing could stop the Gunners from notching up yet another victory. But goals in the 80th and 89th minutes caused Wigan to draw level to force an impressive draw. But the Northerners weren't finished and, in the 90th minute, Charles N'Zogbia fired in the goal that gave them a (what had looked like) highly improbable 3–2 victory.

You'd have thought that that was the greatest comeback of all time but I suggest you'd be wrong.

For the really 'greatest comeback', we have to go all the way back to 1957 and a League match between Charlton Athletic (at home) and Huddersfield Town.

At half-time Huddersfield were 2–0 up. In the second-half, things went even worse for Charlton who had been playing with ten men since the 20th minute (a player had gone off injured and there were no substitutes in those days): after 70 minutes, Charlton were 5–1 down. You wouldn't fancy their chances.

However, Charlton scored a couple of goals and it suddenly became a matter of 'game on' as both teams seemed to stop defending and go on the attack instead. With minutes to go, Charlton took the lead 6–5, but Huddersfield scored again and, with four minutes to go, the scoreline stood at 6–6. Then, just as the referee was about to blow for full time, Charlton scored the winner. They had gone from 5–1 down to 7–6 winners in the space of just twenty minutes. If only one could have been there...but, of course, many of the (home) fans left after 70 minutes – not wanting to see their side take any more punishment. Bet they never left a game early again.

Incidentally, Huddersfield Town are the only team to score six goals in a league match and still lose.

THE HUMAN BODY

We all have unworkable muscles which were once used to move our ears.

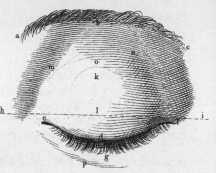

The valves of the human heart are as thick as a single piece of tissue paper.

The permanent teeth that come through to replace your baby teeth are called succedaneous teeth.

The average human body contains enough potassium to fire a toy cannon.

It takes about 20 seconds for a red blood cell to circle the whole body.

The human heart beats once from the left-hand side and once from the right in alternate motions.

If all your DNA were stretched out, it would reach to the moon and back several thousand times.

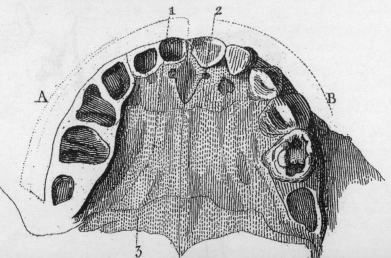

The human body contains enough carbon to make 900 pencils.

The average adult has between 40 and 50 billion fat cells.

The human body contains enough phosphorous to make 2,200 match heads.

The largest human organ is the skin, with a surface area of about 2.32 square metres.

Women have more taste buds than men.

Children have more taste buds than adults.

Babies are born without kneecaps. Kneecaps develop when the child is between two and six years old.

Not all our taste buds are on our tongue; about 10 per cent are on the palate and the cheeks.

Humans are the only primates that don't have pigment in the palms of their hands.

The human kidney consists of over 1 million little tubes with a total length of about 40 miles in both kidneys.

The lens of the eye continues to grow throughout a person's life.

One out of 20 people has an extra rib.

Our skin is only about as deep as the tip of a ballpoint pen.

Fig. 3

TYPES OF BOWLING IN CRICKET

Beamer: an illegal delivery that reaches the batsman at around head height without bouncing.

Bouncer: a fast short pitched delivery that rises up near the batsman's head.

Daisy cutter: when a ball rolls along the pitch or bounces more than twice.

Declaration bowling: poor bowling – typically full tosses and long hops – to allow the batsmen to score runs quickly and encourage the opposing captain to declare.

Dot ball: a delivery bowled without any runs scored off it (so called because it's recorded in the score book with a single dot).

Full toss: a delivery that reaches the batsman without bouncing – making it fairly easy to play as the ball doesn't have the chance to deviate off the pitch.

Googly: a deceptive delivery by a spin bowler.

Jaffa: a well bowled, practically unplayable delivery.

Long hop: like a bouncer but without the lift so the batsman has a lot of time to see the ball and play an attacking shot.

Loosener: a poor delivery bowled at the start of a bowler's spell.

Yorker: a (usually fast) delivery that is pitched very close to the batsman, bouncing underneath his bat or on his toes. A well-pitched fast yorker is almost impossible to keep out.

OFFICIAL US STATE SPORTS

Nine of the fifty US states have 'official sports'.

Alaska has 'mushing' (covers all sports where dogs pull sleds on snow).

Hawaii has surfing and outrigger canoeing.

Maryland has jousting (a contest between two knights mounted on horses using lances) and lacrosse.

Massachusetts has basketball.

Minnesota has hockey.

New Hampshire has skiing.

South Dakota, Texas and Wyoming all have rodeo; Texas also has American football.

GIANT-KILLING FEATS

FOOTBALL

South Africa 2, France 1 (2010)

Egypt 1, Italy 0 (2009)

Senegal 1, France 0 (2002)

Wrexham 2, Arsenal 1 (1992)

Woking 4, West Bromich Albion 2 (1991)

Cameroon 1, Argentina 0 (1990)

Sutton 2, Coventry City 1 (1989)

Wimbledon 1, Liverpool 0 (1988 – FA Cup final)

Altrincham 2, Birmingham City 1 (1986)

AFC Bournemouth 2, Manchester United 0 (1984)

Algeria 2, West Germany 1 (1982)

Exeter City 4, Newcastle United 0 (1981)

Harlow 1, Leicester City 0 (1980)

Colchester United 3, Leeds United 2 (1971)

North Korea 1, Italy 0 (1966)

Leyton Orient 3, Everton 1 (1952)

USA 1, England 0 (1950)

Yeovil Town 2, Sunderland 1 (1949)

CRICKET

Because there is only
a small pool of Test-
playing nations, there is
no scope for giant-killing,
but the one-day (or 20/20)
tournaments, where the non-Test
playing countries are allowed to play,
offer the possibility of huge upsets.
Here are a few.

Zimbabwe beat Australia (1983)

Kenya beat Sri Lanka (2003)

Ireland beat Pakistan (2007)

The Netherlands beat England
(2009)

KEEPIE UPPIE

The men's record for the longest keepie uppie was set by Briton Dan Magness, who kept a football off the ground for 24 hours at London's Covent Garden in May 2009. No one was counting but it was estimated that he hit the ball 250,000 times. The record he broke had been set in August 2003 by Brazilian Martinho Eduardo Orige, who kept a football in the air for 19 hours and 30 minutes.

The women's record was set in July 1996 by Brazilian Cláudia Martin who managed 7 hours and 5 minutes.

Dan Magness set another keepie uppie record in January 2010 when he walked 30 miles doing keepie uppie without letting the ball touch the ground. On his journey, he visited all the Premier League stadiums in London, starting his journey at Fulham's Craven Cottage and ending it at Tottenham Hotspur's White Hart Lane.

Jan Skorkovsky ran the 1990 Prague Marathon in 7 hours 18 minutes 55 seconds while doing keepie uppie – again without the ball ever touching the ground.

However, the most famous display of keepie uppie was probably in the 1967 England vs Scotland international. Scotland were leading 3–2 against the World Cup holders and the Scottish midfielder 'Slim' Jim Baxter tauntingly played keepie uppie in front of the English defence in order to waste time and, yes, to show off his incredible skills.

PUNNY SPORTS STARS' AUTOBIOGRAPHIES

By George (George Foreman)

Life Swings (Nick Faldo)

Gray Matters (Andy Gray)

Biting Talk (Norman Hunter)

Opening Up (Mike Atherton)

It's Knott Cricket (Alan Knott)

Big Fry (Barry Fry)

Time To Declare (Michael Vaughan)

Watt's My Name (Jim Watt)

Managing My Life (Alex Ferguson)

No Holding Back (Michael Holding)

Heading For Victory (Steve Bruce)

Nine Lives (Matt Dawson)

It's All About A Ball (Alan Ball)

Right Back To The Beginning (Jimmy Armfield)

Hell Razor (Neil Ruddock)

Maine Man (Tony Book)

Banks of England (Gordon Banks)

Playing For Keeps (Alec Stewart)

The Real Mackay **(Dave Mackay)**

WONDERFULLY NAMED SOCCER PLAYERS

Einar Aas (Norway)

Chiqui Arce (Paraguay)

Andrei Arshavin (Russia).

Tunji Banjo (Nigeria)

Segar Bastard (England)

Erich Beer (Germany)

Frank Belt (England)

Oh Beom-Seok (South Korea)

Regi Blinker (Holland)

Danny Boffin (Belgium)

Mansour Boutabout (Algeria)

Bongo Christ (Zaire)

Norman Conquest (Australia)

Carlos Costly (Honduras)

Francis Cuggy (England)

Harry Daft (England)

Steve Death (England)

Jay DeMerit (US)

Paul Dickov (Scotland)

Danny Diver (Scotland)

Mario Eggimann (Switzerland)

Charlie Faultless (Scottish referee)

Dean Gerken (England)

Bernt Haas (Switzerland)

Mun In-Guk (North Korea)

Gareth Jelleyman (Wales)

Daniel Killer (Argentina)

Zoltan Kiss (Hungary)

Lars Lagerback (Sweden)

Mario Licka (Czech Republic)

Modest M'Bami (Cameroon)

Jean-Jacques Misse-Misse (Cameroon)

Johnny Moustache (Seychelles)

John Nutter (England)

Emmanuel Panther (Scotland)

Brian Pinas (Holland)

Prince Polley (Ghana)

Razvan Rat (Romania)

Adigun Salami (Nigeria)

Emald Scattergood (England)

Shane Sheriff (Australia)

Danny Shittu (Nigeria)

Dieter Stinka (Germany)

Orlando Trustfull (Holland)

Mario Turdo (Argentina)

Lopez Ufarte (Spain)

Kick van der Vall (Holland)

Rafael van der Vaart (Holland)

Ricardo Virtuoso (Brazil)

Barry Wardrobe (England)

Georgie Welcome (Honduras)

Wolfgang Wolf (Germany)

THE WISEST THING EVER SAID
ABOUT FOOTBALL

'Football is a game in which a handful of fit men run around for one and a half hours watched by millions of people who could really use the exercise.' (Unknown)

THE WISEST THING EVER SAID
ABOUT HORSE RACING

'Horse sense is the thing a horse has which keeps it from betting on people.' (W.C. Fields)

AROUND THE WORLD (2)

In 2006, the retired aircraft carrier USS Oriskany was sunk to the bottom of the Gulf of Mexico to create the word's largest artificial reef and diving centre.

The world's average school year is 200 days per year. In the US, it is 180 days; in Sweden, 170 days, in Japan, 243 days.

There isn't a single person living in Iceland whose ancestors <u>didn't</u> come from another country.

The world's largest car park is in West Edmonton Mall in Edmonton, Canada. It has space for over 20,000 vehicles.

In Ivrea, Italy, the people celebrate the beginning of Lent by throwing oranges at one another.

The population of Colombia doubles every 22 years.

Peru has more pyramids than Egypt.

According to a survey, Mumbai – formerly Bombay – is the world's rudest city.

Beijing boasts the world's largest Kentucky Fried Chicken restaurant.

An estimated 57 per cent of journeys made in the Dutch city of Groningen are on bicycle.

Parmesan is the most shoplifted product in Italy.

The Chinese government recently introduced a 5 per cent chopstick tax to preserve its forests.

Some African tribes refer to themselves as 'motherhoods'.

The top six countries for the highest proportion of houses with five rooms or more are all English-speaking.

In Ethiopia, both males and females of the Surma tribes shave their heads as a mark of beauty.

A third of Africa's population survives on less than $1 a day.

In Alaska, one in 200 collisions between a car and a moose results in the death of a driver or passenger.

A sultan's wife is called a sultana.

Slovakia is the geographical centre of Europe. The Krahule hill near the mining town of Kremnica in Slovakia, is the geographic centre of Europe.

Slovenia is situated at the crossroads of central Europe. The Krahule hill near the mining town of of Kremnica in Slovakia is the exact geographical centre of Europe.

There are more than 1 million Lithuanians living in the United States, Canada, South America, the United Kingdom, Poland, Germany and Australia.

Almost 5 million Hungarians live outside Hungary.

More than 7 million Greeks or persons of Greek origin live outside Greece.

Madrid, the capital, is in the precise centre of Spain.

Vietnam is shaped like a massive 'S'.

Mali is shaped like a butterfly.

Floor-cleaning products in Venezuela have ten times the pine fragrance of British floor-cleaners, as Venezuelan women won't buy a weaker fragrance.

The University of Al-Karaouine, Morocco, is the world's oldest university still open. It was founded in the year 859 AD and it's still running.

In Qatar, the separation of men and women extends to places of prayer, government offices, shops and even lifts.

In Japan, they have a problem with karoshi – which literally means 'death from overwork'. The high pressure of the Japanese workplace has led to a number of deaths from stress-related disorders. This could have something to do with the fact that the average Japanese worker reportedly takes only half of his or her holiday time each year.

Women in Senegal spend an average of 17.5 hours a week just collecting water.

In the United Arab Emirates, people from other countries have to return to their country of origin once they get to retirement age.

On average, the people of India spend more time reading than any other people in the world.

In Afganistan, it used to be against the law to play Chopin's music on the banjo.

In Ancient Peru, if a woman found an odd-looking potato, she had to push it into the face of the nearest man.

There's an island in Thailand named after James Bond.

There is a town in the Cayman Islands called Hell. They have a post office there so tourists can send a postcard from Hell. There's also a town in Norway called Hell.

Although Somalia is named after its people, Somalis also live in many neighbouring countries due to the partitioning of eastern Africa by colonial powers.

Indonesia is known as 'The Emerald of the Equator' because 45 per cent of the country is covered by forests.

As well as their given names, many Somalis also have a nickname based on their time of birth, where they come in the family or even on their appearance.

Tristan da Cunha's wonderfully named capital, Edinburgh of the Seven Seas, is often nicknamed 'The Settlement'.

There's a saying in Nicaragua that 'Everyone's a poet in Nicaragua'.

In Sweden, näver is a traditional craft that involves drying and weaving strips of the soft inner bark from a birch tree. This is then used to make bags and backpacks.

In Switzerland, every citizen is legally required to have access to a bomb shelter.

Workers at the Matsushita Electric company in Japan beat dummies of their foremen with bamboo sticks to let off steam.

In the mountains of Albania an announcement of a birth, a death or a marriage is passed from one house to another by a gunshot or a shout that echoes through the mountains.

Mexico City is in the crater of a super volcano.

Tattooing was very important in Samoa and there were ceremonies devoted to it. Tattoos were applied using the jagged end of combs. The comb would be dipped in ink and then etched into the man's arm.

Deep in the jungles of South America a tribe of primitive people was discovered. Everyone in the tribe had forgotten how to make fire and therefore they carefully guarded piles of burning embers. If all their fires went out, they would have been doomed to living without fire.

The Maldives is the world's lowest country. It's also the flattest, with the highest point only reaching 2.5 metres. The Maldives risks disappearing completely as a result of rising sea levels.

THE SECRET OF SUCCESS

At age 4 success is . . . not peeing in your pants.

At age 12 success is . . . having friends.

At age 17 success is . . . having a driving licence.

At age 20 success is . . . having sex.

At age 35 success is . . . having money.

At age 50 success is . . . having money.

At age 60 success is . . . having sex.

At age 70 success is . . . having a driving licence.

At age 75 success is . . . having friends.

At age 80 success is . . . not peeing in your pants.

CATS

Cats have the largest eyes of all mammals (proportional to their size).

Cats can't survive on a vegetarian diet.

Cats have better memories than dogs. Tests conducted by an American university concluded that a dog remembers things for 5 minutes, while a cat can remember things for 16 hours.

Rome has more homeless cats per square mile than any other city in the world.

Cats are the most popular pets in America.

There are over six million cats in the UK. The most popular breeds in the UK are Persian long hair, Siamese and British short hair. The collective name for a group of cats is a 'clowder'.

The average lifespan of a cat is between 13 and 17 years (depending on the breed and the gender) although the oldest age a cat has ever reached is 34 years.

The normal temperature of a cat is 38.6°C.

The domestic cat is the only species of cat able to hold its tail vertically while walking.

Cats sleep 16 to 18 hours per day.

All cats step with both left legs, then both right legs, when they walk or run. The only other animals to do this are the giraffe and the camel.

Famous cat lovers in history include author Raymond Chandler, Dr Samuel Johnson and Sir Winston Churchill, the former Prime Minister, who used to sleep with his cat in the bed next to him.

Famous cat haters include composer Johannes Brahms, The Queen, French dictator Napoleon Bonaparte and James Boswell (Dr Johnson's biographer).

Domestic cats purr at about 26 cycles per second, the same frequency as an idling diesel engine.

Cats miaow to us but they don't mlaow to each other.

A purring cat doesn't necessarily mean a contented cat. Cats will also purr if they are in pain.

In 1963 the French launched a cat called Feliette into space.

The average cat costs its owner £7,000 over its lifetime (compared with £20,000 for a dog).

The average cat consumes about 127,750 calories a year, nearly 28 times its own weight in food and the same amount again in liquids.

Cats can suffer from a range of 258 different genetic diseases.

The largest cat litter recorded is 19 – although four were still-born.

In Australia, a credit card was issued to a cat named Messiah. Its owner wanted to test the bank's security system.

A cat year is equal to about five human years.

Domestic cats kill more than 57 million creatures a year in the UK – over half of which are birds.

Cats were used on board ship in both World Wars and in the trenches of the first World War to help get rid of rats.

The people of East Anglia used to mummify cats and place them in the walls of their homes to ward off evil spirits.

Since housecats are clean and their coats are dry and glossy, their fur easily becomes charged with electricity. Sparks can sometimes be seen if their fur is rubbed in the dark.

Cats need to consume a substance called tryptophan, which is found in milk, eggs and poultry, in order to sleep well. Without it, they can become insomniacs.

A cat's jaws can't move sideways.

During World War 2 a cat named Oscar served on the German battleship *Bismarck*. When the *Bismarck* was torpedoed, Oscar was rescued by a British sailor from HMS *Cossack*. Five months later HMS *Cossack* was sunk but Oscar was rescued by HMS *Ark Royal*. Just three weeks later a German U-boat destroyed *Ark Royal* and Oscar was rescued again. Oscar was then left to live on land and died peacefully many years later.

When the Black Death swept across Europe in the fourteenth century, it was a long time before the true cause was understood. One theory was that cats caused the plague, and so thousands were slaughtered. This made the problem worse. The cats had been helping keep houses clear of the real culprits: rats. Over five years, 25 million people died of the plague in Europe.

A LITERARY TOP 10

ONE Day (David Nicholls)

The TWO Faces of January (Patricia Highsmith)

THREE Men In A Boat (Jerome K. Jerome)

FOUR Beauties (H.E. Bates)

FIVE Little Pigs (Agatha Christie)

The SIX Sacred Stones (Matthew Reilly)

The SEVEN Pillars of Wisdom (T.E. Lawrence)

EIGHT Black Horses (Ed McBain)

NINE Tailors (Dorothy L. Sayers)

Starter For TEN (David Nicholls)

GENUINE SONG TITLES

I'd Rather Be A Lobster Than A Wiseguy **(Edward Madden and Theodore F. Morse, 1907)**

(Potatoes Are Cheaper – Tomatoes Are Cheaper) Now's The Time To Fall In Love (Al Lewis And Al Sherman, 1931)

Hey Young Fella Close Your Old Umbrella **(Dorothy Fields and Jimmy McHugh, 1933)**

Who Ate Napoleons With Josephine When Bonaparte Was Away (written by Alfred Bryan and E. Ray Gotz in 1920)

Aunt Jemima And Your Uncle Cream of Wheat **(Johnny Mercer and Rube Bloom, 1936)**

Come After Breakfast, Bring 'Long Your Lunch And Leave 'Fore Supper Time (J. Tim Bryman, Chris Smith and James Henry Burris, 1909)

I Love To Dunk A Hunk of Sponge Cake (Clarence Gaskill, 1928)

Caldonia (What Makes Your Big Head So Hard) (Fleecie Moore, 1946)

All The Quakers Are Shoulder Shakers Down In Quaker Town (Bert Kalmar, Edgar Leslie and Pete Wendling, 1919)

(GENUINE) PURCHASES MADE BY LOTTERY WINNERS

Helicopter lessons

A fishing lake

A football club

A piece of the moon

A giant chess set

A castle

An operation to have ears pinned back

A racehorse

An 18-hole golf course

Breast enlargments

THE LATE, GREAT TOMMY COOPER

I went to the doctor's the other day and I said, 'Have you got anything for wind?'

So he gave me a kite.

Man goes to the doctor with a strawberry growing out of his head. The doctor says, 'I'll give you some cream to put on it.'

I went to buy some camouflage trousers the other day but I couldn't find any.

I bought some HP sauce the other day. It's costing me 6p a month for the next 2 years.

Last night I dreamed I ate a ten-pound marshmallow, and when I woke up the pillow was gone.

I cleaned the attic with the wife the other day. Now I can't get the cobwebs out of her hair.

'Doctor, I can't pronounce my F's, T's and H's'. 'Well you can't say fairer than that then.'

Police arrested two kids yesterday, one was drinking battery acid, the other was eating fireworks. They charged one and let the other one off.

My dog was barking at everyone the other day. Still, what can you expect from a cross-breed?

A woman told her doctor, 'I've got a bad back'. The doctor said, 'It's old age'. The woman said, 'I want a second opinion.' The doctor says, 'OK. You're ugly as well.'

A guy walks into a pub with a lump of asphalt on his shoulder. He says to the barman, 'give us a pint and one for the road.'

A man walked into the doctor's and says 'I've hurt my arm in several places'. The doctor says, 'Well, don't go there any more.'

I'm on a whisky diet. I've lost three days already.

Went to the corner shop – bought four corners.

I went to the doctor's the other day, and he said, 'Go to Bournemouth, it's great for 'flu'. So I went, and I got it.

Went to the paper shop – it had blown away.

So I rang up my local swimming baths. I said 'Is that the local swimming baths?' He said 'It depends where you're calling from.'

I told my mum that I'd opened a theatre. She said, 'Are you having me on?' I said, 'Well, I'll give you an audition, but I'm not promising you anything.'

I fancied a game of darts with my mate. He said, 'Nearest the bull goes first.' He went 'Baa' and I went 'Moo'. He said 'You're closest.'

I've lost three days already

PEOPLE WHO APPEARED IN CROSSROADS

Malcolm McDowell (as Crispin Ryder)

Stephen Rea (Pepe Costa)

Max Wall (Walter Soper)

Sue Nicholls (Marilyn Gates)

Johnny Briggs (Cliff Leyton)

Lynda Baron (Phoebe Tompkins)

Diane Keen (Sandra Gould)

Stan Stennett (Sid Hooper)

Trevor Bannister (Keith Willet)

Gabrielle Drake (Nicola Freeman)

Arnold Ridley (Rev. Guy Atkins)

Larry Grayson (wedding car chauffeur)

Elaine Paige (Caroline Winthrop)

Nicholas Ball (Ray Coppins)

Jess Conrad (Philip Bailey)

Jeffrey Holland (Mike Hawkins)

Don MacLean (Cy Townsend)

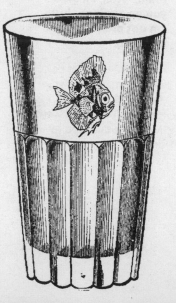

PEOPLE WHO BOUGHT ISLANDS

Mel Gibson (Mago Island, Fiji)

Johnny Depp (Little Hall's Pond Cay, Bahamas)

Nicolas Cage (Leaf Cay, Bahamas)

Celine Dion (Ile Gagnon, Quebec)

Eddie Murphy (Rooster Cay, Bahamas)

David and Frederick Barclay (Brecqhou, Channel Islands)

David Copperfield (Musha Cay, Bahamas)

Bill Gates (Forsyth Island, New Zealand)

John Wayne (Taborcillo, Panama)

Bear Grylls (St Tudwal's West, Wales)

John Lennon (Dorinish Island, County Mayo, Ireland)

Ricky Martin (Angra dos Reis, Brazil)

Diana Ross (Taino, French Polynesia)

Robin Williams (Pender Harbor, British Columbia, Canada)

Michael Ondaatje (Mahone Bay, Ireland)

GONE WITH THE WIND

Margaret Mitchell spent ten years working on *Gone With the Wind*. Working titles included: 'Tote the Weary Load', 'Not In Our Stars', 'Bugles Sang True', 'Ba Ba Black Sheep' and 'Tomorrow is Another Day.' She took her eventual title from the 13th line of the Ernest Dowson poem, *Cynara* – 'I have forgot much, Cynara. Gone with the wind.'

To date, the novel has outsold every hardback book published, with the exception of the Bible. It is also the longest novel transcribed in Braille.

Many people were dismissive of the film's chances of success. Victor Fleming, the film's director (after George Cukor was sacked) said, 'This picture is going to be one of the biggest white elephants of all time.' Gary Cooper, who turned down the role of Rhett Butler, said, 'I'm just glad it'll be Clark Gable who's falling on his face and not Gary Cooper.'

Hattie McDaniel won the Best Supporting Actress – the first black person to win an Oscar.

Clark Gable's bad breath wasn't improved by the whisky he regularly drank or the false teeth he wore, and Vivien Leigh hated having to kiss him.

Clark Gable's personal script for *Gone With The Wind* sold at auction for $244,500 in 1996.

Four hundred actresses tested for the role of Scarlett but only Paulette Goddard and Vivien Leigh were filmed in colour for their auditions.

Racial segregation laws in Georgia prevented black cast members from attending the Atlanta premiere of the film. Clark Gable threatened to boycott the premiere but Hattie McDaniel convinced him to go. Leslie Howard didn't attend.

Leslie Howard felt he was too old for the role of Ashley Wilkes and complained that his costumes made him look like 'a fairy doorman' at a hotel.

Of the four principal actors, three (Leslie Howard, Vivien Leigh and Clark Gable), died relatively young. Olivia de Havilland, the only one who remains alive, was the only one of the four to die in the film.

GENUINE COMPLAINTS RECEIVED BY TRAVEL COMPANIES

'I think it should be explained in the brochure that the local store does not sell proper biscuits like custard creams or ginger nuts.'

'We booked an excursion to a water park but no one told us we had to bring our swimming costumes and towels.'

'We found the sand was not like the sand in the brochure. Your brochure shows the sand as yellow but it was white.'

'We bought 'Ray-Ban' sunglasses for five euros (£3.50) from a street trader, only to find out they were fake.'

'I compared the size of our one-bedroom apartment to our friends' three-bedroom apartment and ours was significantly smaller.'

'The brochure stated: 'No hairdressers at the accommodation'. We're trainee hairdressers – will we be OK staying here?'

'There are too many Spanish people. The receptionist speaks Spanish. The food is Spanish. Too many foreigners.'

'We had to queue outside with no air conditioning.'

'It is your duty as a tour operator to advise us of noisy or unruly guests before we travel.'

There's no air conditioning outside...

'I was bitten by a mosquito – no one said they could bite.'

'My fiancé and I booked a twin-bedded room but we were placed in a double-bedded room. We now hold you responsible for the fact that I find myself pregnant. This would not have happened if you had put us in the room that we booked.'

'It's lazy of the local shopkeepers to close in the afternoons. I often needed to buy things during "siesta" time – this should be banned.'

'On my holiday to Goa in India, I was disgusted to find that almost every restaurant served curry. I don't like spicy food at all.'

'The beach was too sandy.'

'Topless sunbathing on the beach should be banned. The holiday was ruined as my husband spent all day looking at other women.'

'No one told us there would be fish in the sea. The children were startled.'

'It took us nine hours to fly home from Jamaica to England. It only took the Americans three hours to get home.'

... and this beach is too sandy!

ALL THE GRAHAM GREENE NOVELS THAT WERE TURNED INTO FILMS

The Quiet American (1958 and 2002)

The End of The Affair (1955 and 1999)

The Human Factor (1979)

England Made Me (1973)

Travels With My Aunt (1972)

The Comedians (1967)

Our Man In Havana (1959)

A Gun For Sale (1942 and 1957)

The Heart of The Matter (1953)

The Man Within (1947)

The Power And The Glory (1947)

Brighton Rock (1947 and 2010)

The Confidential Agent (1945)

The Ministry of Fear (1944)

Stamboul Train (1934)

NB: *The Third Man* was written specifically for the screen and was later turned into a novel.

EXPRESSIONS WE GET FROM BASEBALL

Ballpark figure – approximate number

Cover all the bases – ensure safety

Curveball – a surprise

Double header – two contests/events held on the same day

Playing hardball (as in 'he's playing hardball with us') – as opposed to softball

Heavy hitter – a powerful person

Home run – a total success (opposite of strike out)

Left field (as in 'that idea came out of left field') – unusual or unexpected

The majors (as in 'to be playing in the majors') – at the top, in the big or major league.

Play ball – go along with something; start

Rain check (as in 'to take a rain check') – do something at a later date

Step up to the plate – to rise to the occasion

Three strikes and you're out – you get two chances before you're held to account

Touch base (as in 'let's touch base later') – to talk later to see that all is well

Whole new ball game – an altered situation

LET'S TOUCH BASE

REALLY SHORT WARS

Britain against Zanzibar (1896) – 38 minutes

Six-Day War (Israel against various Arab countries) (1967) – 6 days

India against Pakistan (1971) – 13 days

Serbia against Bulgaria (1885) – 14 days

Georgia against Armenia (1918) – 24 days

China against Vietnam (1979) – 27 days

Greece against Turkey (1897) – 30 days

Second Balkan War (Bulgaria against Serbia and Greece) (1913) – 32 days

Poland against Lithuania (1920) – 37 days

The Falklands War (Britain against Argentina) (1982) – 42 days

SPANISH CIVIL WAR REPUBLICANS

Ernest Hemingway

James Robertson Justice

Laurie Lee

George Orwell

Claud Cockburn

Arthur Koestler

SPANISH CIVIL WAR FASCISTS

Ezra Pound

Evelyn Waugh

Gertrude Stein

J.R.R. Tolkien (inasmuch as the Fascists were protecting his beloved Catholic Church)

Roy Campbell

'LAWS'

Brooks' law: Adding manpower to a late software project makes it later.

Clarke's three laws – First law: When a distinguished but elderly scientist states that something is possible, he is almost certainly right. When he states that something is impossible, he is very probably wrong. **Second law:** The only way of discovering the limits of the possible is to venture a little way past them into the impossible. **Third law:** Any sufficiently advanced technology is indistinguishable from magic.

Parkinson's law: Work expands so as to fill the time available for its completion.

Dilbert principle: The worst workers are systematically moved to the place where they can do the least damage ... which is management.

Goodhart's law: When a measure becomes a target, it ceases to be a good measure.

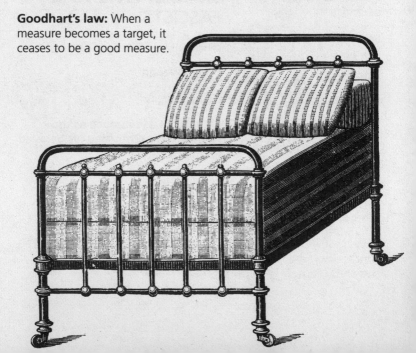

Hanlon's razor: Never attribute to malice that which can be adequately explained by stupidity.

Herblock's law: If it's good, they'll stop making it.

Hofstadter's law: It always takes longer than you expect, even when you take into account Hofstadter's law.

Hutber's law: Improvement means deterioration.

Occam's razor: When two explanations are offered for a phenomenon, the simpler (full) explanation is preferable.

Peter principle: In a hierarchy, every employee tends to rise to his level of incompetence.

Roemer's law: If you build a hospital bed, it will be filled.

Rothbard's law: Everyone specializes in their own area of weakness.

Segal's law: A man with a watch knows what time it is. A man with two watches is never sure.

Skitt's law: Any post correcting an error in another post will contain at least one error itself.

Stigler's law: No scientific discovery is named after its *true* discoverer (named by statistician Stephen Stigler who attributed it to the sociologist Robert K. Merton thus proving his own law).

Sturgeon's law: Nothing is always absolutely so.

Sturgeon's revelation: 90 per cent of everything is crud.

Sutton's law: Go where the money is (named after bank robber Willie Sutton, who, when asked why he robbed banks, is claimed to have answered, 'Because that's where the money is.').

ALL THE FEMALE NOBEL LITERATURE LAUREATES

1909 Selma Lagerlöf

1926 Grazia Deledda

1928 Sigrid Undset

1938 Pearl Buck

1945 Gabriela Mistral

1966 Nelly Sachs

1991 Nadine Gordimer

1993 Toni Morrison

1996 Wislawa Szymborska

2004 Elfriede Jelinek

2007 Doris Lessing

2009 Herta Müller

AMERICAN GANGSTERS AND THEIR NICKNAMES

Wilbur Underhill: Mad Dog

Ellsworth Johnson: Bumpy

Russell Clark: Boobie

Alvin Karpis: Old Creepy

George Kelly: Machine Gun

Vincent Drucci: The Schemer

Giovanni Brusca: The Pig

Kate Barker: Ma Barker

Stefano Magaddino: The Undertaker

Aladena Fratianno: Jimmy the Weasel

Joseph Bonanno: Joe Bananas

Edna Murray: Rabbits

BUTTERFLIES, MOTHS AND CATERPILLARS

A caterpillar has twelve eyes.

The caterpillar of the polyphemus moth can eat 86,000 times its birth weight in less than two months.

The fastest *Lepidoptera* are the sphinx moths. They have been recorded at speeds of 60 kilometres per hour (37 mph).

Some moths survive by drinking the salty tears of cattle.

Most butterflies fly by day while most moths fly by night.

Humans, if they are very sensitive to taste can detect sweetness in a solution of one part sugar to 200 parts water. Some moths and butterflies can detect sweetness when the ratio is 1 to 300,000.

The monarch butterfly has evolved an effective means of survival: it's become poisonous to the birds that attack it.

The Queen Alexandra's
birdwing butterfly lives
in the rain forests of Papua,
New Guinea and has a wingspan that approaches
30 centimetres.

**It is the larvae of moths that damage cloths, not
the moths themselves.**

The silkworm moth is the only truly domesticated insect – it would
cease to exist without human care.

**The North American black and orange monarch butterfly is the
only insect known to be capable of flying over 2,500 miles –
flying between continents in its migration.**

The male lesser emperor moth is able to detect the female
lesser emperor moth at a distance of up to 6.8 miles.

The ghost moth can whistle through its tongue.

The giant atlas moth, the biggest moth, is so huge – with a
wingspan of well over 30 centimetres – that it's often mistaken for
a bat when it's flying.

The markings on the atlas moth's front wing tips resemble a snake's head – making it look like an unpleasant proposition to potential predators.

In Britain in the past 10 years, farmland butterflies have declined by 30 per cent.

There are some 18,000 different species of butterfly.

When the skipper caterpillar is threatened by wasps, it scatters its faeces in all directions. It doesn't do this because it's frightened but because it knows that the wasp is more interested in its faeces than it is in the caterpillar itself.

Some caterpillars and larvae have special glands that secrete poison when they are attacked. Predatory birds soon learn to avoid them.

A caterpillar has more than two thousand muscles.

The fluffy puss caterpillar looks harmless but underneath its fluffy hair are poisonous spines. If you touch these, the spines break off and stay in your skin causing sharp pain, then numbness with a rash and blisters.

Moths can smell a single molecule.

Moths are not really attracted to light. Moths fly towards the blackest point, which is behind the light.

ALL THE CHEMICAL ELEMENTS NAMED AFTER PEOPLE

Bohrium: Neils Bohr

Curium: Marie Curie

Einsteinium: Albert Einstein

Fermium: Italian nuclear physicist Enrico Fermi

Gadolinium: Finnish chemist Johann Gadolin

Hahnium: German chemist Otto Hahn

Lawrencium: American physicist Ernest Lawrence

Meitnerium: Lise Meitner

Mendelevium: Siberian chemist Dmitri Mendeleev

Nobelium: Alfred Nobel

Roentgenium: Wilhelm Roentgen

Rutherfordium: New Zealand physicist Ernest Rutherford

Seaborgium: Glenn T. Seaborg

UNFORTUNATE (GENUINE) WEBSITE ADDRESSES

www.therapistfinder.com

www.homesexchange.com

www.whorepresents.com

www.penisland.net

www.goredfoxes.com

www.choosespain.com

www.mp3shits.com

www.penismightier.com

www.molestationnursery.com

www.expertsexchange.com

www.ipanywhere.com

www.speedofart.com

www.gotahoe.com

SOME OF LONDON ZOO'S STARS FROM THE PAST

Obaysch the Hippopotamus – the first to be seen in Europe since the Roman Empire, and the first in England since prehistory.

Jumbo the Elephant – his name was used to describe anything large. He became aggressive in old age and was sold to Phineas Barnum's circus, where he was hit by a train and killed.

Winnie the American Black Bear – he inspired A.A. Milne, who who visited the zoo with his son Christopher Robin, to write the *Winnie The Pooh* books.

Josephine the Great Indian Hornbill – for many years was the oldest animal at the zoo. She lived in the Bird House until her death in 1998 aged 53.

Guy the Gorilla – lived at the zoo from 1947 until his death in 1978.

Brumas – the first polar bear to be born at the zoo. Thought to be a male, it later transpired she was in fact a female.

Chi Chi – in 1958, the zoo's first giant panda.

Goldie the Golden Eagle – became a national celebrity when he escaped for two weeks in 1965 and flew around the roads and trees of Regent's Park.

THE ORDER IN WHICH THE TRACKS ON *SERGEANT PEPPER'S* WERE RECORDED

When I'm Sixty-Four (recording commenced on 6 December 1966)

A Day In The Life (19 January 1967)

Sergeant Pepper's Lonely Hearts Club Band (1 February 1967)

Good Morning Good Morning (8 February 1967)

Being For The Benefit of Mr. Kite (17 February 1967)

Fixing A Hole (21 February 1967)

Lovely Rita (23 February 1967)

Lucy In The Sky With Diamonds (1 March 1967)

Getting Better (9 March 1967)

She's Leaving Home (17 March 1967)

Within You Without You (22 March 1967)

With a Little Help from My Friends (29 March 1967)

Sergeant Pepper's Lonely Hearts Club Band (Reprise) (1 April 1967)

ALL THE PEOPLE FEATURED ON THE COVER OF *SERGEANT PEPPER'S*

ROW 1

Sri Yukteswar Giri (guru)

Aleister Crowley (occultist)

Mae West (actress)

Lenny Bruce (comedian)

Karlheinz Stockhausen (composer)

W.C. Fields (comedian)

Carl Gustav Jung (psychologist)

Edgar Allen Poe (writer)

Fred Astaire (actor)

Richard Merkin (artist)

Huntz Hall (actor)

Simon Rodia (architect)

Bob Dylan (singer/songwriter)

ROW 2

Aubrey Beardsley (artist)

Sir Robert Peel (Prime Minister)

Aldous Huxley (writer)

Dylan Thomas (poet)

Terry Southern (writer)·

Dion (singer)

Tony Curtis (actor)

Wallace Berman (artist)

Tommy Handley (comedian)

Marilyn Monroe (actress)

William Burroughs (writer)

Sri Mahavatara Babaji (guru)

Stan Laurel (comedian)

Richard Lindner (artist)

Oliver Hardy (comedian)

Karl Marx (political philosopher)

H.G. Wells (writer)

Sri Paramahansa Yogananda (guru)

Sigmund Freud (psychologist)

ROW 3

Stuart Sutcliffe (former Beatle)

Max Miller (comedian)

Marlon Brando (actor)

Tom Mix (actor)

Oscar Wilde (writer)

Tyrone Power (actor)

Larry Bell (artist)

Dr David Livingstone (missionary, explorer)

Johnny Weismuller (swimmer, actor)

Stephen Crane (writer)

Issy Bonn (comedian)

George Bernard Shaw (writer)

H.C. Westermann (sculptor)

Albert Stubbins (soccer player)

Sri Lahiri Mahasaya (guru)

Lewis Carroll (writer)

T.E. Lawrence aka
'Lawrence of Arabia'
(soldier and writer)

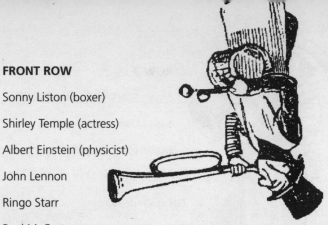

FRONT ROW

Sonny Liston (boxer)

Shirley Temple (actress)

Albert Einstein (physicist)

John Lennon

Ringo Starr

Paul McCartney

George Harrison

Bobby Breen (singer and actor)

Marlene Dietrich (actress)

Diana Dors (actress)

ALL THE PERFORMERS WHO HAVE WON AN OSCAR, A TONY AND AN EMMY

Al Pacino

Vanessa Redgrave

Liza Minnelli

Jason Robards

Maggie Smith

Paul Scofield

Maureen Stapleton

Jessica Tandy

Helen Hayes

Rita Moreno

Sir John Gielgud

Audrey Hepburn

Barbra Streisand (although her Tony was a Special Award)

Jack Albertson

Anne Bancroft

Ingrid Bergman

Shirley Booth

Mervyn Douglas

Jeremy Irons

THE TWENTY WOMEN WITH THE MOST INFLUENTIAL HAIRSTYLES OF ALL TIME*

Jennifer Aniston

Farrah Fawcett

Diana, Princess of Wales

Mary Quant

Marilyn Monroe

Twiggy

Cleopatra

Audrey Hepburn

Queen Elizabeth II

Brigitte Bardot

Madonna

Joanna Lumley

Sharon Stone

Marge Simpson

Joan of Arc

Sophia Loren

Lulu

Sinead O'Connor

Björk

Catherine Zeta-Jones

*According to a poll by Morphy Richards

DARTS PLAYERS AND THEIR NICKNAMES

Phil Taylor: The Power

Eric Bristow: The Crafty Cockney

John Lowe: Old Stoneface

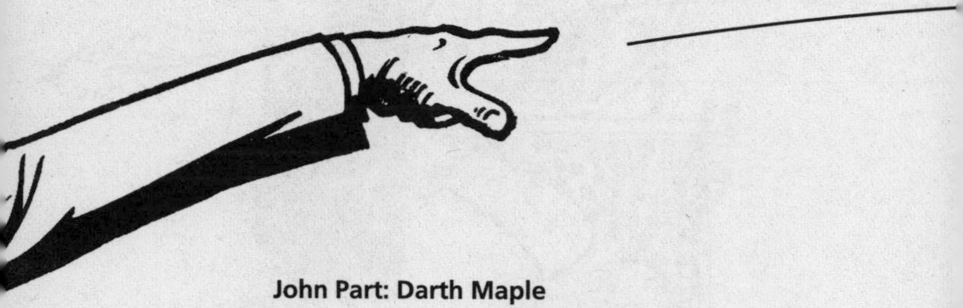

John Part: Darth Maple

Dennis Priestley: The Menace

Martin Adams: Wolfie

Bob Anderson: The Limestone Cowboy

Richie Burnett: The Prince of Wales

Tony David: The Deadly Boomerang

Keith Deller: The Fella

Andy Fordham: The Viking

Ted Hankey: The Count

Les Wallace: McDanger

Martin Atkins: The Assassin

Gary Anderson: The Dreamboy

Bobby George: Bobby Dazzler

Tony West: The Tornado

Simon Whitlock: The Wizard

GENUINE ANNOUNCEMENTS MADE BY AIRLINE STAFF

'Welcome aboard Southwest Flight 245 to Tampa. To operate your seat belt, insert the metal tab into the buckle, and pull tight. It works just like every other seat belt; and if you don't know how to operate one, you probably shouldn't be out in public unsupervised.'

(On a flight with no assigned seating) 'People, people, we're not picking out furniture here, find a seat and get in it.'

'We'd like to thank you folks for flying with us today. And, the next time you get the insane urge to go blasting through the skies in a pressurized metal tube, we hope you'll think of US Airways.'

'Ladies and gentlemen, we've reached cruising altitude and will be turning down the cabin lights. This is for your comfort and to enhance the appearance of your flight attendants.'

'There may be 50 ways to leave your lover, but there are only 4 ways out of this airplane.'

'Thank you for flying Delta Business Express. We hope you enjoyed giving us the business as much as we enjoyed taking you for a ride.'

'In the event of a sudden loss of cabin pressure, masks will descend from the ceiling. Stop screaming, grab the mask, and pull it over your face. If you have a small child travelling with you, secure your mask before assisting with theirs. If you are travelling with more than one small child, pick your favourite.'

'Weather at our destination is 50 degrees with some broken clouds, but we'll try to have them fixed before we arrive. Thank you, and remember, nobody loves you, or your money, more than Southwest Airlines.'

'Your seat cushions can be used for flotation; and, in the event of an emergency water landing, please paddle to shore and take them with our compliments.'

'As you exit the plane, make sure to gather all of your belongings. Anything left behind will be distributed evenly among the flight attendants. Please do not leave children or spouses.'

'Delta Airlines is pleased to have some of the best flight attendants in the industry. Unfortunately, none of them are on this flight.'

'Ladies and gentlemen, if you wish to smoke, the smoking section on this airplane is on the wing and if you can light 'em, you can smoke 'em.'

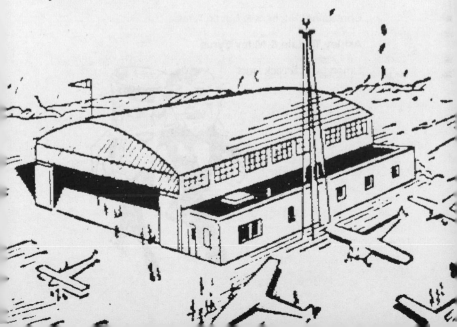

BEST FRIENDS

Liv Tyler & Stella McCartney

Sandi Toksvig & Bonnie Langford

Mylene Klass & Suzanne Shaw

Chris Evans & Danny Baker

Nicole Kidman & Naomi Watts

Ben Affleck & Matt Damon

Courteney Cox & Jennifer Aniston

Sara Cox & Zoe Ball

Graham Gooch & John Emburey

Penelope Cruz & Salma Hayek

Christopher Hitchens & Martin Amis

Ashley Tisdale & Miley Cyrus

Simon Pegg & Nick Frost

PEOPLE WHO HAD/HAVE PERFECT PITCH

Mariah Carey

Chevy Chase

Michael Jackson

Bill Bailey

Ray Charles

Freddie Mercury

Frank Sinatra

Joseph Stalin

Mia Farrow

Dame Julie Andrews

Barbra Streisand

Leonard Bernstein

Spike Milligan

Celine Dion

Tina Turner

Ludwig van Beethoven

PEOPLE WHO POSED AS ARTISTS' MODELS

Lady Emma Hamilton

Charlton Heston

Sir Sean Connery

Lesley Garrett

Quentin Crisp

Anna Chancellor

Juliette Binoche

Miriam Margolyes

WHAT THEIR FATHERS DO/DID FOR A LIVING

Nicolas Sarkozy (Advertising agency boss)

David Mitchell (Lecturer)

Mena Suvari (Psychiatrist)

Amanda Holden (Merchant navy petty officer)

Leona Lewis (Youth worker)

Zac Efron (Engineer)

Susan Boyle (Miner)

Katie Melua (Doctor)

Emily Blunt (Barrister)

Gemma Arterton (Architect)

Kristen Stewart (TV producer)

Robert Pattinson (Car salesman)

Ellen Page (Graphic designer)

Shia LaBeouf (Clown)

January Jones (Gym teacher)

John Bercow (Taxi driver)

Ashton Kutcher (Factory worker)

Holly Willoughby (Manager of a double-glazing company)

Sarah Palin (Science teacher and track coach)

Simon Pegg (Jazz musician and keyboard salesman)

Daniel Craig (Publican)

John Barrowman (Tractor factory manager)

Sir Alan Sugar (Tailor)

Barry McGuigan (Singer)

Robert Wyatt (Journalist)

Len Deighton (Chauffeur)

Koo Stark (Film producer)

Stewart Copeland (CIA agent)

Lesley-Anne Down (Caretaker)

Sir Bruce Forsyth (Garage owner)

Anne Diamond (Scientist)

Gloria Hunniford (Newspaper advertising manager)

Alexander Armstrong (Doctor)

Sir Peter Hall (Stationmaster)

Keith Chegwin (Timber firm rep)

Joe Strummer (Diplomat)

Elaine Paige (Estate agent)

Sir David Puttnam (Photographer)

Frederick Forsyth (Furrier)

Hugh Dennis (Clergyman)

John Stapleton (Co-op manager)

Suggs (Photographer)

Lynn Faulds-Wood (Accountant)

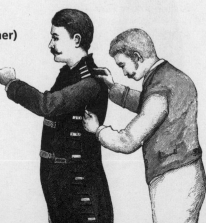

HAD FATHERS WHO WERE HEADMASTERS

Graham Greene

Sir John Mills

Richard Herring

Ioan Gruffudd

Sir Joshua Reynolds

Enoch Powell

Charles de Gaulle

Alexander Kerensky

Matthew Arnold

Jon Snow

WHAT THEIR MOTHERS DO/DID FOR A LIVING

David Mitchell (Lecturer)

Natasha Kaplinsky (Professor of Economics)

Anne Hathaway (Lawyer)

Lindsay Lohan (Investment banker)

Orlando Bloom (Teacher)

Amanda Holden (Secretary)

Simon Cowell (Ballet dancer)

Leona Lewis (Social worker)

Simon Pegg (Civil servant)

Shia LaBoeuf (Ballerina)

Kanye West (University professor)

Lily Allen (Film producer)

Coleen Rooney (Nursery nurse)

Wayne Rooney (Part-time cleaner at the school Coleen attended)

Ellen Page (Teacher)

Zac Efron (Secretary)

Susan Boyle (Shorthand typist)

Gemma Arterton (Cleaner)

David Duchovny (Teacher)

Kirsten Stewart (Script supervisor and film director)

Ellen Page (Teacher)

Holly Willoughby (Air stewardess)

Sarah Palin (School secretary)

Josh Brolin (Wildlife activist)

Emily Blunt (English teacher)

Daniel Craig (Art teacher)

John Barrowman (Singer)

Reese Witherspoon (Professor of Nursing)

Damon Albarn (Theatrical set designer)

Dan Brown (Musician)

David Walliams (Laboratory technician)

Hilary Duff (Music producer)

Mark Ruffalo (Hairstylist)

Russell Brand (Secretary)

Jake Gyllenhaal (Screenwriter)

Anastacia (Actress)

Rhys Ifans (Nursery school teacher)

Ben Affleck (Teacher)

Kevin Bacon (Teacher)

Christian Bale (Circus dancer)

Tyra Banks (Photographer)

Benjamin Bratt (Native American activist)

Adrien Brody (Photojournalist)

Sandra Bullock (Opera singer)

Aled Jones (Primary school teacher)

Vin Diesel (Psychologist)

Kirsten Dunst (Art gallery owner)

Colin Firth (Open University lecturer)

Cuba Gooding Jr (Backing singer)

Phill Jupitus (Artist)

Jay Kay (Jazz singer)

Alicia Silverstone (Airline stewardess)

Dervla Kirwan (Teacher)

Lisa Kudrow (Travel agent)

Laura Linney (Nurse)

Matthew Macfadyen (Actress)

Tobey Maguire (Secretary)

Matthew McConaughey (Teacher)

Kylie Minogue (Ballerina)

Bill Nighy (Psychiatric nurse)

Matthew Perry (Pierre Trudeau's press agent)

Keanu Reeves (Showgirl)

Condoleezza Rice (Pianist)

Mia Sara (Stylist)

David Schwimmer (Attorney)

Christian Slater (Casting director)

Patrick Swayze (Choreographer)

Billy Bob Thornton (Psychic)

Uma Thurman (Model)

Pete Townshend (Singer)

Denzel Washington (Beautician)

Isla Fisher (Novelist)

Matt Lucas (Synagogue worker)

**Franka Potente
(Medical administrator)**

Catherine Tate (Florist)

PEOPLE WHO DROWNED

Jeff Buckley

Le Corbusier

Spalding Gray

Robert Maxwell

Josef Mengele

Percy Bysshe Shelley

Matthew Webb

James Whale

Natalie Wood

Virginia Woolf

THE WAY WE LIVE (2)

Only about 6 per cent of women fail to cry at least once a month, while 50 per cent of men fail to cry that often.

Eight million nappies are thrown away in the UK every day.

In a typical restaurant, customers receive 27 pence worth of food for every pound that they spend.

The average Briton drinks 33 litres of bottled water a year.

The average person speaks almost five thousand words a day – although almost 80 per cent of speaking is self-talk (talking to yourself).

An office chair with wheels will travel about seven and a half miles a year.

A person is more likely to eat twice as much in the company of others as when eating alone.

According to restaurant staff, married men tip better than unmarried men.

Most people who read the word 'yawning' will yawn.

The British use almost twice as much soap as the French.

According to a Canadian researcher, left-handed people are more accident-prone than right-handers and are likely to die younger. The researcher looked at the records of over two thousand ex-professional baseball players and discovered that left-handers over the age of 35 were 2 per cent more likely to die than right-handers of the same age. There were very few left-handers in the group who made it beyond 85 years old. In another Canadian study of left-handers, it was found that 44 per cent of left-handers had been hospitalized within the last five years due to an accident – compared to just 36 per cent of the right-handers.

If you are involved in a car accident, your chances of getting hurt are only one out of ten. If you have an accident on a motorcycle, your chances of getting hurt are nine out of ten.

According to the National Safety Council, bicycles are the most dangerous objects in a typical home. Next on the list are stairs, then doors.

The busiest time for 999 calls is between 10.30 p.m. and midnight (around 6,000 calls per hour).

Almost two-thirds of British people choose a shower rather than a bath.

The average single man is one inch shorter than the average married man.

Perfume is frequently made from – among other things – a slippery, musky substance called ambergris which is vomited up by certain species of whales.

The distances between cities are actually the distances between city halls. When you see a sign 'Manchester – 60 miles', it means it is 60 miles to the city hall in Manchester.

The three most valuable brand names in the world are Marlboro, Coca-Cola, Budweiser, in that order.

Worldwide, coffee is the most popular drink. Altogether we drink 400 billion cups a year.

Only 1.6 per cent of the water on Earth is fresh.

The calendar repeats itself every 14 years.

MEN WHO TRAINED AT SANDHURST

David Niven

James Blunt

Prince Harry

Ian Fleming

Sir Winston Churchill

Louis de Bernières (left after four months)

Antony Beevor

King Abdullah of Jordan

Desmond Llewelyn

The Duke of Kent

Michael Morpurgo

FORMER GOALKEEPERS

Albert Camus

Niels Bohr

Bob Willis

Vladimir Nabokov

Pope John Paul II

Nicky Byrne (Westlife)

Sir Arthur Conan Doyle (for Portsmouth under the pseudonym A.C. Smith)

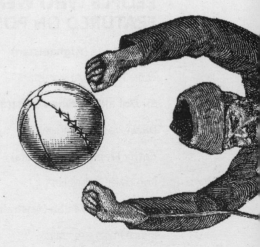

PEOPLE WHO WERE
FEATURED ON POSTAGE STAMPS

Marie Curie (Afghanistan)

Pablo Picasso (Afghanistan)

Sir Donald Bradman (Australia)

Dawn Fraser (Australia)

Cathy Freeman (Australia)

Rod Laver (Australia)

Dame Nellie Melba (Australia)

Prince Philip (Australia)

Dame Joan Sutherland (Australia)

Ian Thorpe (Australia)

Wayne Gretzky (Canada)

Marshall McLuhan (Canada)

Pierre Trudeau (Canada)

Louis Armstrong (Gabon)

Nat King Cole (Gabon)

Christopher Dean (Gabon)

Hermann Hesse (Gabon)

Aung San Suu Kyi (Gabon)

Mark Spitz (Gabon)

Winston Churchill (Germany)

Friedrich Engels (Germany)

Mahatma Gandhi (Germany)

The Bee Gees (Isle of Man)

Karl Marx (Germany)

**Dame Kiri Te Kanawa
(New Zealand)**

PEOPLE WHO WERE FEATURED ON AMERICAN STAMPS

Bud Abbott, Louisa May Alcott, Louis Armstrong, Desi Arnaz, Arthur Ashe, George Balanchine, James Baldwin, Lucille Ball, Theda Bara, Ethel Barrymore, John Barrymore, Lionel Barrymore, Count Basie, Jack Benny, Irving Berlin, Leonard Bernstein, Humphrey Bogart, Clara Bow, Fanny Brice, Pearl S. Buck, James Cagney, Hoagy Carmichael, Enrico Caruso, John Cassavetes, Charlie Chaplin, Patsy Cline, Nat King Cole, John Coltrane, Gary Cooper, Lou Costello, Bing Crosby, James Dean, Cecil B. DeMille, Jack Dempsey, Emily Dickinson, Walt Disney, Wyatt Earp, W. C. Fields, Henry Fonda, Clark Gable, Greta Garbo, Judy Garland, George Gershwin, Ira Gershwin, Benny Goodman, Martha Graham, Cary Grant, Woody Guthrie, Bill Haley, Oliver Hardy, Lorenz Hart, Moss Hart, Edith Head, Jim Henson, Sir Alfred Hitchcock, Billie Holiday, Buddy Holly, Edward Hopper, Harry Houdini, Chester 'Howlin' Wolf' Burnett, Robert Johnson, Scott Joplin, Frida Kahlo, Boris Karloff, Buster Keaton, Grace Kelly, Jerome Kern, Stan Laurel, Vivien Leigh, Alan Jay Lerner, Sinclair Lewis, Charles Lindbergh, Harold Lloyd, Frank Loesser, Frederick Loewe, Joe Louis, Bela Lugosi, Henry Mancini, Rocky Marciano,

Hattie McDaniel, Clyde McPhatter, Herman Melville, Johnny Mercer, Ethel Merman, Glenn Miller, Charlie Mingus, Margaret Mitchell, Thelonious Monk, Marilyn Monroe, Audie Murphy, Ogden Nash, Annie Oakley, Eugene O'Neill, Jesse Owens, Charlie Parker, Dorothy Parker, ZaSu Pitts, Cole Porter, Elvis Presley, Man Ray, Otis Redding, Paul Robeson, Edward G. Robinson, Sugar Ray Robinson, Bessie Smith, John Steinbeck, Dr Seuss, Ritchie Valens, Rudolph Valentino, Andy Warhol, Muddy Waters, John Wayne, Orson Welles, Hank Williams, Tennessee Williams, Tom Wolfe, Malcolm X

PEOPLE WHO WERE FEATURED ON IRISH STAMPS

Thomas Alva Edison, Albert Einstein, Oscar Wilde, Marie Curie, Roy Keane, David O'Leary, Bono, The Edge, Phil Lynott, Adam Clayton, Larry Mullen Jr, Rory Gallagher, Van Morrison, Gay Byrne, Samuel Beckett, Seamus Heaney, Darren Clarke, Paul McGinley, Eamonn Darcy, Ronan Rafferty

ONLYs (2)

The Channel Islands were the **only** British soil occupied by German troops in World War 2.

Until 1896, India was the **only** source for diamonds in the world.

Lebanon is the **only** country in the Middle East that doesn't have a desert.

Liechtenstein and Uzbekistan are the **only** two doubly landlocked countries in the world (this means that they're both entirely surrounded by landlocked countries).

The armadillo is the **only** animal – apart from man – that can catch leprosy.

Bangladesh has a unique system of transfer of power. It's the **only** country where, at the end of the tenure of a government, power is handed over to members of a civil society for three months who run the general elections and then transfer the power to elected representatives.

Bangkok is Thailand's **only** city.

Of the world's top ten most unhealthy countries, the **only** one not in Africa is Afghanistan.

The **only** dog in a Shakespeare play is Crab, in *The Two Gentlemen of Verona*.

There is **only** one person in all recorded history who has been killed by a meteorite. A man named Manfredo Settala from Milan in Italy in 1680. He was 80 years old.

Alaska is the **only** US State that can be typed on one row of keys (the middle row).

The **only** mammal species in which the female is normally taller than the male is the okapi, a type of antelope.

Henry VII was the **only** British King to be crowned on the field of battle.

There are **only** seven different surnames on the island of Tristan da Cunha.

New Hampshire is the **only** US state where adults don't have to wear seat belts in cars.

The Comedy of Errors is the **only** Shakespeare play which doesn't have a song in it.

The United States and the Phillippines are the **only** countries that allow bounty hunting.

Sailing is the **only** sport that has a triangular course.

An Austrian man named Adam Rainer (1899–1950) is the **only** man in recorded human history ever to have been both a dwarf and a giant. At the age of 21, he was just 3ft 10½in but then he had growth spurts that saw him grow to an incredible 7ft 8in.

The armadillo is the **only** animal that can walk underwater.

The honeybee is the **only** insect that produces food eaten by us. It's also the only insect that can be moved for the express purpose of pollination and it's also the **only** insect to leave its stinger behind when it stings (thus causing its own death).

The praying mantis is the **only** insect that can turn its head 360 degrees. It's also the only creature on Earth with just one ear.

The midge is the **only** insect that can survives the sub-zero temperatures of the Antarctic.

The firefly is the **only** insect in the world that produces its own energy.

Five countries in Europe touch **only** one other: Portugal, Denmark, San Marino, Vatican City and Monaco.

STARTED OUT WITH ANNA SCHER

Kathy Burke, Pauline Quirke, Linda Robson, Patsy Palmer, Susan Tully, Phil Daniels, Gillian Taylforth, Jesse Birdsall, Dexter Fletcher, Gary Kemp, Martin Kemp, Sid Owen, Natalie Cassidy

THE HUMAN CONDITION (2)

We can live four times as long without food as we can without water.

Constant exercising can be just as bad for a person as no exercise at all. The human body needs 24 hours without exercise about once a week in order to cleanse itself of lactic acid and other waste products.

In an average day the average adult spends 77 minutes eating.

The sound of a snore can be almost as loud as the noise of a pneumatic drill.

Someone's gender can be guessed with 95 per cent accuracy just by smelling their breath.

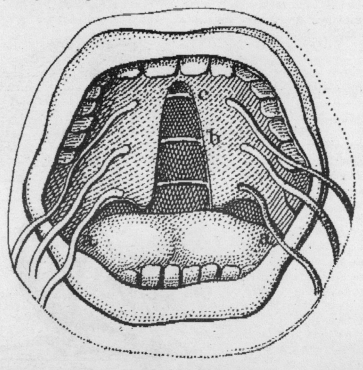

The average cough comes out of your mouth at 60 miles per hour.

If one identical twin grows up without a given tooth coming in, the second identical twin will usually also grow up without the tooth.

You can't bend your little finger without moving the finger next to it.

Humans can't taste water – although some animals can. We taste the chemicals and impurities in the water but not the water itself.

Happy events – like family celebrations or evenings with friends – boost the immune system for the following two days.

You can't sneeze in your sleep. You also have no sense of smell when asleep.

Beards are the fastest growing hairs on the human body. If the average man never trimmed his beard, it would grow to nearly 10 metres in his lifetime.

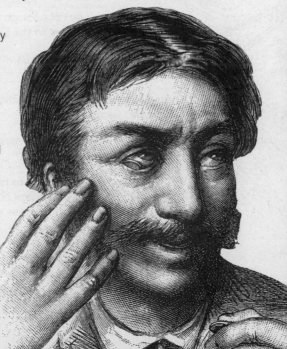

Human sweat contains a chemical that is the same as wasp poison.

A blond beard grows faster than any other colour beard.

Vegetarian women are more likely to give birth to baby girls than to baby boys.

Eighty-five per cent of people can curl their tongue into a 'U' shape.

People with initials that spell out GOD or ACE are likely to live longer than people whose initials spell out words like APE, PIG or RAT.

Your heart rate can rise as much as 30 per cent during a yawn.

Your body gives off enough heat in half an hour to bring a litre of water to the boil.

Your ears secrete more earwax when you're afraid than when you're relaxed.

Your body is creating and killing 15 million red blood cells per second.

Mouth ulcers are the most common human affliction.

During his or her lifetime, the average human will grow 590 miles of hair.

When you're wide awake, alert and mentally active, you're still never more than 25 per cent aware of what various parts of your body are doing.

Half of all people who have ever smoked have now quit.

Girls learn to talk earlier, use sentences earlier, and learn to read more quickly than boys.

The pupil of the eye expands as much as 45 per cent when a person looks at something pleasing.

Only 1 per cent of bacteria cause disease in humans.

The mineral content, porosity and general make-up of human bone is nearly identical to some species of South Pacific coral. The two are so alike that plastic surgeons are using the coral in facial reconstructions, to replace lost human bone.

The sensitivity of the human eye is so keen that on a clear moonless night a person standing on a mountain can see a match being struck as far as 50 miles (80 kilometres) away.

On any one square centimetre of our skin there are some eight million microscopic animals. We even have microscopic mites living in our eyelashes.

The tips of fingers and the soles of feet are covered by a thick, tough layer of skin called the stratum corneum.

Sweat glands are little coiled up ducts. If you stretched them out and lined up all of the sweat glands in one human end to end, the line would be nearly two thousand miles long.

Most peoples' legs are slightly different lengths.

It takes only 15 watts of electricity going through a human body to stop the heart. Common light bulbs run on about 25 to 75 watts of electricity.

The knee is the most easily injured of all the joints in the body.

Parasites count for 0.01 per cent of our body weight.

The type specimen (i.e. the best example) for the human species is the skull of Edward Drinker Cope, an American palaeontologist of the late 1800s.

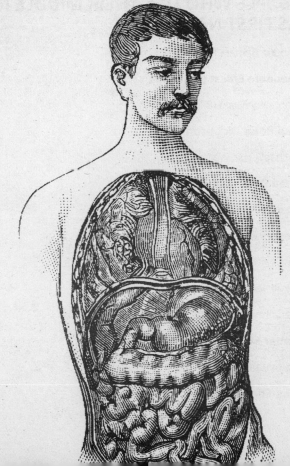

PEOPLE WHO USE THEIR MIDDLE NAMES AS FIRST NAMES

Daphne Barbara Follett

Theodore Ernest (Ernie) Els

Stephen William (Billy) Bragg

Paul Bruce Dickinson

Michael Louis Walsh

Jared Drake Bell

Andreas Nikolaus (Niki) Lauda

Frederick Charles (Charlie) George

John Michael Stipe

Clyde Jackson Browne

Maria Linda Ronstadt

Walter Menzies Campbell

Walter Stacy Keach

John Eric Morecambe

TEETOTALLERS

Daniel Radcliffe, Bruce Willis, Tony Benn,
Griff Rhys-Jones, Chris Eubank, David Bailey,
Sol Campbell, Lenny Henry, Alastair Campbell,
Frank Skinner, Michael York, Tracey Ullman,
Davina McCall, George W. Bush, Naomi Campbell, Anne
Robinson, David Beckham, Tony McCoy, Padraig Harr
ington, Peter Beardsley, Johnny Depp, David Letterman,
Jimmy Nail, Jennifer Lopez, Donald Trump

PEOPLE NAMED AFTER SOMEONE/ SOMETHING FAMOUS

Mariah Carey (after the song *They Called the Wind Mariah* from the 1969 film Paint Your Wagon)

January Jones (after January Wayne, a character in Jacqueline Susann's *Once Is Not Enough*)

Lewis Hamilton (after Carl Lewis)

Orlando Bloom (after the seventeenth-century British composer Orlando Gibbons)

DIED DURING FILMING

Heath Ledger (*The Imaginarium of Dr Parnassus*, 2008)

Marilyn Monroe (*Something's Got To Give*, 1962)

James Dean (*Giant*, 1955)

Jean Harlow (*Saratoga*, 1937)

John Candy (*Wagons East*, 1994)

Bruce Lee (*Game of Death*, 1973)

Brandon Lee (*The Crow*, 1993)

Roy Kinnear (*Return of The Musketeers*, 1989)

River Phoenix (*Dark Blood*, 1993)

Vic Morrow (*The Twilight Zone*, 1982)

Natalie Wood (*Brainstorm*, 1981)

ANAGRAMS

ERROR ON BIDET – Robert De Niro

ORDER IN YAWN – Winona Ryder

SCREEN ANNOY – Sean Connery

BIG LEMONS – Mel Gibson

BRAIN CREEPS ON – Pierce Brosnan

SOME TASK – Kate Moss

BLOB RECREATION – Robbie Coltrane

ANGRY BOILS – Gaby Roslin

NO, I DECLINE – Celine Dion

HMM. A SNOT POEM – Emma Thompson

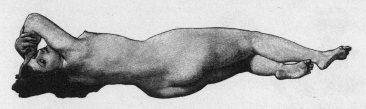

I LIKE 'EM YOUNG – Kylie Minogue

DIET? TREMBLE. – Bette Midler

REVIEW AGONY SURE – Sigourney Weaver

I'M SO CUTER – Tom Cruise

OLD WEST ACTION – Clint Eastwood

ONLY I CAN THRILL – Hillary Clinton

FOUL HARD IN GROIN – Gloria Hunniford

PLAY NOT, LORD – Dolly Parton

SLOVENLY STEEL STAR – Sylvester Stallone

HE'S GROWN LARGE 'N' CRAZED – Arnold Schwarzenegger

GERMANY – Meg Ryan

ANORAK'S IN TOWN – Rowan Atkinson

TWO RED RATS – Rod Stewart

I WARM BILLIONS – Robin Williams

LIBRARY WOMAN – Barry Manilow

CLOSE EVIL SLOT – Elvis Costello

HUGE MAIL WAIL – William Hague

NATIVE NODDY – Danny Devito

INTERNAL SCUM – Martin Clunes

BUM NOT MEAN – Emma Bunton

GOT SO WEIRD – Tiger Woods

CONSIDER NAVEL – Clive Anderson

BORN INSANE? NO – Anne Robinson

EVIL LASS IN EROTICA – Alicia Silverstone

BAND ON ALARM – Damon Albarn

SUPER AMORAL FLIRT – Mariella Frostrup

HEADING LOW – Goldie Hawn

OK, FINE TART, RIDE – Frankie Dettori

INSANE MOLE – Liam Neeson

COOL OGRE IMMINENT – Colin Montgomerie

PORK MESS – Ross Kemp

LENT WORTHY GAWP – Gwyneth Paltrow

AH. POLISHED – Sophie Dahl

NO, I AM CRAZED – Cameron Diaz

ABSENT PREY, SIR – Britney Spears

NOT RISKY GUY – Kirsty Young

GEOLOGY ENCORE – George Clooney

SLICK OR FATAL CHAT – Calista Flockhart

A DRUG IF FOUND – Ioan Gruffudd

RICH IN ALE? GOSH – Charlie Higson

VEINS CRASH – Chris Evans

THEME BAULK – Kate Humble

KILLER ON EARLY – Lorraine Kelly

TALKING ON SEX – Alex Kingston

I DO RAW SULK – Lisa Kudrow

VALID, CAN CALM – Davina McCall

HANG MORON ART – Graham Norton

NICE QUAINT LONER – Caroline Quentin

WE ARE JUST ILL – Julie Walters

CAP STAR TREK WIT – Patrick Stewart

WIN MIRACLE LIP – Prince William

SO ANGRY OR MAD – Gordon Ramsay

TURNED STINKS – Kirsten Dunst

MAKE HOSTILE – Katie Holmes

MEET JUBILANT RISK – Justin Timberlake

BAD STAR IS BARREN – Barbra Streisand

ADJOINING FLAMES – James Gandolfini

CRASH MUCH EACH MILE – Michael Schumacher

EMPHATIC LIES – Michael Stipe

WOMANLY TIES – Emily Watson

NEVER NOT SICK – Kevin Costner

CLEAR IN HABITS – Christian Bale

HER SLOW CRY – Sheryl Crow

ANIMAL CRANK – Alan Rickman

GROW ACNE GERM – Ewan McGregor

RUES BREAK – Sue Barker

A ZIP SHALL RIP – Zara Phillips

JAIL GENIAL ONE – Angelina Jolie

VALUES SLIM WIN – Venus Williams

THIS INERT RASCAL – Christian Slater

ENVY SICK APE – Kevin Spacey

IN MOCK DENIAL – Nicole Kidman

DON'T REAR DOWN – Edward Norton

RECENTLY SAT CALM – Stella McCartney

IMAGINED UNION – Dannii Minogue

JUST A BROILER – Julia Roberts

STERN LIBEL – Ben Stiller

REPLENISH FAN – Ralph Fiennes

FUN, SEX GALORE – Alex Ferguson

GOD I DO COMPLAIN – Placido Domingo

PAY MR CLEAN-CUT – Paul McCartney

I AM RACY, HEAR? – Mariah Carey

BURSTING PRESENCE – Bruce Springsteen

IN TONE – WHY SHOUT? – Whitney Houston

MOLEST ME – ENJOY – Tommy Lee Jones

I'M A TRUE BOGEY – Tobey Maguire

MORMON IDEAS – Marie Osmond

AMERICAN YELLS 'HI' – Shirley Maclaine

RIGHT FEE IN A FILM – Melanie Griffith

NO REAL CHARM BENEATH – Helena Bonham Carter

RUDE? I'M HYPED – Eddie Murphy

IDEAL SINEWY LAD – Daniel Day-Lewis

DO 'ANNIE' TAKE – Diane Keaton

I AM A PLONKER – NOT SMART – Tara Palmer-Tomkinson

BEST PG – NEVER LIES – Steven Spielberg

FASCINATING FACTS (2)

In France, it's possible to marry a deceased person with the authorization of the President of the Republic – but only in exceptional cases.

In the nineteenth century, a Frenchman named Casimir Polemus survived three shipwrecks (the *Jeanne Catherine*, which was wrecked off Brest on 11 July 1875; the *Trois Frères*, which was wrecked in the Bay of Biscay on 4 September 1880 and *L'Odéon*, which was wrecked off Newfoundland on 1 January 1882. What made this even more extraordinary is that, in each case, he was the only survivor.

In the 1930s, a cult started up on the South Pacific island of Tanna in Vanuatu over cargo that was brought over from the US. The locals thought that the cargo – labelled John Frum Cargo – had been sent by the gods and started worshipping John Frum.

Saparmurat Niyazov, the President of Turkmenistan from 1990 until his death in 2006, declared that those who read *Ruhnama, The Book of The Soul* (his book of moral and spiritual guidance) three times a day would automatically go to heaven. Saparmurat Niyazov was better known as President Turkmenbasy. He changed the name of the month of January to 'Turkmenbasy', and he had a melon named after him.

The Indus river, from which India derived its name, is now entirely in the territory of Pakistan.

There is a street in Italy that is less than half a metre wide.

A Belgian student couldn't afford a party to celebrate his twentieth birthday so he had the bright idea of offering his friends' foreheads for hire to advertisers on an internet auction site. A company paid them all to have its logo painted on their foreheads for the night of the party.

Ethiopia is famous as the country of '13 months of sunshine'. The Ethiopian year is based on the Julian calendar, which has 12 months of 30 days each and a 13th month called Pagume, which has five days (or six in a leap year).

Malta's the nearest Commonwealth country to the UK.

Occasionally people are born with horns. The majority of these horns protrude from people's foreheads, but some people have had horns on their thighs, backs, noses and feet.

A student at Rugby school managed to pop a spot and spray pus over a distance of two metres.

A teenager in India has an unusual party trick. He can drink milk through his nose and squirt it out of his eyes through his tear ducts.

Almost 90 per cent of Uruguayans are of European descent.

The natives of the Solomon Islands claim to be able to kill trees just by shouting at them.

Lake Balkash in eastern Kazakhstan contains two kinds of water: salt water in the east and fresh water in the west.

In Kenya, a person's middle name is based on the time of day at which they were born.

The launching mechanism of a carrier ship that helps planes to take off could throw a pickup truck over a mile.

There's an Argentinian town where horses have to wear a hat if it's too hot.

Only 8.5 per cent of all Alaskans are Inuit.

In Japan some restaurants serve smaller portions to women, even though they charge as much as they do for men's portions.

The smallest bicycle that an adult could ride had wheels made from silver dollars.

In the nineteenth century, a French mime artist accidentally got stuck in his imaginary glass box and starved to death. Think about it.

There was a Togolese man with 17 wives and 60 children.

In Tibet some women have special metal instruments they use for picking their noses.

There is a house in Margate, New Jersey that is made in the shape of an elephant. A home in Norman, Oklahoma is shaped like a chicken.

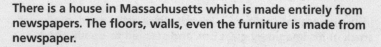

There is a house in Massachusetts which is made entirely from newspapers. The floors, walls, even the furniture is made from newspaper.

Another house, this one in Canada, is made of 18,000 discarded glass bottles.

There was once a devout Hindu who, to demonstrate his mastery over pain, raised his arm above his head and kept it that way for years. He held his arm so still that a bird built a nest in his hand.

Magnetic north is actually a thousand miles away from the North Pole ('True North'). The North Pole is technically is located at 90° N (and any longitude), but magnetic north is currently at 73° N, 100° W.

In the Middle Ages, Lithuania was the biggest country in Europe.

There's only 5.54 centimetres of coastline per person in the world.

Pitcairn Island is the second largest of all the Pitcairn Islands but it's the only one that's inhabited.

There's a Starbucks in South Korea that has five levels.

In Hungary, hot springs are used for central heating in homes.

The game Monopoly was very popular in Cuba but, due to it being considered a game of capitalism, Fidel Castro ordered that all the games be destroyed.

A British man named Dave Cornthwaite took up skateboarding in March 2005. Fourteen months later he became the first person to skate the 1,450km journey from John O'Groats to Land's End.

On a Japanese TV show, a young child was told his mother had just been killed. The producers wanted to see how many seconds it would take before the toddler started crying.

When a Tokyo organized-crime boss was killed in 1978, his killers cooked his hands in a pot of soup. They then served this soup to unwitting people.

The mothers of Oscar Wilde and Franklin D. Roosevelt dressed their sons as girls for the first few years of their lives.

The longest tandem – i.e. extended bicycle – was designed for 35 riders. It was 20 metres long and weighed as much as a small car.

TINNITUS SUFFERERS

Russell Grant, Pete Townshend, Barbra Streisand, Julia McKenzie, Alan Bleasdale, Vincent Van Gogh (which is why, it is now thought, he cut his ear off), Jack Straw, Johnnie Walker

WONDERFULLY TITLED (GENUINE) BOOKS

Proceedings of the Second International Workshop on Nude Mice

The 2009–2014 World Outlook for 60-milligram Containers of Fromage Frais

How to Conduct a One-Day Conference on Death Education

The Large Sieve and its Applications

The Book of Marmalade: Its Antecedents, Its History, and Its Role in the World Today

Oral Sadism and the Vegetarian Personality

Versailles: The View From Sweden

Highlights in the History of Concrete

What Do Socks do?

Japanese Chins

Egg Banjos from Around the World

Greek Rural Postmen and Their Cancellation Numbers

Living with Crazy Buttocks

People Who Don't Know They're Dead: How They Attach Themselves to Unsuspecting Bystanders and What to Do About It

The Stray Shopping Carts of Eastern North America: A Guide to Field Identification

How to Avoid Huge Ships

TWO OF A KIND

PEOPLE WHO WERE FAT AS CHILDREN
Russell Brand

Gok Wan

HAD A BABY IN A HOSPITAL BIRTHING POOL
Emma Thompson

Jerry Hall

DYSPRAXIC
David Bailey

Daniel Radcliffe

EX-*BLIND DATE* CONTESTANT
Nina Wadia

Ed Byrne

AMBIDEXTROUS
James Woods

Maria Sharapova

HAS SUFFERED FROM ULCERS
George Clooney

Gok Wan

LOST A FINGER/THUMB

Rahm Emanuel lost the tip of his middle finger to a meat slicer

Vince Vaughn lost a piece of his thumb in a car crash

BORN WITH EXTRA FINGERS

Brenda Blethyn was born with an extra finger

Gemma Arterton was born with six fingers on each hand

MODELLED FOR TEEN PHOTO-ROMANCE STORIES

Fiona Bruce

Alex Kingston

KEEN ASTRONOMERS

Robson Green

Myleene Klass

SONS OF BISHOPS

Jon Snow

Hugh Dennis

SONS OF PROFESSIONAL FOOTBALLERS

Ricky Hatton (Manchester City)

Alan Carr (Northampton Town)

HEAD BOYS AT SCHOOL
Eric Idle (Royal Wolverhampton School)
Matt Smith (Northampton School For Boys)

HEAD GIRLS AT SCHOOL
Enid Blyton (St. Christopher's School, Beckenham)
Rebecca Hall (Roedean)

ALLERGIC TO CATS
Eli Roth
The Duke of York

DIABETICS
Nick Jonas
Arthur Smith

BLOOD DONORS
Prince Harry
Sophie Ellis-Bextor

HAD A FUSCHIA NAMED AFTER THEM
Kenny Dalglish
Jonny Wilkinson

FATHERS WERE KILLED IN WORLD WAR 2
Sir Garfield Sobers
Gareth Hunt

SUFFERED FROM PSORIASIS
Eli Roth
Dennis Potter

DROPPED OUT OF UNIVERSITY
Rebecca Hall
Charlie Brooker

HAS A TWIN
Ben Whishaw (James)
Duffy (Katy Ann)

WANTED TO BE PRIESTS
James McAvoy
Jack Dee

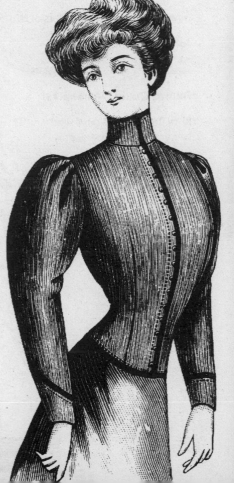

CELEBRITIES IN BANDS

Michael Barrymore (Fine China)

Pat Cash & John McEnroe (The Full Metal Rackets)

Jeff Goldblum (The Mildred Snitzer Orchestra)

Robson Green (The Workie Tickets)

Jeremy Irons (The Four Pillars of Wisdom)

John Simm (Magic Alex)

Jared Leto (30 Seconds To Mars)

Dennis Quaid (The Sharks)

Rhys Ifans (the original lead
singer for The Super Furry
Animals)

Gwen Stefani (No Doubt)

FACTS AND STATS ABOUT THE LONDON UNDERGROUND

The London Underground is the longest and largest underground system in the world. It was also the world's first.

Number of miles travelled by each Tube train each year: 73,500.

Total number of passengers carried on the Tube each year: 1,014 million.

Number of individual passengers carried on the Tube each year: 28 million.

Length of network: 408km/253 miles.

Proportion of the network which is in tunnels: 46 per cent. Thus more of the London Underground is above ground than underground.

Longest continuous tunnel: East Finchley to Morden (via Bank) – 27.8km/17.25 miles.

The first Tube escalator was introduced at Earls Court in 1911. Wooden-legged 'Bumper' Harris was employed to travel up and down it to prove that it was safe.

Station with most escalators: Waterloo has 23 plus 2 passenger conveyors.

Longest escalator: Angel – 60 metres/197 feet.

Shortest escalator: Chancery Lane – 9.1 metres/30 feet.

Deepest lift shaft: Hampstead – 55.2 metres/181 feet.

Shortest lift shaft: Westminster – 2.5 metres/8 feet.

Stations with the most platforms: Moorgate and Baker Street have 10 platforms each.

Passengers enter the Tube system at a rate of 146,000 people an hour.

London Underground's world-famous logo, the roundel – a red circle crossed by a horizontal blue bar – was designed by calligrapher Edward Johnston and first appeared in 1913.

Of the 287 stations on the London Underground, only 29 are south of the Thames.

The shortest distance between stations on the London Underground is that between Leicester Square and Covent Garden on the Piccadilly line – 0.16 miles. Taking into account the stairs etc., it's much quicker to walk.

Green grapes cause more accidents on the London Underground than banana skins.

Just two stations on the London Underground have all five vowels in their names – Mansion House and South Ealing.

Julian Lloyd Webber was London Underground's first official busker.

TATTOOED

Jennifer Aniston (the name of her late dog on her foot)

Fearne Cotton (several – including a fern leaf covering her right hip)

Pixie Geldof (Paula Yates's signature on her wrist)

Danielle Lloyd ('Only God can judge me' in Hebrew down the back of her neck)

Victoria Beckham ('I am my beloved's and my beloved is mine, He who pastures his flock among the lilies' in Hebrew on her neck and back)

Kate Moss (two swallows on her back and an anchor tattoo on her wrist)

Jordan (art on the back of her neck)

Wayne Rooney ('Just Enough Education To Perform' on his forearm)

Scarlett Johansson (the sun setting on the sea with a star in the sky on her forearm)

Joss Stone (flowers on her feet)

Samantha Cameron (dolphin on her ankle)

Lady GaGa (a quote from the German poet Rainer Maria Rilke on her left arm)

Whoopi Goldberg (Woodstock on breast)

EXTRAORDINARY MIDDLE NAMES

Daniel WROUGHTON Craig

Sarah Louise HEATH Palin

Orlando BLANCHARD Bloom

Beyoncé GISELLE Knowles

Michelle LAVAUGHN Obama

Martin OSBORNE Johnson

John SCOT Barrowman

Paul EMERSON CARLYLE Ince

Paul YAW Boateng

Antony CARDEW Worrall Thompson

Willie HUNTER FISHER Carson

NAMES OF FLOWERS AND PLANTS

Dog's-Tooth-Grass

Old Man's Beard

Jack-Go-To-Bed-At-Noon

Witches'-Butter

None So Pretty

Morning Glory

Love-In-Idleness

Devil's Snuffbox

Gill-Over-The-Ground

Elephant's-Ears

SPORT (2)

Polo originated in Central Asia around 2,500 years ago but it was only in 1975 that, for safety reasons, left-handed play was banned.

Table-tennis is the world's biggest participation sport.

Water polo was originally known as water rugby.

Greek gymnast Dimitrios Loundras is the youngest person ever to have taken part in the Olympics. He was just ten years old when he represented his country in the gymnastics at the first modern Olympics in 1896. He lived for another 74 years before dying at the age of 84 in 1970.

I say that Dimitrios Loundras is the youngest competitor but there's speculation that the young French boy who was brought in to cox (i.e. steer) the Dutch pair in the 1900 rowing finals might have been even younger. The Dutch rowers thought that their cox was, at 60 kilograms, too heavy, and so they drafted in a local lad (the Games were held in Paris). So far, so true – and, indeed, there is a photograph in existence of the two oarsmen with the boy after they'd won the gold medal. However, despite much research, no one has ever identified the boy or his age – though it's thought he might have been as young as seven.

The baseball legend Babe Ruth wore a cabbage leaf under his cap to keep him cool.

More athletes than spectators attended the 1900 Paris Olympic Games.

During the original ancient Olympic Games, all wars between the Greek city-states were put on hold until the games were finished.

Jim Thorpe, a part-Native American, became a hero when he won gold medals in 1912 for decathlon and pentathlon, but in 1913 it was revealed that in 1909 and 1910 he had earned $25 a week playing minor league baseball. This infringed his amateur status and he was stripped of his medals by the Amateur Athletic Union. In 1951, Thorpe was portrayed by Burt Lancaster in *Jim Thorpe – All-American*. In 1982, the IOC lifted the ban on Thorpe and the following year, 30 years after his death, his gold medals were given to his children.

The Italian Abdon Pamich won gold for the 50-kilometre walk in the 1964 Games but only after stopping at 38 kilometres to throw up.

Melvin Sheppard, the American who won gold in the 1908 Olympics, had applied to become a policeman but was rejected – due to a 'weak heart'. He went on to win another three Olympic gold medals.

In the final of the 1932 3,000 metres steeplechase, Volmari Iso-Hollo of Finland crossed the finishing line with a 40-metre lead. But because the lap checker had forgotten to change the lap counter after the first lap, there was no tape on the line and the lap counter read '1'. So Iso-Hollo set off on another lap and duly won the race by 75 metres in a race which was, by default, extended to 3,400 metres.

If you throw that, it's war!

No women competed at the first modern Olympic Games because the Games' founder, Baron Pierre de Coubertin, felt that their inclusion would be 'impractical, uninteresting, unaesthetic, and incorrect'.

If a woman watched even one Olympic event in Ancient Greece, she could be executed.

A badminton shuttlecock travels at a speed of over 110 mph.

In horse races, the favourite wins just under than 30 per cent of the time.

Every year some 20 million golf balls are lost in water hazards on British golf courses.

If you hit a bad shot on the tee of the first hole in a game of golf, your opponent might be kind enough to offer you a mulligan. In golf, a mulligan is a retaken shot on the first tee – and *only* on the first tee – after a bad shot.

It is every golfer's ambition to 'score his age' – that's to say, go around a golf course in the same number of strokes (or fewer) as his age. The oldest player to 'score his age' in a game of golf was C. Arthur Thompson (1869–1975) of Victoria, British Columbia, Canada, who carded 103 in 1973.

Sport? It's so uninteresting.

THE SIMPSONS

The Simpsons started out as a short insert on *The Tracey Ullman Show* but soon became a half-hour prime-time show. It is now the longest-running American sitcom as well as the longest-running American animated programme.

Evergreen Terrace, the street the Simpsons live on, is the name of the street the show's creator, Matt Groening, grew up on in Portland, Oregon.

Many of the characters in the show are named after streets in Portland, Oregon. These include Flanders, Kearney, Lovejoy, Quimby and Terwilliger (Sideshow Bob).

Homer's grunt – D'oh – has entered the English dictionary.

The doorknocker on the Simpsons' front door looks a lot like Mr Burns – complete with liver spots and pointy nose.

The Simpsons is the only sitcom to have had 'appearances' from three former Beatles (Paul, George and Ringo).

Initially, Yeardley Smith auditioned for the voice of Bart and Nancy Cartwright for the voice of Lisa. They play them the other way around.

Dan Castellaneta, the voice of Homer, based the voice on his own father's voice.

In the supermarket in the title sequence of *The Simpsons*, Maggie scans as $847.63. This was the average monthly cost of feeding and caring for an American baby.

No one knows where Springfield, the Simpsons' home town, is, and the writers often tease the audience. For example, in one episode, Marge phones an egg-painting company and, when asked for her address, says, '742 Evergreen Terrace, Springfield Ohi–', but continues, 'Oh hiya, Maude,' speaking to the person who has just appeared in her kitchen.

Hank Azaria, the voice for many of the characters, says that most of his voices are just bad celebrity impressions. Moe is Al Pacino while Louie the cop is Sylvester Stallone.

'APPEARED' ON *THE SIMPSONS*

Simon Cowell (Henry)

Sarah Michelle Gellar (Gina Vendetti)

Kim Cattrall (Chloe Talbot)

Lucy Liu (Madam Wu)

Albert Brooks (Tab Spangler)

Liam Neeson (Father Sean)

Alec Baldwin (Caleb Thorn)

Lily Tomlin (Tammy)

Michael York (Mason Fairbanks)

Antonio Fargas (Huggy Bear)

Ricky Gervais (Charles)

Frances McDormand (Melanie Upfoot)

Larry Hagman (Wallace Brady)

Mandy Moore (Tabitha Vixx)

Stacy Keach (Howard K. Duff VII)

Michael Imperioli (Dante Calabresis Jr

Kiefer Sutherland (Jack Bauer)

Steve Buscemi (Dwight)

Jack Black (Milo)

Emily Blunt (Juliet Hobbes)

Colm Meaney (Tom O'Flanagan)

Ellen Page (Alaska Nebraska)

Jodie Foster (Maggie Simpson)

Seth Rogen (Lyle McCarthy)

Anne Hathaway (Princess Penelope)

Sacha Baron Cohen (Tour guide)

Eddie Izzard (Nigel Baker-Butcher)

Hugh Laurie (Roger – credited as as Hugh 'Struck by a' Lorry)

Rachel Weisz (Dr Thurmond)

Martha Stewart (Martha Claus)

Jon Hamm (FBI investigator)

Werner Herzog (Walter Hottenhoffer)

Martin Landau (The Great Raymondo)

PLAYED THEMSELVES ON
THE SIMPSONS

Stephen Sondheim, Lionel Richie, Placido Domingo, Ted Nugent, Jon Stewart, John C. Reilly, Lance Armstrong, Drew Carey, Denis Leary, Jeff Bezos, Matt Groening, Eartha Kitt, Gary Larson, Chris Martin, Simon Cowell, Ellen DeGeneres, Randy Jackson, Rupert Murdoch, Mark Zuckerberg, David Mamet, Halle Berry, Russell Brand, Ricky Gervais, David Copperfield

WEATHER

Mali is the hottest country on Earth.

Greenland is the coldest country.

The Atacama Desert in Chile is the world's driest place. No rainfall has ever been recorded there.

Nights in the tropics are warm because moist air retains the heat well. Desert nights, on the other hand, get cold rapidly because dry air doesn't hold heat to the same degree.

A rainbow can occur only when the sun is 40 degrees or less above the horizon.

In ten minutes, a hurricane releases more energy than all the world's nuclear weapons combined.

The average hailstorm lasts about 15 minutes.

Japan is hit by up to 30 typhoons a year. Winds can reach 200 kilometres an hour and 30 centimetres of rain can fall in 24 hours.

The warmest temperature ever recorded on Antarctica was -16°C.

Russia 'boasts' the lowest recorded temperature in Europe: -68°C in 1933.

Morocco has the lowest recorded temperature in Africa: -24°C in 1935.

The River Nile, the world's longest river, has frozen over twice – once in the ninth century, and again in the eleventh century.

Iraq and the Persian Gulf states have two important winds. The eastern Sharki wind is hot and humid, while the northern Shamal wind brings welcome cooler air during the hot summer.

In Bosnia and Herzegovina, the jugo is a wind that brings rain to various parts of the country.

This is one of those strange-but-true facts worth noting: Argentina not only has the lowest recorded temperature in South America (-33°C in 1907), it also has the highest recorded temperature in South America (49°C in 1905).

Reunion Island endured the worst 24 hours of rain when 183 centimetres fell on 7/8 January 1966.

The wettest place on earth is Tutunendo, Colombia where an average of 1,176 centimetres of rain falls every year.

However, during a twelve-month period in 1860–61, Cherrapunji recorded 2,647 centimetres of rain.

In the Alps, the warm Föhn winds can raise temperatures by as much as 30°C in a few hours. This has the effect of melting the ice and causing avalanches. It can also increase the risk of forest fires, so when it's blowing, some Swiss mountain villages forbid smoking.

In Seville in Spain on 4 August 1881, the temperature reached 50°C – the hottest in the history of Europe.

The highest temperature ever recorded anywhere in the world was in Al' Aziziyah, Libya, on 13 September 1922, when the thermometer climbed to a mind-boggling 57.8°C.

Brunei's lowest recorded temperature is 21°C.

A one-day weather forecast requires about 10 billion mathematical calculations.

In Bangladesh in 1988, 92 people were killed by giant hailstones weighing up to 1kg.

When Anders Celsius, the creator of the temperature scale that bears his name, first developed his scale, he made freezing 100 degrees and boiling 0 degrees (i.e. the wrong way round). Since no one dared point this out to him, his fellow scientists waited until Celsius died to change the scale.

One centimetre of rain is equal to 10 centimetres of snow.

THUNDER & LIGHTNING

Two-thirds of the people struck by lightning survive.

An average bolt of lightning is less than one inch thick. The electricity is 30 million volts.

Thunderstorms can approach as fast as 50 mph.

Rocket launches, nuclear explosions and volcanic eruptions can all trigger lightning.

Lightning doesn't always produce thunder

When fashionable Parisian women of the late eighteenth century went out in blustery weather, they wore a lightning rod attached to their hats.

In 1994, an Austrian woman was killed when her underwired bra was struck by lightning.

Between the years 1967 and 1977, there were thunderstorms in the Ugandan town of Tororo for 250 days a year – that's more than two-thirds of the time.

At any one moment, there are about 1,800 thunderstorms on Earth.

The gurnard, a fish found in Florida, grunts when a thunderstorm is brewing, and is said to be more reliable than weather-forecasters.

Grunt

THE HUMAN LIGHTNING ROD

Roy Sullivan was a park ranger in Virginia's Shenandoah National Park. Between 1942 and 1977, Sullivan was hit by lightning on no fewer than 7 different occasions and – no less incredibly – he survived each time. As a result, he earned the nicknames the Human Lightning Conductor and the Human Lightning Rod and was recognized by the *Guinness Book of World Records* as the person struck by lightning more recorded times than any other person.

All these strikes were documented by the superintendent of Shenandoah National Park and were verified by doctors. Sullivan said that he'd been hit other times too – the first time as a child: he was helping his father to cut wheat in a field, when a thunderbolt struck the blade of his scythe. However, because he didn't have any proof, he didn't ask for it to be added to his official tally.

You probably might guess that he died from the seventh and final strike but you'd be wrong. In fact, he shot himself in 1983 at the age of 71.

Anyway, here for the record are Sullivan's seven strikes.

Strike #1: 1942. He was hiding from a thunderstorm in a fire lookout tower that didn't have a lightning rod. The tower was hit seven or eight times and so Sullivan ran out and received what he reckoned to be his worst lightning strike, which burned a strip all along his right leg, hit his toe and left a hole in his shoe.

Strike #2: 1969. After 27 years of being lightning-free, Sullivan was hit while driving his truck on a mountain road. A vehicle's metal body normally protects people but, this time, the lightning hit nearby trees and was deflected into the open window of the truck. The strike knocked Sullivan unconscious and burned off his eyebrows, eyelashes and most of his hair. The uncontrolled truck kept moving until it stopped near a cliff edge.

Strike #3: 1970. Sullivan was struck in his garden. The lightning hit a nearby power transformer and from there jumped to his left shoulder, searing it.

Strike #4: 1972. Sullivan was working inside the ranger station in Shenandoah National Park when a lightning strike set his hair on fire. At this point, he was starting to think he was jinxed and would be struck even if he were in a crowd of people.

Strike #5: 1973. By now, Sullivan was entitled to feel unlucky. Out on patrol in the park, Sullivan saw a storm cloud forming and drove away quickly. When he finally thought he had outrun it, he decided it was safe to leave his truck but he was struck by a lightning bolt that he later said he actually saw hit him. The lightning set his hair on fire, moved down his left arm and left leg and crossed over to his right leg just below the knee. Still conscious, Sullivan crawled to his truck and poured the can of water, which he always kept there, over his head.

Strike #6: 1976, Sullivan was struck by a bolt of lightning that injured his ankle.

Strike #7: 1977. Sullivan was fishing when a lightning bolt hit the top of his head and travelled down, burning his chest and stomach.

SURVIVED NERVOUS BREAKDOWNS

Dave Gorman, Thandie Newton, Jennifer Lopez, Susan Boyle, Miranda Hall, Ken Russell, Rupert Brooke, Sir Isaac Newton, John Lennon, Jon Pertwee, Michael Barrymore, Sir Denis Thatcher, Sir Peter Hall, Vince Hill, Fiona Fullerton, Terry Scott, Dame Catherine Cookson, Frankie Howerd, Dora Bryan, Sir Richard Hadlee, Alastair Campbell, James Herriot, Samantha Janus, Jeremy Brett, Eric Porter, Mike Yarwood, Spike Milligan, Donny Osmond, Walt Disney, Marie Curie, Tony Slattery, Sir Noel Coward, Bill Oddie

HAD PUBS NAMED AFTER THEM

Rebecca Adlington (The Adlington Arms)

Fred Trueman (Fiery Fred in Yorkshire)

Jack Walker (Uncle Jack's in Blackburn)

Lord Harold Wilson (Pipe and Gannex in Liverpool)

Sir Henry Cooper (Henry Cooper in London)

Sir Tom Finney (Tom Finney in Preston)

General Sir Jeremy Moore (The General Moore in Plymouth)

Prince Philip (Duke of Edinburgh in Bacton, Norfolk)

Sir Alf Ramsey (Sir Alf Ramsey in Tunbridge Wells, Kent)

Stan Laurel (The Stan Laurel Inn in Ulverston)

Horatio Nelson (Lord Nelson in Burnham
Thorpe, Norfolk)

**Rupert Brooke (The Rupert Brooke,
Rugby)**

Dean Macey (The Silver Decathlete
in Canvey Island)

DIED IN THE BATHROOM

Judy Garland

Elvis Presley

King George II

Lenny Bruce

Catherine The Great

GUEST EDITORS

Eva Herzigová – *Mirror Woman*

Marco Pierre White – *Caterer And Hotelkeeper*

Bono – *Vanity Fair*

Kylie Minogue – *Vogue (Australia)*

Rowan Williams – *The New Statesman*

David Cameron – *The Big Issue*

Jamie Oliver – *The Big Issue*

Trudie Styler – *The Big Issue*

AMERICANS AND THEIR CLASSMATES' RATINGS

Kevin Federline – Most Likely to Be on *America's Most Wanted*

Ryan Phillippe – Best Smile

Jack Nicholson – Class Clown

Cybill Shepherd – Most Attractive

Teri Hatcher – Most Likely to Become a Solid Gold Dancer

Natalie Portman – Most Likely to be a Guest on Jeopardy

Dennis Hopper – Most Likely to Succeed

Rosie O'Donnell – Class Clown

Joan Allen – Most Likely to Succeed

Matthew McConaughey – Most Handsome

Oprah Winfrey – Most Popular

HEALTH

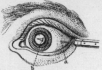

According to researchers, when patients are brought in 'dead on arrival', the people who work in hospital emergency rooms are more likely to make resuscitation attempts on the good-looking patients than the ugly ones.

In a survey, one out of every four second opinions failed to confirm the original doctor's opinion.

There is a disease called hypertrophy of the tongue that can make the tongue so large that it no longer fits into a person's mouth.

People who are chronically ill never yawn.

Leontiasis – or lion face – is a rare condition in which the facial and cranial bones in the skull overgrow. This can lead to total blindness due to compression of the optic nerve.

Necrotizing fasciitis is a flesh-eating disease caused by a strain of flesh-eating bacteria.

The letters 's', 'p' and 't' – all the consonants in the word 'spit' – produce the sounds most likely to cause someone to spit and therefore pass on viruses like colds and flu.

How do doctors know for certain that someone is dead? There are machines that can test for brain activity but what if a machine isn't available? In that case, there are other reliable methods which include: pouring freezing water in the person's ear; poking something in their eye; poking something down their throat; grinding knuckles into the base of their spine.

Nepal and Benin have the fewest hospitals per person in the world: just 3 for every 10,000 people.

Monaco has the most hospitals and the most hospital beds per person with 163 for every 10,000 people.

Monday is the day of the week when the risk of a fatal heart attack is greatest. A ten-year Scottish study found that 20 per cent more people die of heart attacks on Mondays than on any other day of the week. It's thought to be due to a combination of too much fun over the weekend and the stress of going back to work.

In an experiment, a computer program diagnosed people with various problems. It was right in 98 per cent of cases. By contrast, the (real-life) doctors were right in just 78 per cent of cases.

The longest recorded 'bout' of hiccups lasted for 65 years.

The longest recorded sneezing fit lasted for 978 consecutive days (nearly three years).

Over 90 per cent of diseases are caused or complicated by stress.

Prior to the use of drugs like penicillin, mouldy slices of bread were sometimes used to stop wounds from becoming infected.

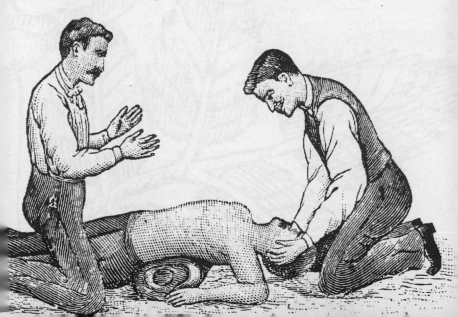

PEOPLE WHO HAD ROSES NAMED AFTER THEM

Pele, Prince William, Heidi Klum, LeAnn Rimes, Gary Player, The Princess Royal, Dolly Parton, Barbra Streisand, Princess Caroline of Monaco, Charlotte Rampling, Chris Evert, Camilla, Duchess of Cornwall, Liv Tyler

PEOPLE WITH FAMOUS STEP-PARENTS

Mark Ronson – Mick Jones (of Foreigner)

Josh Brolin – Barbra Streisand

Kate Hudson – Kurt Russell

Carrie Fisher – Dame Elizabeth Taylor

Julian Lennon – Yoko Ono

Sienna Miller – Kelly Hoppen

ANIMALS (2)

When a lion has eaten its fill, it carries its head high. This is well known in the animal kingdom – so much so that a well-fed lion can walk head-up through a herd of antelope without scaring them. However, if the lion's head is low, the antelope know it's feeding time and scarper.

The last known wild wolf in Britain was killed in Scotland in 1743.

A jackrabbit can travel more than 3.6 metres in one bound.

The male fox will mate for life, and if the female dies, he remains single for the rest of his life. However, if the male dies, the female will hook up with a new mate.

Cows produce 20 per cent of all methane released into the atmosphere.

Male marmoset monkeys put on weight in sympathy with their pregnant mates.

Rabbits are more closely related to horses than they are to rodents or mice.

Beavers were once the size of bears.

A bear has 42 teeth.

Pumas can leap a distance of about 18 metres.

A female ferret can die if she goes into heat and can't find a mate.

Human birth-control pills work on gorillas.

There are about 1.5 million hedgehogs in the UK.

When a hippopotamus dies, other hippos surround the corpse and lick it for a whole day – only leaving the corpse when hungry crocodiles get too numerous to deter.

When a pair of rhinos feels threatened, they stand back to back, confronting their enemies from opposite directions.

The long-nosed bandicoot has a pouch on its back.

The orangutan eats very slowly and can take 20 minutes to chew a single piece of fruit.

Beavers mate for life.

The star-nosed mole is the fastest eating mammal in the world. Using its fleshy tentacles, it can eat a meal of worms in 227 milliseconds.

Animals evolved legs to walk underwater, not on land. Some types of fish appear to use their fins to walk along the seabed.

Hedgehogs can climb trees (their spines protect them from injury if they fall).

Unlike most cats, tigers love the water and can easily swim three or four miles.

WHAT THEY DID BEFORE BECOMING FAMOUS

Orlando Bloom – Clay pigeon trapper at a skeet shooting range

Beyoncé Knowles – Swept up hair at her mother's salon

Keith Richards – Worked as a ball boy at a tennis club

Amy Adams – Worked in a Hooters restaurant

Matthew McConaughey – Shovelled chicken manure in Australia

Gwen Stefani – Mopped floors at a Dairy Queen

James Brown – Racked balls at a poolhall

James Stewart – Magician's assistant

Tom Cruise – Paperboy

Dara O Briain – Children's TV presenter on Irish TV

Bill Murray – Sold chestnuts outside a grocery store.

Johnny Depp – Pen salesman

John Barrowman – Shovelled coal for an Illinois
power company

Susan Boyle – Trainee cook

Damon Albarn – Worked as a tea boy at the Beat Factory studio

Ken Dodd – Coal delivery assistant

Sir Michael Caine – Cement mixer, driller

Rutger Hauer – Electrician

Bob Newhart – Accountant

**Anthea Turner – Worked for the AA's information and
breakdown service**

Mickey Rourke – Sold pretzels

Roger Daltrey – Sheet metal worker

Ringo Starr – Barman

Anita Dobson – Insurance clerk

Burt Lancaster – Circus acrobat

Malcolm McDowell – Coffee salesman

Belinda Carlisle – Petrol–pump attendant

Nicole Appleton – Lake lifeguard

Diane Keaton – Photographer

Keanu Reeves – Managed a pasta shop in Toronto, Canada.

Brendan Cole – Builder

Robert Pattinson – Model (between the ages of 12 and 16)

FORMER TEACHERS

Dame Vivienne Westwood, Gene Simmons, Art Garfunkel, Mr T (PE), Stephen King, Tom O'Connor, Gareth Hale, J.K. Rowling (in Portugal)

WHAT THEY ORIGINALLY INTENDED TO BE

Lily Allen – Florist (and she studied horticulture)

Simon Pegg – Vet

Alesha Dixon – PE teacher

Lee Mack – Jockey

Nick Berry – Professional footballer

Mike Read – Singer

Georgie Fame – Professional Rugby League player

Gareth Hale – Vet

William Baldwin – Professional baseball player

Zeinab Bedawi – Doctor

Kate O'Mara – Concert pianist

Caroline Quentin – Ballerina

Rachel de Thame – Ballerina

THE EARTH

One third of all the fresh water on Earth is in Canada.

The lifetime of the sun's light is estimated at 109 years.

All the land mass of the Earth – and more – could fit into the Pacific Ocean.

There have been fewer people below 2km in the sea than have been on the moon.

It takes 8.5 minutes for light to get from the sun to Earth.

New Zealand's South Island is the oldest exposed surface on Earth.

The lowest place on Earth is around the Dead Sea where it's 400 metres below sea level.

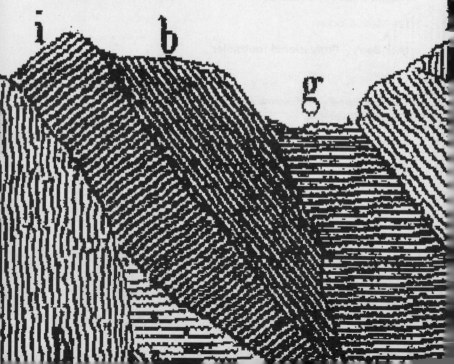

The most common elements in Earth's crust are oxygen, silicon and iron, in that order.

The Red Sea is the world's warmest sea, with an average temperature of 25ºC.

The deepest spot in the ocean (and therefore on Earth) is the Mariana Trench in the Pacific Ocean. Its maximum depth is 11 kilometres or 6.8 miles. Contrast that with the highest point on Earth (on top of Mount Everest) which is 'only' 8.85 kilometres high.

The Earth gets 100 tons heavier every day due to falling space dust.

The Earth's crust has an average depth of 24km.

One third of the world's land surface is desert.

Every gallon of seawater contains more than 100 grams of salt.

The Pacific Ocean, the biggest ocean, is three times larger than Asia, the biggest continent.

Two minor earthquakes occur every minute.

Less than 2 per cent of the water on Earth is fresh.

Lake Manitou on Manitoulin Island in the middle of Lake Huron in Canada is the largest lake on an island within a lake in the world.

More than 75 per cent of the countries in the world are north of the equator.

Over one million Earths would fit in the sun.

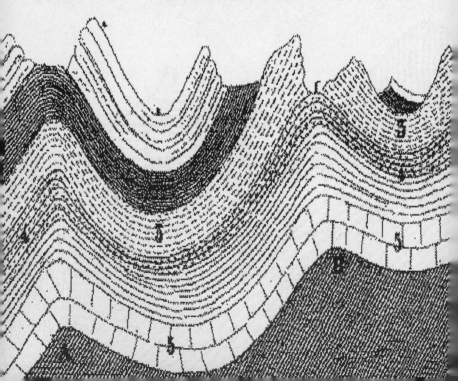

The Sutter Buttes in California is the smallest mountain range on Earth.

The Amazon rainforest produces half the world's oxygen supply.

Of all the land on earth, 7.6 per cent is currently being farmed but twice as much more land *could* be farmed.

The volume of the Earth's moon is the same as the volume of the Pacific Ocean.

The are more than 20 million trillion litres of water on Earth. This is the same quantity of water as there was 4 billion years ago.

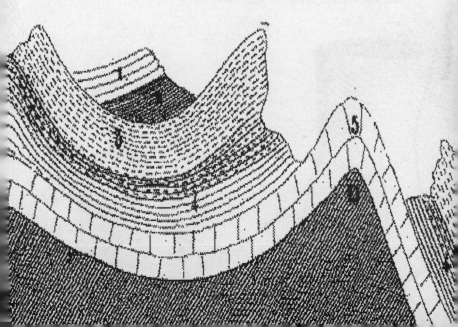

SCIENCE AND NATURE

A hardboiled egg will spin. An uncooked or softboiled egg will not.

Sound at the right vibration can bore holes through a solid object.

Airports at higher altitudes require a longer airstrip.

A ball of glass will bounce higher than a ball of rubber. A ball of solid steel will bounce higher than one made entirely of glass.

The microwave was invented after a researcher walked by a radar tube and a chocolate bar melted in his pocket.

Grapes explode when you put them in the microwave.

The only thing that can destroy a diamond is intense heat.

Cut an onion in half, rub it on the sole of your foot and an hour later you'll taste onion in your mouth.

Sound moves faster through water than it does through air.

A combustion engine wastes 75 per cent of the chemical energy contained in petrol.

The metal with the highest melting point is tungsten, at 3,410°C.

The estimated temperature at the centre of the Earth is around 4,100°C.

For an experiment in maternal attachment, scientists raised three groups of monkeys. Some were raised by their mother. Some were raised by a stationary bottle covered with fur. The last group were raised by a bottle also covered with fur that was remotely controlled and acted rather like a real mother. The monkeys with the moveable-bottle mother grew up nearly as normal as those raised with a real mother, but those with a stationary mother gradually became mad.

Thirty thousand monkeys were used in the massive three-year effort to classify various types of polio.

In the 1970s, scientists successfully transplanted a monkey's head on to another monkey's body.

Nine out of every ten scientists who ever lived are alive today.

A comet's tail always points away from the sun.

Helium is the element with the lowest boiling point.

There are more atoms in a single grain of sand than there are grains of sand on the beach.

Gemstones contain several elements – except the diamond, which is all carbon.

The reason why bubbles are round is because this is the most efficient shape that soap film can take for the amount of air trapped inside.

Just one litre of used motor oil can ruin one million litres of fresh water.

The strength of early lasers was measured in Gillettes – the number of razor blades a given beam could puncture.

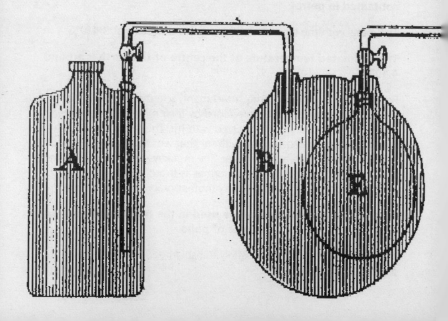

There is the same quantity of water on Earth today as there was 4 billion years ago.

About 20 per cent of the Earth is permanently frozen.

Two sugar cubes rubbed together will spark.

In 1978, a temperature of 70 million degrees Celsius was generated at Princeton University in the US. It was during an experiment and it remains the highest man-made temperature ever.

The degree sign (°) is thought to be an ancient representation of the sun.

The deepest bore hole drilled in the world was 17,400 metres deep (Azerbaijan, 2002).

The deepest bore hole drilled in the ice was 3,053 metres (Greenland, 1993).

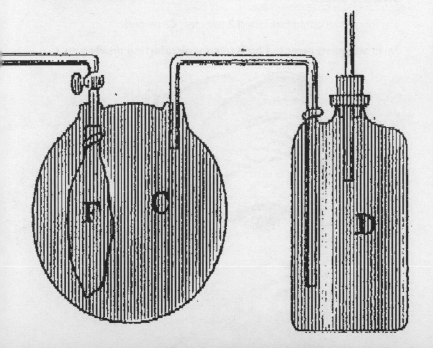

FARTS AND FARTING

If you farted continuously for six years and nine months, enough wind would be produced to equal the energy of an atomic bomb.

Less than 1 per cent of a fart is made up of stinky stuff but that's smelly enough to make it unpleasant.

The average fart releases 100g of gases.

Farts contain gases such as carbon dioxide and methane that contribute to global warming.

An 11-year-old American boy farted 217 times in five minutes on a radio call-in show.

In Ancient Japan, public contests were held to see who in a town could break wind loudest and longest. Winners were awarded prizes.

The longest recorded fart lasted 2 minutes, 42 seconds.

Farts are mostly created by bacteria microfarting inside you.

Parp!

Women fart three times more often than men but are much better at disguising it. Men, on the other hand, are much more likely to boast about their farting. A serious study on the differences between the sexes when it comes to farting found that, when fed exactly the same food, women produce more concentrated gas than men – in other words, they produced 'a greater odour intensity'.

It is known that gas escaping from a corpse can make it sound as if someone is farting after death. One man wrote to *Bizarre* magazine to say that he's eating lots of fruit and vegetables so he can go out with a bang when he dies. He added that his mother, a nurse, said that skinny people made the loudest farts.

Farts have been clocked at three metres per second.

The most famous farter of all time was Le Pétomane, a Frenchman whose real name was Joseph Pujol. Originally a baker, he used to entertain his customers by imitating musical instruments by farting.

Parp!

He took to the stage and adopted his new name. His act was phenomenally successful in Paris towards the end of the nineteenth century with his highlights including the sound effects of cannon fire and thunderstorms, as well as playing 'O Sole Mio and La Marseillaise on an ocarina (an ancient flute-like 'wind' instrument) through a rubber tube in his bottom He could also blow out a candle from several yards away. He even farted his impression of the 1906 San Francisco earthquake.

Later in life, he retired from performing and returned to bakery, opening a biscuit factory. He died in 1945, aged 88 and was buried in the cemetery of La Valette-du-Var, where his grave can still be seen today. The Sorbonne university offered his family a large sum of money to study his body after his death, but the family refused the offer.

Le Pétomane has a modern successor in a British 'flatulist' named Paul Oldfield who goes by the stage name Mr Methane and claims to be the only performing professional flatulist in the world. His 'rectal rumblings' include playing the British national anthem. On New Year's Eve, he farts the count down to midnight and then performs *Auld Lang Syne*.

The story of an unintentional flatulist was reported in *Scientific American* a few years ago. A 24-year-old man went to a hospital in Wales complaining of weird crackling sounds coming from pockets of air trapped under his skin. The sounds came from all over his body, including his bottom, 'providing a built-in whoopee-cushion effect.' It turns out that he had inflated a large number of balloons for a party earlier that day. His vigorous blowing had obviously caused this extraordinary effect.

Parp!

The Yanomami, an Indian tribe in South America, use farting as a greeting.

Flatulence runs in families, because they have a genetic tendency to harbour similar intestinal parasites as well as an inclination to eat the same types of foods.

The average person farts 14 times a day.

NOMS DE PLUME

Saki (Hector Munro)

Lewis Carroll (Charles Lutwidge Dodgson)

John Le Carré (David Cornwell)

George Sand (Amandine Dupin)

Molière (Jean-Baptiste Poquelin)

Mark Twain (Samuel Langhorne Clemens)

Sapper (Cyril McNeile)

George Orwell (Eric Blair)

Voltaire (François Marie Arouet)

James Herriot (James Alfred Wright)

ORGANS PRESERVED AFTER DEATH

Albert Einstein's brain

Percy Bysshe Shelley's heart

Galileo's finger

Lenin's brain

Joseph Haydn's head

Dr David Livingstone's heart

George Washington's tooth

King Richard II's jawbone

Thomas Hardy's heart

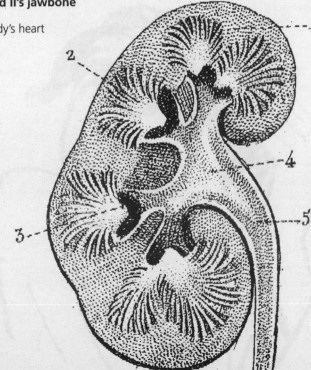

DYSLEXIC

Orlando Bloom, Lara Flynn Boyle, Marcus Brigstocke,
Pablo Picasso, Guy Ritchie, Babe Ruth, Quentin Tarantino,
Lindsay Wagner, Benjamin Zephaniah, Noel Gallagher,
Sir Anthony Hopkins, Jay Leno, Mika, Zoe Wanamaker,
Holly Willoughby

UNIMAGINATIVE FIRST NAMES

Eddie Edwards

Kris Kristofferson

Neville Neville (Gary and Phil's father)

Jerome K. Jerome

Bobby Robson

Dave Davies

Magnus Magnusson

Bev Bevan

Sirhan Sirhan

Boutros Boutros-Ghali

PURE TRIVIA (2)

In 1379, a Mr and Mrs Coke of Yorkshire named their daughter 'Diot' (a short form of Dionisia, the modern-day name Denise).

Diet Coke was invented in 1982.

Pearls melt in vinegar.

Twenty per cent of all the people in the whole history of mankind who have lived beyond the age of 65 are alive today.

If Barbie – whose full name is Barbara Millicent Roberts – were lifesize, she would have a neck twice the length of a normal human's neck.

In Victorian times fire engines were pulled by horses. The horses were stabled on the ground floor of the fire stations, which had circular staircases to stop them trotting upstairs.

Alan Mullally is the only England Test cricketer to have four of the same letters in his surname.

At 2 minutes past 8 o'clock in the evening of 20 February 2002, the time was, for sixty seconds only, in perfect symmetry: 2002, 2002, 2002. Or, to be more precise: 20.02, 20/02, 2002. At 12 minutes past 9 o'clock in the evening of 21 December 2112, the same symmetry will exist: 2112, 2112, 2112. Or: 21.12, 21/12, 2112.

Henry Ford was the man who started the Ford Motor Company but he never had a driving licence.

Kleenex tissues were originally used as filters in gas masks.

In 1933, Mickey Mouse got 800,000 fan letters.

Until 1687, clocks only had an hour hand.

You can make nine hexagonal pencils with the same amount of wood it takes to make eight round ones.

If 20-a-day smokers inhaled a week's worth of nicotine they would die instantly.

On average, a drop of Heinz tomato ketchup leaves the bottle at a speed of 25 miles per year.

The nineteenth-century French writer Guy de Maupassant hated the Eiffel Tower so much that he regularly used to eat lunch in the Tower's restaurant – because that was the one place in Paris he wouldn't have to look at it.

King Mongut of Siam had 9,000 wives. Before dying, he was quoted as saying he only loved the first 700.

The bubbles in Guinness beer sink to the bottom rather than float to the top as in other beers.

In Shakespeare's *Antony and Cleopatra*, Cleopatra plays billiards.

Henry I, King of England from 1100 to 1135, decreed that the distance between his nose and the tip of the index finger on his outstretched arm should be known as one yard (slightly shorter than a metre). He is also credited with creating the first zoo.

Microsoft once threatened a 17-year-old boy called Mike Rowe with a lawsuit after he launched a website called MikeRoweSoft.com.

The 1912 Olympic Games were held in Stockhom but there was no boxing as, under the (then) Swedish law, boxing was not allowed.

Only 6 per cent of the autographs in circulation from members of the Beatles are believed to be real.

The only one of his sculptures Michelangelo signed was *The Pietá*, completed in 1500.

The largest number of horses assembled for a film was 8,000 for King Vidor's epic *War and Peace* (1956).

The seventeenth-century French Cardinal Mazarin never travelled without his personal chocolate-maker.

The biro, invented by Hungarian refugee Lásló Biro, was first used by the US air force in World War 2. On 9 October 1945, it was put on sale to the public in a New York department store. Over 5,000 people crammed in to buy biros at the costly sum of $12.50 each. Full-page ads promised people the pen would work equally well at at altitude or ground level, underwater or on dry land.

Picasso could draw before he could walk and his first word was the Spanish word for pencil.

The shortest stage play is Samuel Beckett's *Breath* – 35 seconds of screams and heavy breathing.

In 1973, a Swedish confectionery salesman named Roland Ohisson was buried in a coffin made of chocolate.

A French man named Michel Lotito ate 128 bicycles, 15 supermarket trolleys, six chandeliers, two beds and a pair of skis.

The world's longest engagement lasted 67 years. Octavio Guillen and Adriana Martinez were 15 when they got engaged and 82 on their wedding day.

The chihuahua is the world's smallest breed of dog but it's named after the biggest state in Mexico.

Lord Byron had four pet geese that he took with him everywhere he went.

If all the Lego in the world were evenly distributed, we would each receive 30 pieces.

The people killed most often during bank robberies are the robbers.

SPORTING HEROES

In 1928, the Welsh international rugby union player Harry Jarman spotted a runaway coal truck heading towards a group of children playing. Without a thought for his own safety, he threw himself in front of the children and saved them – but at the cost of his own life.

The great Liberian international footballer George Weah paid for all his team's uniforms and other expenses so that Liberia could compete in the 1996 African Nations Cup.

Having been a pilot in the first World War, the Frenchman Robert Benoist became a Grand Prix motor racing driver. On the outbreak of World War 2, he and two other racing drivers escaped to England where they joined the SOE (Special Operations Executive) and became secret agents in order to return to France to assist the French Resistance. Parachuted into France, Captain Benoist helped organize sabotage cells and moved weapons from air-drops in the forest to his home for storage and distribution. However, the Gestapo, the German secret police caught him but while being driven to Gestapo headquarters, Benoist leaped from the moving vehicle and escaped, eventually being smuggled back to Britain via the French underground.

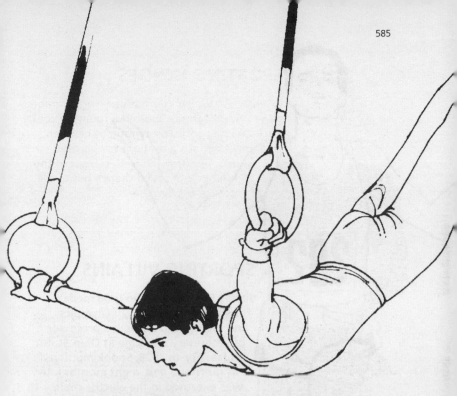

Benoist insisted on returning to France for a second mission and then a third. On this occasion, he was captured and, on 11 September 1944, executed.

After the war, the Coupe Robert Benoist automobile race was held in Paris in his memory and a street was named after him.

At the 1904 Olympics, the American gymnast George Eyser won six medals – even though his left leg was made out of wood.

Jeff Hall, who played football for Birmingham City and England, died of polio just two weeks after being taken ill in March 1958. The publicity surrounding his death helped to persuade people to participate in a mass inoculation scheme to combat the awful disease. So a man who was a sporting hero in life (England never lost a game in which he played) became an even greater hero in death.

SPORTING VILLAINS

James Snook won two gold medals for shooting at the 1920 Olympics and went on to become a professor of veterinary medicine at Ohio State University. In 1928, Snook murdered his girlfriend and, eight months later, was executed in the electric chair.

Leslie Hylton was a fast bowler who played in six Test matches for the West Indies between 1935 and 1939. In 1955, he was hanged for murdering his wife. He is the only Test cricketer to have been executed.

In the 1912 Olympic marathon, the two South African runners Kennedy McArthur and Charles Gitsan were well ahead of the field when, on the understanding that McArthur would wait for him, Gitsan stopped for a drink of water. McArthur, however, didn't honour his word and carried on running to win the race.

In the 1988 Olympics, the Canadian runner Ben Johnson won the 100 metres in a world record time of 9.79 seconds. Shortly afterwards he tested positive for steroid use and was stripped of his medal.

In 1930, Alex Villaplane captained France to victory in the very first match of the very first World Cup. Fourteen years later, he was shot by a French firing squad for collaborating with the Nazis.

There was a scandal at the 1980 Boston Marathon when an amateur runner named Rosie Ruiz appeared from out of nowhere to win the women's race. Marathon officials became suspicious when it was found that Ruiz didn't appear in race videotapes until near the end of the race. A subsequent investigation decided that Ruiz had skipped most of the race and blended into the crowd about one mile from the finish line, where she then ran to her apparent victory. Ruiz was officially disqualified.

ANCIENT ROME

Romans used powdered mouse brains as toothpaste.

In Ancient Rome, they used to use urine to clean laundry. To make sure they had a regular supply (urine, not laundry), people would leave containers in the street for other people to pee in.

Libya has many important Roman archaeological sites – including wells that still provide water.

Nero had a slave whose job it was to be a 'glutton' and had to eat *everything* that was put in front of him – including human flesh.

Nero made Christians into human candles and burnt them at his parties.

The Circus Maximus in Rome could hold up to 250,000 people (an equal number again, could view the games from the adjoining hills).

The idea of separate cubicles for toilets is a relatively modern invention; the Romans sat down together in large groups.

WRITERS AND BOOKS

The UK publishes more books than any other country in the world.

Virginia Woolf and Lewis Carroll wrote their books standing up.

John Milton used 8,000 different words in *Paradise Lost*.

The world's longest non-fiction work is *The Yongle Dadian*, a 10,000-volume encyclopaedia produced by 5,000 scholars during the Ming Dynasty in China six hundred years ago.

Moby Dick sold 50 copies during its writer Herman Melville's lifetime.

Greek philosopher Aristotle wrote *Meteorology* in the fourth century BC: it remained the standard textbook on weather for 2,000 years.

French author Michel Thaler published a 233-page novel which had no verbs.

The American poet Emily Dickinson wrote more than 900 poems but only four were published in her lifetime.

Jonathan Coe's *The Rotters' Club* contains a 13,955-word sentence – the longest sentence in literature.

The British writer Rudyard Kipling, who died in 1936, wrote only in black ink.

Hans Christian Andersen was so terrified of being killed in a fire that he always carried a piece of rope with him so that he could escape any building that was alight.

In 1097, Trotula, a midwife of Salerno, wrote *The Diseases of Women* – it was used in medical schools for 600 years.

Pope Benedict XVI had his library of 20,000 books photographed shelf by shelf so they could be reassembled in the Vatican in precisely the same order.

It is estimated that of the millions of cookery books owned in Britain, more than a third have never been opened.

Cleopatra wrote a book on cosmetics. One of the ingredients was burnt mice.

The Bible is the most shoplifted book in the US.

In 1898 (14 years before the Titanic sank), Morgan Robertson wrote a novel called *Futility*. This fictitious novel was about the largest ship ever built hitting an iceberg in the Atlantic Ocean.

Scarlett O'Hara, the heroine of Margaret Mitchell's *Gone with the Wind*, was originally named Pansy.

The first draft of John Steinbeck's *Of Mice And Men* was eaten by his dog.

Bambi was originally published in 1929 in Germany.

Before settling on the name of Tiny Tim for the name of his character in *A Christmas Carol*, Charles Dickens considered – and rejected – Little Larry, Puny Pete and Small Sam.

Lewis Carroll's 'You Are Old, Father William' in *Alice's Adventures in Wonderland* is a parody of Robert Southey's 'The Old Man's Comforts and How He Gained Them.'

With 72 million books, the Library of Congress in Washington DC, US is the largest library in the world.

Apart from the Bible, the world's most translated book is *Don Quixote*.

In 1955, a book was returned to Cambridge University library – 288 years overdue.

Leo Tolstoy's wife copied his manuscript of *War And Peace* seven times – by hand.

There is approximately one library book for every single person on Earth.

During the US Civil War, all the officers in the confederate army were given copies of *Les Misérables* by Victor Hugo to carry with them at all times because their leaders believed that the book symbolised their cause.

Meanwhile, Victor Hugo wrote *The Hunchback of Notre Dame* in just six months – using (or so it is claimed) a single bottle of ink.

T.E. Lawrence (also known as Lawrence of Arabia) had to rewrite *Seven Pillars of Wisdom* – in full – after losing his only manuscript while changing trains at Reading station in 1919.

THINGS SAID ABOUT BOOKS

'Books are for people who wish they were somewhere else' (Mark Twain)

'Books are the quietest and most constant of friends; they are the most accessible and wisest of counsellors, and the most patient of teachers' (Charles W. Eliot)

'Books, the children of the brain' (Jonathan Swift)

'I cannot live without books' (Thomas Jefferson)

'The book you don't read can't help' (Jim Rohn)

'The proper study of mankind is books' (Aldous Huxley)

'A bookstore is one of the only pieces of evidence we have that people are still thinking' (Jerry Seinfeld)

'Books are the carriers of civilization. Without books, history is silent, literature dumb, science crippled, thought and speculation at a standstill' (Henry David Thoreau)

'You know you've read a good book when you turn the last page and feel a little as if you have lost a friend' (Paul Sweeney)

'Some books are undeservedly forgotten; none are undeservedly remembered' (W. H. Auden)

'A room without books is like a body without a soul' (Cicero)

BOOKS REJECTED BY PUBLISHERS

A Time To Kill **(John Grisham)**

A River Runs Through It (Norman MacLean)

The War of The Worlds **(H.G. Wells)**

Jonathan Livingston Seagull (Richard Bach)

Gone With The Wind **(Margaret Mitchell)**

Carrie (Stephen King)

Watership Down **(Richard Adams)**

The Kon Tiki Expedition (Thor Heyerdahl)

The Peter Principle **(Laurence J. Peter)**

The Enormous Room (ee cummings. cummings self-published this, dedicating it to the 15 publishers who had rejected it.)

WROTE CHILDRENS' BOOKS

Julianne Moore (*Freckleface Strawberry*)

Dionne Warwick (*Say A Little Prayer*)

Steve Martin (*The Alphabet from A to Y with Bonus Letter Z*)

John Travolta (*Propeller One-Way Night Coach: A Fable for All Ages*)

LL Cool J (*And The Winner Is...*)

BANNED BOOKS

Catcher In The Rye (J.D. Salinger): **banned in Boron, California in 1989 because of the word 'goddamn'. It was also banned in another US state because of the words 'hell' and 'for Chrissake'. This is probably the most famous work of fiction never to have been turned into a feature film.**

The Adventures of Tom Sawyer (Mark Twain): banned by several London libraries (in politically correct Labour-controlled boroughs) in the mid-1980s on account of the book's 'racism' and 'sexism'.

My Friend Flicka (Mary O'Hara): **banned from schoolchildren's reading lists in Clay County, Florida in 1990 because the book contains the word 'bitch' to describe 'a female dog'.**

Black Beauty (Anna Sewell): banned by the African country Namibia in the 1970s because the government took offence at the 'racist' title.

The Scarlet Pimpernel (Baroness Orczy): banned by the Nazis – not because of its language or its theme (though Leslie Howard starred in an anti-Nazi film entitled *Pimpernel Smith*) – but because Baroness Orczy was Jewish. Other authors banned by the Nazis for the same reason included Erich Maria Remarque, Thomas Mann, Sigmund Freud and Marcel Proust. Authors banned by the Nazis because of their political sentiments included Ernest Hemingway, Upton Sinclair and Jack London.

Noddy (Enid Blyton): banned by several British libraries in the 1960s – along with other Enid Blyton books – because they weren't thought to be 'good' for children.

The Grapes of Wrath (John Steinbeck): banned from schools in Iowa, USA in 1980 after a parent complained that the classic novel – by the Nobel Prize-winner – was 'vulgar and obscene'. Steinbeck's other famous novel, *Of Mice And Men*, has also been banned in other US states for similar reasons.

The Irish have done more than their share of banning: All of Steinbeck and Zola's novels were banned in Ireland in 1953 for being 'subversive' and/or 'immoral'. Other books once banned by the Irish include *Brave New World* (Aldous Huxley), Elmer Gantry (Sinclair Lewis) and *The Sun Also Rises* (Ernest Hemingway).

Billy Bunter books (Frank Richards): banned from British libraries in the 1970s in case it led children to tease overweight schoolmates. In more recent years, other politically correct institutions have banned the books because of the black character, Hurree Ramset Jam Singh, known to all his pals as 'Inky'.

On The Origin of Species (Charles Darwin): banned in several US states (especially in the Christian Fundamentalist south) through the years – but particularly before World War 2 – owing to the fact that Darwin didn't accept the Bible's account of Creation. Incredibly, Desmond Morris's *The Naked Ape* has been banned from one or two US libraries on the same basis. Darwin's book was also banned by the USSR because it was 'immoral'.

FLUENT IN FOREIGN LANGUAGES

Sting (Portuguese)

Sian Williams (Japanese)

Dom Joly (Arabic and French)

Christoph Waltz (English and French)

Carey Mulligan (German)

Mick Fleetwood (Norwegian)

WORLD WAR 2 POWs

Clive Dunn, Denholm Elliott,
Robert Kee, Angus Maude,
Sam Kydd, Donald Pleasance,
Roy Dotrice, The Earl of Harewood,
Ronald Searle, E.W. Swanton,
Klaus Kinski, Eric Lomax,
Bert Trautmann

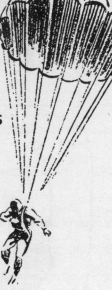

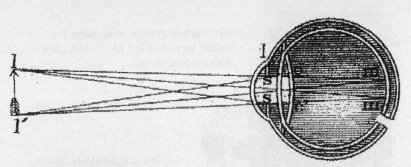

ASTRONOMY

The Sun is only one of 120 million stars in our galaxy.

The centre of the Earth has a liquid core as hot as the Sun's surface.

The Earth travels 12 million miles a day.

A day on Jupiter is approximately 9 hours, 50 minutes and 30 seconds long at the Equator.

The Sun is 300,300 times bigger than the Earth.

Average wind speed on Jupiter is 225 miles per hour.

Most stars shine for at least 10 billion years.

The Earth is the densest planet in the solar system.

A manned rocket reaches the Moon in less time than it once took a stagecoach to travel the length of England.

The winds on Saturn blow at 1,200 miles per hour – ten times faster than a strong Earth hurricane.

The number of UFO sightings increases when Mars is nearest Earth.

Every 11 years the magnetic poles of the Sun switch, in a cycle called 'Solarmax'.

Five planets can be seen with the naked eye: Jupiter, Mars, Mercury, Saturn and Venus.

The Sea of Waves, the Sea of Cleverness, the Sea of Clouds and the Sea of Islands can all be found on the moon.

Galileo went totally blind – probably because of his constant gazing at the sun through his telescope.

In the 1660s, French astronomer Adrien Auzout once considered building a telescope that was three hundred metres long. He thought the magnification would be so great he would see animals on the moon.

The moon weighs 81,000 trillion tons (approximately.)

19367 Pink Floyd is an asteroid between Mars and Jupiter (this minor planet was named in honour of the band).

Halley's comet last appeared in 1986 and won't appear again until 2061.

Two objects have struck the Earth with enough force to destroy a whole city. Each object, one in 1908 and again in 1947, struck regions of Siberia. Not one human being was hurt either time.

The surface speed record on the moon is 10.56 miles per hour. It was set in a lunar rover.

Organist William Herschel discovered the planet Uranus in 1781 with the first reflecting telescope that he built. He named it Georgium Sidium in honour of King George III of England, but in 1850 it was renamed Uranus in accordance with the tradition of naming planets after Roman gods.

If it were possible to drive through space at 75mph (120 km/h), you could reach the sun in a little over 142 years. But at that same speed it would take more than 38 million years to reach the nearest star.

In 1989, the space shuttle *Discovery* carried 32 fertilized chicken eggs into orbit.

The tail of the Great Comet of 1843 was 330 million kilometres long. (It will return in 2356.)

Summer on Uranus lasts for 21 years – but so does winter.

The pressure at the Earth's inner core is 3 million times the pressure at the surface.

It takes 8 minutes 12 seconds for sunlight to reach Earth.

For every extra kilogram carried on a space flight, 530 kilograms of excess fuel is needed at lift-off.

During a total solar eclipse the temperature can drop by 6°C.

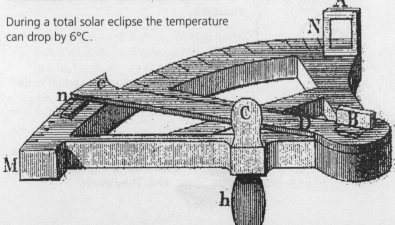

SOCCER (2)

In 1952, Charlie Tully scored both of Northern Ireland's goals in a 2–2 draw with England, one of them from the corner flag. Tully achieved this feat again the following year for Celtic in a Scottish Cup match against Falkirk. He took a corner and swung the ball directly into the net. The referee, presuming that the ball must have been placed away from the corner spot, ordered Tully to retake the corner. Tully did so and once again placed the ball into the net directly from the corner.

During a match played in Paraguay between Sportivo Ameliano and General Caballero, a total of 20 red cards were shown.

A first-class soccer game has an average of 85 throw-ins – almost one a minute.

In 1964, 350 football fans died in a riot after an equalizer by Peru was disallowed. The referee said afterwards, 'Anyone can make a mistake.'

Aston Villa played their first-ever game in March 1875 against a rugby team called Aston Brook St Mary's. The first half was played under rugby rules, the second under soccer rules. I can find no record of which team won – if indeed either side did.

In 1980, the Liberian team playing against Gambia were threatened with the firing squad if they lost. They drew.

Tottenham Hotspur didn't have a single player sent off in a Football League match between 27 October 1928 and 4 December 1965.

In 1958–59, the Gateshead United team contained two players whose name was Ken Smith. For identification purposes the Football League designated them Ken Smith 1 and Ken Smith 2. All very straightforward – until Gateshead beat Carlisle United with Ken Smith 1 scoring twice and Ken Smith 2 scoring once. The result in the paper read Gateshead 3 (K. Smith 1 (2), K. Smith 2 (1)).

In 1996, Ali Dia was struggling to make a living in the lower reaches of French football. So he decided to try his luck in England. He was turned down by a couple of League clubs but he managed to sign semi-professional terms with non-league Blyth Spartans. This was probably just about his level but Dia wanted more so he launched an audacious bid to get into a Premiership club.

He got in touch with Southampton boss, Graeme Souness, and (wrongly) claimed that he had 13 caps for Senegal and that he was related to Liberian superstar striker George Weah (he wasn't). However, a phone call from someone pretending to be Weah was enough to convince the Saints to hand him a contract. Dia was lined up to play in a reserve game but after that was cancelled he was thrown straight into the deep-end with a place on the bench against Leeds. When the great Matt Le Tissier was injured after half an hour there was great excitement in the crowd as the new signing, the cousin of the great George Weah, came on to the field.

It turned out that the man who had pretended to be George Weah on the other end of the phone had actually been Dia's agent. Southampton – obviously – cancelled his contract.

When Rangers lost 3–2 to Hibs in the Scottish Cup quarter-final in 1896, keeper John Bell took it very personally. Blaming himself for the defeat, he changed without speaking to anyone, and walked away from the ground, never to return.

King Carol of Romania selected his country's squad for the 1934 World Cup.

In 1954, Chelsea were playing Leicester City, in a game they won 3–1. It is their second

goal that is of interest for it was an own goal ... but not *any* own goal. No, this own goal was officially recorded as a 'shared own goal' as two Leicester City defenders, while trying to clear the ball, both simultaneously kicked the ball into their own net.

Sheffield United are known as the Blades, a nickname which used to belong to Sheffield Wednesday.

The most isolated ground in the Football/Premier Leagues belongs to Carlisle United who are 58 miles from their nearest neighbour, Newcastle United. At the opposite end of the scale, up in Scotland, Dundee and Dundee United are only some 200 metres apart.

Doncaster Rovers were originally formed in 1879 to play a match against the Yorkshire Institute for the Deaf and Dumb.

The entire Southport team was hypnotized before a game against Watford in 1975. They lost 2–1.

On the first day of the 1950/51 season, all the promoted clubs lost, all the relegated clubs won and the newly elected clubs drew.

AC Milan was founded in 1899 by a British man named Alfred Edwards – and that's why they call themselves Milan (the English version of the city) rather than the Italian 'Milano'.

DOGS

Noseprints are the most reliable way to identify dogs.

Two dogs (a Pomerian – name unknown – and a pekinese called Sun Yat Sen) survived the sinking of the *Titanic*.

Toy-breed dogs live longer than large breeds.

The oldest breed of dog is the saluki.

A dog can suffer from tonsillitis, but not appendicitis. It doesn't have an appendix.

A collie/Staffordshire terrier crossbreed dog swallowed a knife that was only slightly smaller than itself ... and lived to tell the tale. Kylie, 45 centimetres long, swallowed the 38cm bread knife with the sharp end in her stomach and the blunt end sticking out of her mouth.

Every dog except the chow has a pink tongue – the chow's tongue is jet black.

In an American Animal Hospital Association poll, 33 per cent of dog owners admitted that they talked to their dogs on the phone or left messages on an answering machine when they were away.

The basenji is the only dog that doesn't bark.

Macadamia nuts are toxic to dogs.

Dachshunds were bred to fight badgers in their dens.

The heaviest dog ever recorded was an Old English mastiff named Zorba which weighed in at a massive 155kgs.

If unfolded and laid out flat, the membranes in a dog's nose would be larger than the dog itself.

While drug-sniffing dogs are trained to bark like crazy, and go 'aggressive' at the first whiff of the right powder ... bomb-sniffing dogs are trained to go 'passive' lest they set off a motion sensor or a noise sensor or any number of other things that might result in a bomb going off.

As a result of inbreeding, three out of every ten Dalmatians suffer from a hearing disability.

The average lifespan of a dog is between 8 and 15 years, depending on the breed.

Every hour, 12,500 puppies are born in the United States.

The largest amount of money left to a dog was £15 million – to a poodle in 1931 by one Ella Wendel of New York.

Toy poodles were once used as hand warmers by the aristocracy.

Dogs don't need to eat citrus fruit because they make their own vitamin C.

They sell toupees for dogs in Japan.

Dogs eat rabbit droppings and they also eat cat poo because of its high protein content.

Dogs have very powerful ears. This explains why they don't like going out in the rain. It's not just that they don't like getting wet: the rain amplifies sound and actually hurts a dog's ears.

According to hospital figures, one in 350 people get bitten by dogs every year.

On the other hand, nearly two-thirds of dog owners admit to kissing their dogs. Of these, some 45 per cent kissed them on the nose, 19 per cent on the neck, 7 per cent on the back, 5 per cent on the stomach and 2 per cent on the legs. An additional 29 per cent listed the place they kiss their dog as 'other'.

Eight per cent of dogs will bite somebody before they die.

The breeds most likely to bite are German shepherds, chows and poodles.

The breeds least likely to bite are golden retrievers, labradors and Old English sheepdogs.

People who used to sleep with their dog in the bed next to them include the Duke of Windsor, General Custer and Elizabeth Barrett Browning.

There are some 7 million dogs in the UK. The most popular breeds are labradors, alsatians, west highland white terriers and golden retrievers.

The name 'poodle' derives from the German *pudeln*, meaning 'to splash in water.'

A 'seizure alert' dog can alert its owner when he or she is about to have an epileptic seizure.

Dogs can be trained to smell the presence of autism in children.

At the end of World War 1, the German government trained the first guide dogs to assist blind war veterans.

The most popular names for dogs in the UK are Sam, Trixie, Polly and Spot.

The most intelligent dog breeds are (in order): border collie, poodle, alsatian and golden retriever.

'A dog teaches a boy fidelity, perseverance and to turn round three times before lying down.' (Robert Benchley)

'I loathe people who keep dogs. They are cowards who haven't got the guts to bite people themselves.' (August Strindberg)

'That indefatigable and unsavoury engine of pollution, the dog.' (John Sparrow)

'The censure of a dog is something no man can stand.' (Christopher Morley)

PEOPLE WHO HAD A DOG AS THEIR BEST MAN OR BRIDESMAID

Sir Elton John

David Furnish

John Peel

Ashley Jensen

David Hasselhoff

Rolf Harris

Robbie Williams (even had his dogs dressed as bridesmaids)

CHANGED CITIZENSHIP

Warren Mitchell (from British to Australian)

Joe Bugner (from British to Australian)

Martina Navratilova (from Czech to American)

Nadia Comaneci (from Romanian to American)

Yehudi Menuhin (from American to British)

Greta Scacchi (from British to Australian)

Andrew Sachs (from German to British)

Zola Budd (from South African to British to South African)

Ivan Lendl (from Czech to American)

Allan Lamb (from South African to British)

John Huston (from American to Irish)

T.S. Eliot (from American to British)

Josephine Baker (from American to French)

Sir Anthony Hopkins (from British to American)

Jane Seymour (from British to American)

Sheena Easton (from British to American)

David Soul (from American to British)

Christopher Hitchens (from British to American)

Tracey Ullman (from British to American)

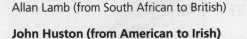

BATS

There is a bat that
lives on scorpions
and is immune to their
stings.

**African heart-nosed bats
can hear the footsteps
of a beetle on sand 2
metres away.**

Bats, like people, usually give
birth to one baby at a time. Twins
are rare.

**For their size, bats are the slowest
reproducing mammals on earth,
producing only one baby a year. This makes
them vulnerable to extinction.**

90 per cent of all bats in the world are tiny, and
weigh less than 25 grams.

**Vampire bats don't suck blood. They bite, then lick up the flow.
They need about 2 tablespoonfuls of blood a day, which they
can extract in about 20 minutes.**

Bats are voracious eaters – devouring as many as 600 bugs an hour
through the night every night.

**A bat colony of 5 million bats is capable of eating more than
25,000 kilograms of moths in a single night.**

The fruit bat can eat 2 kilos of fruit in a single session – so a group of
them can easily strip an orchard of all its fruit.

**Mexican free-tailed bats sometimes fly 3 kilometres high to
feed or to catch tailwinds that carry them over long distances at
speeds of almost 100 kilometres an hour (60 mph).**

The leg bones of a bat are so thin that no bat can walk.

Bats are the only mammals that can fly. There is a 'flying squirrel', but it only glides on outstretched skin flaps.

Plants that are dependent on bats for pollination include dates, figs, cashews, avocados, cloves, mangoes, breadfruit, carob and almost every tropical night-blooming plant.

The giant bats called flying foxes, which live in Indonesia and elsewhere, have wingspans of almost 2 metres.

Bats are not blind, are far too smart ever to become entangled in human hair and seldom transmit diseases to other animals or humans.

Ninety per cent of all bats in the world are tiny and weigh less than 1 ounce.

Baby bats are born upside down and are caught by their mother's wings.

Bats can eat from one-half to three-quarters their weight per evening.

Male epauletted bats have pouches in their shoulders, which contain large patches of white fur that they flash to attract mates.

Vampire bats use rivers to navigate as they have such a powerful sense of smell they can scent animal blood even underwater and can use it to guide them where they want to go.

COUNTRIES WITH MORE THAN A HUNDRED LANGUAGES

Papua New Guinea: 820 languages

Indonesia: 742

Nigeria: 516

India: 427

US: 311

Mexico: 297

Cameroon: 280

Australia: 275

China: 241

Democratic Republic of the Congo: 216

Brazil: 200

Philippines: 180

Malaysia: 147

Canada: 145

Sudan: 134

Chad: 133

Russia: 129

Tanzania: 128

Nepal: 125

Vanuatu: 115

Myanmar: 113

Vietnam: 104

THE ROMAN NAMES FOR COUNTRIES AND REGIONS

Latin Name	Current Name
Aegyptus	Egypt
Armorica	Brittany
Belgica	Belgium and The Netherlands
Britannia	Britain
Caledonia	Scotland
Cambria	Wales
Cornubia	Cornwall
Dania	Denmark
Finnia	Finland
Gallia	France
Germania	Germany
Helvetia	Switzerland
Hibernia	Ireland
Hispania	Spain
Islandia	Iceland
Judaea	Israel
Lusitania	Portugal
Norvegia	Norway
Tingitania	Morocco
Tripolitana	Libya

THE CLEANEST COUNTRIES IN THE WORLD

Finland

Norway

Sweden

Iceland

Canada

Switzerland

Austria

Australia

New Zealand

Ireland

COUNTRIES AND THEIR MOTTOS

Andorra: *Unity Is Strength*

Aruba: *One Happy Island*

El Salvador: *God, Union And Freedom*

Gabon: *Union, Work, Justice*

Germany: *Unity, Right And Freedom*

Ghana: *Freedom And Justice*

Greece: *Freedom or Death*

Guam: *Where America's Day Begins*

Guatemala: *Freedom*

Haiti: *Liberty, Equality, Fraternity*

India: *Truth Will Win Out*

Iraq: *Unity, Liberty, Socialism*

The Ivory Coast: *Union, Discipline, Work*

Jamaica: *Out Of Many, One Country*

Jordan: *God, The Homeland, The King*

Kenya: *Let Us All Move Forward Together*

Libya: *Liberty, Socialism, Unity*

Liechtenstein: *God, Prince, Homeland*

Luxembourg: *We Stay As We Are*

Madagascar: *Fatherland, Liberty, Justice*

Malawi: *Unity And Freedom*

Malaysia: *Unity Is Strength*

Mali: *One People, One Aim, One Faith*

Morocco: *God, The Homeland, The King*

The Netherlands: *I Shall Uphold*

New Zealand: *Onward*

Nicaragua: *God, Homeland And Honour*

Niger: *Fraternity, Work, Progress*

Nigeria: *Unity And Faith*

Pakistan: *Unity, Faith, Discipline*

Paraguay: *Order And Progress*

Peru: *Stable And Happy Through The Unity Of All*

Portugal: **The Good Of The Nation**

Senegal: **One People, One Aim, One Faith**

Sierra Leone: **Unity, Freedom, Justice**

Singapore: **Go Ahead, Singapore**

South Africa: **Unity Is Strength**

St Kitts and Nevis: **Country Above Self**

Suriname: **Justice, Piety, Faith**

Syria: **Unity, Liberty, Socialism**

Tanzania: **Independence And Work**

Thailand: **Homeland, Religion, King**

Togo: **Work, Freedom, Homeland**

Trinidad and Tobago: **Together We Aspire, Together We Achieve**

Tunisia: **Liberty, Order, Justice**

Uganda: **For God And My Country**

US: **In God We Trust**

Vietnam: **Independence, Freedom, Happiness**

Yemen: **God, The Homeland, The Revolution**

Zambia: **One Zambia, One Nation**

Zimbabwe: **Unity, Freedom, Industry**

COUNTRIES THAT STILL HAVE THE DEATH PENALTY

Belarus, China, Cuba, Egypt, India, Indonesia, Iran, Iraq, Japan, Jordan, Kazakhstan, Kuwait, Lebanon, Malaysia, Nigeria, Rwanda, Saudi Arabia, Singapore, Somalia, Syria, Taiwan, United Arab Emirates, US, Vietnam, Zimbabwe

THE COUNTRIES WITH THE BIGGEST RAIL NETWORKS

US: 228,999 kilometres

Russia: 85,542 kilometres

India: 63,465 kilometres

China: 62,200 kilometres

Canada: 57,671 kilometres

Argentina: 35,753 kilometres

Germany: 34,228 kilometres

Brazil: 29,314 kilometres

France: 29,286 kilometres

Mexico: 26,662 kilometres

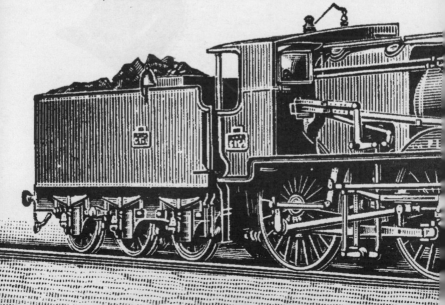

Ukraine: 22,001 kilometres

Japan: 20,052 kilometres

South Africa: 20,047 kilometres

Poland: 19,599 kilometres

Italy: 16,751 kilometres

UK: 16,208 kilometres

THE ONLY COUNTRIES WITH MORE THAN A MILLION KILOMETRES OF ROADS

US: 6,430,366 kilometres

India: 3,383,344 kilometres

China: 1,870,661 kilometres*

Brazil: 1,751,868 kilometres

Japan: 1,183,000 kilometres

Canada: 1,042,300 kilometres

*It's estimated that, by 2050, China's road network will cover over 4 million kilometres.

Tuvalu has just 8 kilometres of roads in total while, of the developed countries, Monaco has the fewest with just 50 kilometers.

The world's longest international highway or motorway is the Pan-American Highway, which connects many countries in the Americas. It's just under 48,000 kilometres long.

The longest national highway within a single country is Australia's Highway 1, which is over 20,000 kilometres long and runs almost the entire way around the country's coastline. With the exception of Canberra (which is inland) it links all the capital cities – although Brisbane and Darwin are not directly connected.

The world's widest highway or motorway is the Katy Freeway (part of Interstate 10) in Houston, Texas. Some sections have up to 26 lanes – although some of these lanes are restricted for use by different categories of driver or vehicle.

When it comes to the highest number of unrestricted lanes, the highway/motorway with the most is Highway 401 which runs through Ontario in Canada. It has 18 unrestricted lanes.

LONG PLACE NAMES

Moretonhampstead in Devon boasts the longest one-word place name in England.

Llanfairpwllgw

There is a place in Wales that has the longest officially recognized place name in the United Kingdom: Llanfairpwllgwyngyllgogerychwyrndrobwllllantysiliogogogoch.

This translates into English as 'The church of St. Mary in the hollow of white hazel trees near the rapid whirlpool by St Tysilio's of the red cave'.

lgogerychwyrndrobwllllantysiliogogogoch

Llanfairpwllgwyngyllgogerychwyrndrobwllllantysiliogogogoch. com is the longest single word (without hyphens) .com domain name in the world.

Taumatawhakatangihangakoauauotamateapokaiwhenuakitanatahu is the name of a hill in the Hawke's Bay region of the North Island of New Zealand. At 85 letters, this is the longest geographical name in the world. It translates into English (from Maori) as 'the summit where Tamatea, the man with the big knees, the climber of mountains, the land-swallower who travelled about, played his nose flute to his loved one'. The locals, not surprisingly, call it simply Taumata.

The full ceremonial name of Bangkok is in fact the world's longest place name. In full, it's Krung Thep Mahanakhon Amon Rattanakosin Mahinthara Yuthaya Mahadilok Phop Noppharat Ratchathani Burirom Udomratchaniwet Mahasathan Amon Piman Awatan Sathit Sakkathattiya Witsanukam Prasit. Thai children have to learn this and recite it in school. Poor them.

In Webster, Massachusetts there is a lake called Chargoggagoggmanchauggagoggchaubunagungamaugg. It's also known as Webster Lake.

There's a village in Ireland called Muckanaghederdauhaulia. In English this means 'pig-marsh between two seas'.

ALL THE UNESCO WORLD HERITAGE SITES IN THE UK

Castles and Town Walls of King Edward in Gwynedd

Durham Castle and Cathedral

Giant's Causeway and Causeway Coast

Ironbridge Gorge

St Kilda

Stonehenge, Avebury and Associated Sites

Studley Royal Park including the Ruins of Fountains Abbey

Blenheim Palace

City of Bath

Frontiers of the Roman Empire

Westminster Palace, Westminster Abbey and St Margaret's Church

Canterbury Cathedral, St Augustine's Abbey and St Martin's Church

Henderson Island

Tower of London

Gough and Inaccessible Islands

Old and New Towns of Edinburgh

Maritime Greenwich

Heart of Neolithic Orkney

Blaenavon Industrial Landscape

Historic Town of St George and Related Fortifications, Bermuda

Derwent Valley Mills

Dorset and East Devon Coast

New Lanark

Saltaire

Royal Botanic Gardens, Kew

Liverpool – Maritime Mercantile City

Cornwall and West Devon Mining Landscape

MOVIES

More popcorn is sold during scary movies than during comedies.

'Smithee' is a pseudonym that film-makers use when they don't want their names to appear in the credits.

For the 1959 thriller *The Tingler*, theatres were rigged with buzzers under the seats to scare viewers at key moments in the film.

The movie *Earthquake* featured Sensurround, which shook the theatre seats.

The most used line in the movies is 'Lets get out of here.'

In the film *ET*, the sound of ET walking was made by someone squishing their hands in jelly.

Kevin Spacey requests a ping-pong table in his room whenever he's on location.

Napoleon Bonaparte is the historical figure most often portrayed in movies.

In *The Bridge On The River Kwai* (1957), Alec Guinness – who won an Oscar for his role – had his name spelt with just one 'n' in the final credits.

In 1920, 57 per cent of Hollywood movies billed the female star above the leading man. In 1990, only 18 per cent had the leading lady given top billing.

When English-language films are dubbed in Poland, all the voices are dubbed by a male actor. So the viewer ends up watching women and children talking with the voice of one man.

The Exuma Islands have been the location for James Bond films, not once, but twice.

All the films nominated for Best Picture in 1999 were set more than 50 years before the films were released. The winner was *Shakespeare in Love*; the other nominees were *Saving Private Ryan*, *Life Is Beautiful*, *The Thin Red Line* and *Elizabeth*.

PEOPLE WHO WERE ADOPTED

Newt Gingrich, Joe Cole, Jeanette Winterson, Chanelle Hayes, Wendy James, Fatima Whitbread, Edward Albee, Wesley Clark, Steve Jobs, J.C. Chasez, Faith Hill, Melissa Gilbert, Lee Majors, Kristin Chenoweth, Gary Coleman, Bo Diddley, Jamie Foxx, Brian Moore, Caroline Wyatt, Jean Genet, Buffy Sainte-Marie

INVENTORS

Eddie van Halen (belt buckle that grips the back of his guitar freeing his hands to play another instrument)

Terry Venables (the Manager board game)

Jack Johnson (held three patents – two to do with cars: an improved adjustable wrench and an anti-theft device. The first patent was filed while Johnson was in jail at Leavenworth)

Michael Jackson (moonwalk boots)

Gary Burghoff (enhanced fish attractor device)

Danny Kaye (paper party squeakers)

Marlon Brando (tuning device for conga drums; mobile home that could sink into the ground out of the path of hurricanes)

LANGUAGES

There are a staggering 7,000 languages in the world. Mandarin is the most widely spoken, followed by English and then Spanish. Even though Russia is one of the biggest countries in the world, there are only 145 million people who have Russian as their first language. Japan, which is tiny by comparison, has 122 million who speak Japanese as their first language. But only a million Japanese bother to learn a second language. Compare them to the 65 million people who have French as their first language: 80 per cent of those people have learned to speak another language.

The Albanian alphabet was invented as recently as 1908. It contains 36 letters but no 'w'.

The German language combines words to make composite words. So, for example, the single German word for 'Favourite break-time sandwich' is 'Lieblingspausenbrotte'.

There are 32 letters in the Polish alphabet, including three variations of the letter Z.

The Lao language has no words ending in 's'. So they call their country Lao instead of Laos.

There's a Mexican language named Zoque which withered away until there were just two people in the whole world who spoke it. The trouble was that those two men – both in their seventies – hated each other and so refused to speak to one another.

The Lozi language of Zambia has at least 40 words meaning 'woman'. Each describes a woman at a particular stage in life. For example, an unmarried woman, a newlywed, just arrived in her husband's village, a widow etc.

Nearly half of all Germans are fluent in English, but only 3 per cent of Germans speak French fluently.

In Bulgaria, shaking the head from side to side means yes and nodding up and down means no.

Because of the mix of cultures and languages, many Mauritians are multilingual. A person might speak Bhojpuri at home, French to a supervisor at work, English to a government official and Creole to friends.

The Cambodian alphabet has 72 letters.

In Hungary, the word 'szia' can be used to mean either 'hello' or 'goodbye' when it's said to an individual. This probably explains why Hungarians whose English isn't that good will sometimes say 'hello' instead of 'goodbye' when they're leaving.

The Paraguay football team speaks the indigenous language of Guarani on the pitch so that the opposing team can't work out what they're saying.

The Scandinavian languages have two genders, one for living things and the other for all the rest.

Some African languages have up to 20 'genders.'

Some three hundred languages are spoken in London, the world's most cosmopolitan city.

The Japanese language doesn't have genders but it does have different ways of speaking for men and women.

The language of Manx is taught in almost every school on the Isle of Man.

Sanskrit is considered as the mother of all higher languages.

Over 800 different languages are spoken in Papua New Guinea. With a population of just over six million people, that's about one language for every 7,500 people. The result of this is that there are villages within five miles of each other which speak different languages.

Asia has the most languages and the most speakers, accounting for 61 per cent of all language speakers in the world.

In the Netherlands, they have a wonderful expression of amazement that translates as 'That breaks my clog'. The sturdy wooden clog is still worn by some Dutch farmers because it is waterproof in damp fields.

Rather than merely saying 'goodbye,' an Irish person might say 'safe home.'

Luxembourg has its own language – Luxembourgish – which is also sometimes spoken in parts of Belgium, France and Germany.

In the northern province of Friesland in the Netherlands, the children learn Frisian, the local language, as well as Dutch and English.

The Filipino language reflects the importance of rice to the Filipino people. Their language has several words for rice – e.g. including words to cover rice that is harvested but not cleaned, rice that is still cooking in a pot and rice that is ready to eat.

UNUSUAL NAMES GIVEN TO CHILDREN

Ignatius – Cate Blanchett

Sunday – Nicole Kidman

Banjo Griffiths-Taylor – Rachel Griffiths

Reignbeau Rhames – Ving Rhames (like Rainbow)

Buddy Bear, Petal Blossom Rainbow, Poppy Honey and Daisy Boo – Jamie Oliver

Kai – Wayne and Coleen Rooney

Aviana Olea – Amy Adams

Aphra Kendal – Gyles Brandreth

Jesse James Louis – Jon Bon Jovi

Sistine Rose – Sylvester Stallone

True – Forest Whitaker

Victoria Kafka – Tommy Lee Jones

Aurelius Cy – Elle Macpherson

Kenya – Quincy Jones and Nastassja Kinski

Homer (after Gere's father) – Richard Gere

Audio Science Sossamon – Shannon Sossamon

Jaz Agassi – Andre and Steffi Agassi

Emerson Rose – Teri Hatcher

Roan and Laird – Sharon Stone

Princess Tiaamii – Jordan and Peter Andre

Mingus – Helena Christensen

Queen Elizabeth – Boxer Manny Pacquiao

FORMER PRESIDENTS OF THE OXFORD UNION

Sir Edward Heath, Tony Benn, Sir Robin Day, William Waldegrave, Michael Heseltine, Sir Jeremy Isaacs, Brian Walden, Gyles Brandreth, Tariq Ali, Jeremy Thorpe, Paul Foot, Susan Kramer, Alan Duncan, Michael Crick, William Hague, Boris Johnson, Michael Gove, Peter Jay, Benazir Bhutto

FORMER PRESIDENTS OF THE CAMBRIDGE UNION

Clare Balding, Sir Norman St John Stevas, Douglas Hurd, Sir John Nott, Sir Leon Brittan, John Gummer, Michael Howard, Kenneth Clarke, Norman Lamont, Arianna Huffington, Ann Mallalieu, Chris Smith, Peter Bazalgette, Bernard Jenkin

APPEARED ON UNIVERSITY CHALLENGE AS COMPETITORS

Lord Julian Fellowes (Magdalene College, Cambridge)

David Aaronovitch (Manchester)

Christopher Hitchens (Balliol College, Oxford)

Charles Moore (Trinity College, Cambridge)

Dr David Starkey (Fitzwilliam College, Cambridge)

SOME DEADLY AUSTRALIAN CREATURES

The blue-ringed octopus – one bite or squirt causes paralysis. Death follows in minutes.

The 'sea wasp' or box jellyfish – the survival rate from its sting is almost zero. Death follows in four minutes.

The taipan snake is 180 times more venomous than the king cobra – one bite could kill a person within three seconds.

The tiger snake – death occurs within 12 hours. Anti-venom is available but it must be used within 30 minutes of the bite. One snake has enough venom to kill 118 sheep.

The funnel-web spider – one of the most dangerous spiders in the world. The bite of the male can kill a person in 15 minutes. There have been no deaths since the anti-venom was found.

Textile cone shells – underwater creature with up to 12 darts, each of which has enough poison to kill someone. Death follows in minutes.

Irukandji jellyfish – this has poisonous tentacles. Swimmers, if stung, can suffer a heart attack and drown.

The great white shark – this is the most dangerous of the many sharks in Australian waters. It kills in seconds with just one snap of its awesome teeth.

Redback spider – the bite of the female can kill. There have been no deaths since the anti-venom was found.

PEOPLE WHO RELEASED SOLO ALBUMS

Eddie Murphy (*Love's Alright*, 1993)

Kurt Russell (*Kurt Russell*, 1970)

Honor Blackman (*Everything I've Got*, 1965)

Scarlett Johansson (*Anywhere I Lay My Head*, 2008)

David Hemmings (*David Hemmings Happens*, 1967)

Jack Palance (*Palance*, 1970)

Dennis Weaver (*Celebrities Songs*, 1974)

Goldie Hawn (*Goldie*, 1972)

Bruce Willis (*Heart of Soul*, 1990)

Sally Field (*The Star of 'The Flying Nun'*, 1967)

Clint Eastwood (*Cowboy Favorites*, 1959)

Leonard Nimoy (*Two Sides of Leonard Nimoy*, 1968)

John Le Mesurier (*What Is Going To Become of Us All*, 1976)

Bette Davis (*Miss Bette Davis*, 1976)

George Hamilton (*By George*, 1966)

Dame Barbara Cartland (*Album of Love Songs*, 1978)

Chevy Chase (*Chevy Chase*, 1980)

James Brolin (*James Brolin Sings*, 1974)

Richard Chamberlain (*Richard Chamberlain Sings*, 1964)

Albert Finney (*The Albert Finney Album*, 1977)

Jack Lemmon (*A Twist of Lemmon*, 1958)

Rock Hudson (*Pillow Talk*, 1959)

Anthony Quinn (*In My Own Way...I Love You*, 1969)

Burgess Meredith (*Songs From How The West Was Won*, 1963)

Sidney Poitier (*Poitier Meets Plato*, 1964)

Uri Geller (*Uri Geller*, 1975)

Cybill Shepherd (*Cybill Does It...To Cole Porter*, 1974)

MIKE THE HEADLESS CHICKEN

Mike the Headless Chicken – also known as Miracle Mike – was a speckled rooster that lived for 18 months after its head had been cut off. Sounding like a Disney character, he was thought by many people to be a hoax, but the bird was taken by its owner to the University of Utah in Salt Lake City to establish its authenticity.

This is how Mike came to become the most famous chicken in the world. On 10 September 1945, farmer Lloyd Olsen of Fruita, Colorado was sent out to the back yard by his wife to bring back a chicken so that she could cook it for her mother who was coming for dinner.

Olsen chose a five-and-a-half-month-old cockerel named Mike and tried to decapitate it with his axe. He nearly succeeded but the axe missed the jugular vein, leaving one ear and most of the brain stem intact.

Despite this, Mike was still able to balance on a perch and walk clumsily; it even attempted to preen and crow, although it could do neither. Mr Olsen was impressed by Mike and decided to let him live. He fed Mike a mixture of milk and water via an eyedropper and also gave him small grains of corn. Mike occasionally choked on his own mucus which the Olsen family would clear using a syringe.

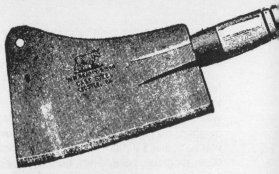

Being semi-headless didn't stop Mike from putting on weight: at the time of his partial beheading he weighed one kilogram. By the time he died two years later, he weighed three times that amount.

Mike soon became famous and began a career of touring sideshows in the company of such other creatures as a two-headed calf. Mike was on display to the public for an admission cost of 25 cents. At the height of his popularity, Mike earned his owner $4,500 a month and was valued at $10,000. Of course, this success resulted in a wave of copycat chicken beheadings, but no other chicken lived for more than a day or two.

After he died, it was discovered that the axe blade had missed the carotid artery and a clot had prevented Mike from bleeding to death. Although most of the head was severed, most of its brain stem and one ear was left on the body. Since basic functions (breathing, heart-rate, etc) as well as most of a chicken's reflex actions are controlled by the brain stem, Mike was able to remain quite healthy.

CELEBRITIES AND THE ALIASES THEY'VE USED

Sir Elton John (Lillian Lollipop, Lord Choc Ice, Lord Elpus, Binky Poodleclip, Fanny Beaversnatchclit)

Bruce Dickinson (Iffy Boatrace.)

Lenny Kravitz (Pepper La Bijou)

Drew Barrymore (Anita Mentor)

Mischa Barton (Marianne Antoinette)

Courtney Love (Mary Magdalin)

Kylie Minogue (Sue Denim)

Hilary Swank (Leslie Schevendecker)

Freddie Mercury (Lord Fickle)

John Lennon (Winston O'Boogie)

Ringo Starr (Mr Monaco)

Britney Spears (Alotta Warmheart, Mrs Diana Prince, Queen of the Fairy Dance, Mrs. Abra Cadabra)

RELIGIOUS CONVERSIONS

The Duchess of Kent (Protestant to Catholic)

Felicity Kendal (Christian to Jewish)

Cat Stevens/Yusuf Islam (Christian to Muslim)

Hayley Mills (Christian to Hare Krishna)

Chris Eubank (Christian to Muslim)

John Gummer (Protestant to Catholic)

Tina Turner (Christian to Buddhist)

Dame Elizabeth Taylor (Christian to Jewish)

Bob Dylan (Jewish to Christian to Jewish)

Bobby Fischer (Jewish to Christian)

Boris Pasternak (Jewish to Christian)

Carroll Baker (Christian to Jewish)

Jim Croce (Christian to Jewish)

Sammy Davis Jr (Christian to Jewish)

Marilyn Monroe (Christian to Jewish)

Eleanor Parker (Christian to Jewish)

Johnny Vaughan (Protestant to Catholic)

Delia Smith (Protestant to Catholic)

Ann Widdecombe (Protestant to Catholic)

Tom Hanks (Protestant to Greek Orthodox)

Pat Sharp (Christian to Jewish)

DOLPHINS

Dolphins can jump 6 metres above the water surface.

Dolphins can reach speeds of 60 kilometres per hour (37mph).

In 340 BC Aristotle observed that dolphins gave birth to live young that were attached to their mother by umbilical cords. For this reason, he considered dolphins and related creatures to be mammals. Twenty-four centuries later, biologists agreed with him.

Ganges river dolphins are virtually blind. All they can 'see' is the direction and intensity of light. This is one of the reasons why they swim on one side, with one flipper trailing in the muddy riverbed.

Dolphins swim in circles while they sleep with the eye on the outside of the circle open to keep watch for predators. After a certain amount of time, they reverse and swim in the opposite direction with the opposite eye open.

Handicapped dolphins
can survive independently.
A blind, deaf and mute
bottlenose was found aged nine in
Californian waters. It was monitored for seven
years and managed perfectly well without
normal communication.

Bottlenose dolphins can mimic the sounds other dolphins make underwater.

Dolphins jump out of the water to conserve energy as it's easier to move through the air than through the water.

RATS AND OTHER RODENTS

Rats prefer boiled sweets to cheese.

Rats multiply so quickly that in 18 months, two rats could have over a million descendants.

Rats can swim for a half a mile without resting, and they can tread water for three days.

A mouse's tail is as long as its body. It's also scaly to help the mouse grip when climbing.

A mouse's incisors never stop growing. They're ground down by all the gnawing a mouse does. If it weren't for that, their incisors could grow up to 13cm a year.

The world's largest rodent is the capybara. A huge semi-aquatic rodent which only lives in South America and looks like a giant guinea pig, it can weigh more than 45 kgs and grow to more than 1.25 metres long. Its name means 'master of the grasses' and it eats up to 3.6 kgs of grass and aquatic plants every day.

The capybara can be found wild in much of South America in densely forested areas near bodies of water (they're semi-aquatic). The only time they're found further afield is when they escape from captivity – which is why one was found in the River Arno in Florence, Italy in 2008.

The largest order of mammals, with about 1,700 species, is that of the rodent. Bats are second, with about 950 species.

A rat will find its way through a maze more easily if you play Mozart to it.

Squirrels might live for 15 or 20 years in captivity, but their lifespan in the wild, where they fall victim to disease, malnutrition, predators, cars and humans, is much shorter.

Rats are omnivorous, which means they eat almost any kind of food, including dead and dying members of their own species.

In an experiment, rats were able to distinguish between Japanese and Dutch – even when they were played backwards.

Naked mole rats live longer than any other rodent – 28 years on average, which is seven times longer than ordinary mice of the same size.

The kangaroo rat doesn't drink water.

The Mojave ground squirrel, found mainly in the American West, hibernates for eight months a year.

Mice will nurse babies that are not their own.

Rats can't vomit.

Before going into its winter hibernation, a dormouse breathes at the rate of 260 breaths a second.

A squirrel can use its tail as a parachute should it fall from a tree. The tail can also be used to cushion a hard landing, and to communicate with other squirrels.

During the 1962 Test match between England and Pakistan at Edgbaston, a mouse stopped play.

The word 'squirrel' comes from the Greek word meaning 'shadow-tailed,' because the squirrel uses its tail to keep warm or shade itself from the sun.

The heart of a mouse beats 650 times per minute.

A pair of mice can produce five hundred offspring in a year.

The mouse is the most common mammal in the US.

Rats have been trained to sniff out landmines. They have a nose for them, and are too light to trigger off an explosion.

In the first World War, rats were often sent into tunnels behind enemy lines to check for poisonous gas.

Like humans, mice have seven neck vertebrae.

There is a type of rat poison, made from white corn meal, peanut butter and treacle, which causes the rat to die of constipation.

An ancient cure for bedwetting was to eat fried mice.

A mouse has more bones than a human: mouse – 225, human – 206.

INSECTS

There are 200 million insects for every human being on Earth.

Adult earwigs can float in water for up to 24 hours.

Termites do more damage in the US every year than all the fires, storms and earthquakes combined.

In Germany, there's a flea that lives and breeds only in beer mats.

A queen bee lays a number of eggs from which successor queen bees will emerge. However, one of these queens will destroy all the others and reign alone.

Centipedes always have an uneven number of pairs of legs.

Amazon ants can do nothing except fight, so they steal the larvae of other ants and then keep them as slaves.

Every year, insects consume 10 per cent of the world's food supply.

Each of a dragonfly's eyes contains 30,000 lenses.

Male ants develop from unfertilized eggs. Queen and worker ants are developed from fertilized eggs.

There are 3,000 types of lice.

Cockroaches can detect movement as small as 2,000 times the diameter of a hydrogen atom.

The blood of insects is yellow. (The blood of mammals is red and the blood of lobsters is blue.)

Bees are born fully grown.

Female earwigs can't distinguish their own eggs from those of other earwigs and so steal any eggs they find.

Cockroaches break wind every 15 minutes. Even after they die, they carry on releasing methane gas for another 18 hours.

Ants evolved from wasps more than 100 million years ago.

The jaw of the trap-jaw ant snaps shut more than 2,000 times faster than the blink of an eye.

A 13-year-old boy in India produced winged beetles in his urine after hatching the eggs in his body.

If you teach a leech how to go through a maze and then cut it up and feed it to another leech the second leech immediately knows how to go through that maze.

If two flies were left to reproduce without predators or other limitations for one year, the resulting mass of flies would be the size of the Earth.

A large swarm of locusts can eat up to 85,000 tons of corn a day.

There are up to 8 million worms in the soil of each hectare of forest.

Flatworms split into two new worms after mating. That's how they reproduce.

Termite nests are sometimes used in the construction industry because the dirt is dust-free.

When it's startled by a possible predator, an ant raises its abdomen. This sends a signal to other ants in the colony, and all the other ants raise their abdomens too.

In the nineteenth century, a man in Nebraska in the US watched a swarm of Rocky Mountain locusts (now extinct). He reported that the swarm averaged a half-mile in height (some locusts were higher than a mile) and was 100 miles wide and 300 miles long. The swarm moved at about 5 mph in the air and continued to pass for six hours. Having worked out the number of locusts per square metre, he was able to calculate that the swarm had consisted of some 124,000,000,000 locusts. That's 124 billion locusts, each capable of devouring their own body weight in crops and vegetation.

Female tarantulas have been known to live for up to 30 years. Males rarely live longer than a few months.

Burying beetles are unusual among insects in that both the males and females take care of their offspring.

In 2002, an ant colony was found on the Ishikari coast of Hokkaido in Japan which covered an area of 2.7 square kms. Inside that colony were 306 million worker ants and 1 million queens living in 45,000 interconnected nests. Not unreasonably, it was thought to be the biggest ant colony in existence. But, more recently, a colony measuring 100 kms wide was found underneath Melbourne in Australia, while it's thought that there's a kind of super-colony of connected nests right across Europe that might stretch to almost 6,000 kms.

The sexton (or burying) beetle can smell a rotting corpse from up to a mile away.

The fastest insect in the world is the dragonfly which is capable of speeds up to 50 mph. It can hover, fly backwards, turn around in mid-air, and land wherever it wants to in an instant.

Killer ants are predatory; they have been called the fiercest predators on Earth. These ants kill more creatures than all other bigger predators combined. They attack en masse when their mounds are disturbed, and can kill animals many times their size – even deer.

There are some species of insects for which a male of the species has never been found.

If we humans had the same relative jumping ability as a flea, we would be able to achieve 215 metres in the long jump and 140 metres in the high jump.

Hard ticks can expand to 30 mms to accommodate all the blood they need to survive.

Cockroaches have teeth in their stomachs.

Ants live in an ant colony which consists of a series of underground chambers, connected to each other and the surface of the earth by small tunnels. Incredibly, there are rooms for nurseries and food storage. The colony is built and maintained by huge numbers of worker ants who carry tiny bits of dirt in their mandibles and deposit them near the exit of the colony (forming the 'anthill'), where they can be used as required.

The tropical stick bug – or the walking stick – can change colour in response to changes in humidity, light intensity and temperature.

The longest insect ever recorded is also the longest creature ever recorded. In 1864, a bootlace worm measuring 55 metres was washed up on the shore in Scotland. Even at their usual length – of 30 metres – bootlace worms are incredibly long, although they're rarely thicker than 1 centimetre.

Between them, honey bees travel a distance equal to twice around the world in order to gather enough nectar to make 400 grams of honey.

Wasps don't have any way of storing food for the winter, which is why their colonies only last for one season. Each colony starts to break up in the autumn and the workers die of cold.

Slugs lose water very quickly from their soft, unprotected bodies – which is why they live in damp places where they won't dry out.

Fire ants have adapted to cope with flooding. When water levels in their nests rise, they form a huge ball with the workers on the outside and the queen inside. The ball floats until it reaches higher ground and safety.

If it's being attacked, the katydid – a type of grasshopper – can shed a leg to escape.

Some species of cockroach are capable of remaining alive for a month without food, and are able to survive on almost anything (such as the glue on the back of postage stamps). Some can go without air for nearly an hour by slowing down their heart rate. In one experiment, cockroaches were able to recover from being submerged underwater for half an hour.

Every year, insects eat about a third of our planet's total food crop.

The strongest insect is the rhinocerous beetle which is so powerful it can carry 850 times its own weight.

Dung beetles can move mountains of manure that are 100 times heavier than them.

The female of most insect species is generally larger than the male of the species.

Insect flatulence may account for one-fifth of all the methane put out by our planet.

Some cockroaches are so fast they can run 50 times their own body length per second.

The African giant cricket eats human hair.

Leeches can drink up to five times their weight in blood.

All insects have three body parts – a head, a thorax, and an abdomen. They also have six (jointed) legs and two antennae which they use as sensors.

A fly's eyes don't have any eyelids so flies rub their eyes with their feet to keep them clean.

Giant ants can be used in medicine. They're sometimes used to stitch wounds. The ant's mandibles leave the edges of the wound stitched together.

Flowers use ultraviolet patterns to attract insects for pollination purposes.

Clever spiders use silk that reflects ultraviolet light, thereby attracting insects that think they are seeing harmless flowers.

If an insect intrudes into a beehive, honey bees can amass and vibrate their bodies together. The heat this creates literally cooks the insect intruder to death.

An insect's worst enemies are other insects. Of the millions of insects that are not vegetarian, most feed on other insects.

Over one million insect species have been discovered by scientists, and they think that there might be ten times that many that haven't been named yet.

With over 300,000 different species, one out of every four animals on Earth is a beetle.

The tarantula flicks hairs at its prey and this is enough to cause an allergic reaction which enables the tarantula to capture and then eat its poor victim.

The female firefly attracts males by flashing her light at them. When the males turn up, the females eat them.

Soldier termites can't feed themselves and so they must be fed by the workers.

APPEARED IN SOAPS

David Walliams (fake registrar at the wedding of Alfie Moon and Kat Slater in EastEnders)

Michael Palin (surfer in Home And Away)

Dame Judi Dench (as Pru Forrest in The Archers)

Boris Johnson (as himself in EastEnders)

DNA

Identical twins have one hundred per cent identical DNA.

We share our DNA with other people/things to the following extent:

99.9 per cent with every other human being

98.4 per cent with chimpanzees

92 per cent with dolphins

90 per cent with other animals

70 per cent with slugs

44 per cent with fruit flies

26 per cent with yeast

18 per cent with lettuce

GOLDFISH

The common goldfish is the only creature that can see both infra-red and ultra-violet light.

The oldest known goldfish was Goldie, who lived for 45 years after being won at a fairground in 1960.

If a goldfish is exposed to a loud noise, it can take a month for its hearing to go back to normal.

Humans have three colour receptors in their eyes, while goldfish have four.

SHARKS

Some sharks swim in a figure of eight when threatened.

The nurse shark spends much of its time in caves.

Sharks are older than dinosaurs, as shown by their fossil records.

Many sharks lay soft-shelled eggs but hammerhead sharks give birth to live young that are miniature versions of their parents. Young hammerheads emerge head first, with the tip of their hammerhead folded back to make the birth easier.

Females of some shark species give birth to only two young at a time.

Hammerhead sharks are expert at catching stingrays, on which they feed. The great distance between the eyes and nostrils of the shark may be what gives it such an ability.

Bull sharks have been known to pursue their victims on to land.

Sharks have an additional sense which enables them to detect bioelectrical fields given off by other sea creatures, and to navigate by detecting changes in the Earth's magnetic field.

A shark can swallow anything half its size in a single gulp, but when it comes to eating larger prey they have to twist and turn, which can sometimes lead them to bite their own bodies.

The biggest egg in the world is laid by a shark.

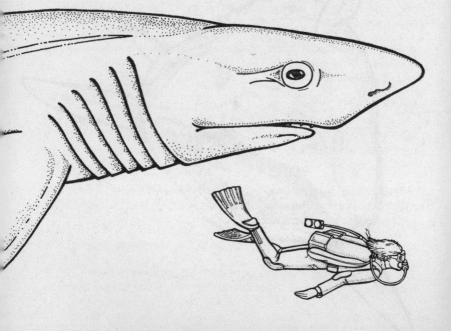

Sharks have no bones. They consist of cartilage, muscle and teeth.

The largest great white shark ever caught measured over 11 metres and weighed 10,900 kilograms. It was found in a herring weir in New Brunswick in 1930.

A 330 kilogram mako shark caught off Bimini in the Bahamas contained in its stomach a 54 kilogram swordfish – with the sword still intact.

Most hunting sharks prefer prey that's weak or helpless because it's easier to catch. That's why sharks are good at smelling blood – it tells them when an animal (or person) is injured. Sharks usually give their prey a fatal bite, then leave it to bleed to death. They then return to feed on the body.

Sharks can be dangerous even before they are born. A scientist was bitten by a sand tiger shark embryo while he was examining its pregnant mother.

About ten times more men than women are attacked by sharks.

The embryos of tiger sharks fight each other while in their mother's womb, the survivor being the baby shark that is born.

Sharks are the only creatures that never get sick. As far as is known, they are immune to every known disease including cancer.

Sharks in Greenland eat reindeer when they fall through the ice.

Sharks sometimes eat fish caught in fishing boats' nets before they can be pulled to the surface.

A sharks's stomach has the capacity to stretch so that the shark can consume large amounts of food quickly.

In 2004, while snorkelling in Australia, Luke Tresoglavic was bitten by a small wobbegong carpet shark that refused to let go. He had to swim to the shore and then drive to get help...with the shark still attached to his leg.

A shark has six senses. Besides vision, hearing, touch, taste and smell, sharks can also sense the tiny amounts of electricity given off by other animals.

The cookie-cutter shark is so aggressive it even attacks nuclear submarines.

Bull sharks have been known to kill hippos in rivers.

Sharks have very strong jaws. They can bite other animals in half – even those with tough shells, such as turtles.

The basking shark's liver, which accounts for up to a quarter of its whole body weight, runs the entire length of the abdominal cavity and is reckoned to play a role in keeping it buoyant.

Probably the the worst ever shark attack was in 1945, during World War 2. A US warship was torpedoed and sank in the South Pacific, leaving a thousand crew members in the water. Before they could be rescued, over six hundred of them had been eaten by sharks.

A great white shark bit off undersea photographer Henri Bource's leg while he was diving off Australia in 1964. He was soon back at work in the same job, and four years later another shark bit his artificial leg.

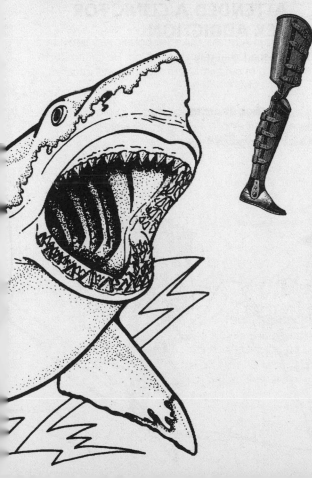

ATTENDED A CLINIC FOR SEX ADDICTION

Michael Douglas

Rob Lowe

Billy Bob Thornton

David Duchovny

SPORTING FIRSTS

The first English Football League game to be broadcast live on radio was Arsenal v. Sheffield United in 1927. To help listeners visualize the action, the BBC employed a grid system, published in the *Radio Times*, that divided the pitch into squares. And that's how we get the saying 'back to square one.'

Coincidentally, the Gunners were also involved in the first live coverage of a soccer match on television. In 1937, an exhibition match between Arsenal's first team and their reserves was televised live.

The first female jockey to ride in the Grand National was Charlotte Brew in 1977 on Barony Fort (which refused at the fourth fence from home). In 1982, Geraldine Rees became the first female jockey to complete the race when she finished eighth on Cheers. The race awaits its first female winner – although Jenny Pitman has had successes as a trainer with Corbiere (1983) and Royal Athlete (1995).

In 2003–4, Arsenal became the first club to win the Premiership without losing a single game.

In 2010, Spain became the first European country to win a World Cup held outside Europe. The final – in which Spain beat Holland – was also the first final between two monarchies (and didn't the Spanish Queen love it.)

The first marathon was run in 490 BC by Pheidippides, a Greek soldier, who ran from Marathon to Athens (about 25 miles) to tell the Athenians about the battle the Greeks had fought with the invading Persians. Poor old Pheidippides arrived in Athens exhausted and with bleeding feet. After telling the townspeople of the Greeks' success in the battle, he promptly fell down dead. In 1896, at the first modern Olympic Games, it was decided to hold a race of approximately the same distance in honour of Pheidippides's marathon run.

The 2006 FIFA World Cup was the first World Cup where the first and last goals of the tournament were scored by defenders.

In tennis, the Grand Slam is achieved by winning the Singles Championships at the French Open, Wimbledon, the US Open and the Australian Open in the same calendar year. The first man to achieve this feat was the American Don Budge in 1938; the first woman was the American Maureen Connolly in 1953. Since then, only Rod Laver (1962 and 1969), Margaret Court (1970) and Steffi Graf (1988) have achieved this feat.

In 1901 Tottenham Hotspur – then not even in the Football League – won the FA Cup and, at the celebration dinner, became the first club to tie (blue and white) ribbons on the handles of the trophy, a practice which has since become a custom.

The first international cricket match took place in 1844 and involved neither England nor Australia. It was held between the US and Canada in New York, and Canada won by 23 runs.

The first international Test match took place in 1877 and did involve Australia and England. Played in Melbourne, it finished with Australia winning by 45 runs. 100 years later, in 1977, a centenary Test match between the two countries was played in Melbourne. Australia beat England by 45 runs – the precise same margin by which they had won the inaugural match 100 years earlier.

Going back to that first Test in 1877, Australia's Charles Bannerman set a number of records. He faced the first ball in Test Cricket, scored the first run, the first four and the first century. He ended up scoring 165 not out in Australia's total of 245 all out – his innings constituting over two-thirds (67.34 per cent) of the team's total. Incredibly, this is still the highest per centage by a batsman in a completed Test innings.

Incidentally, Charles Bannerman also went on to become the first Australian to score a century in England (though it wasn't in a Test match).

But that's not all. The first radio broadcast of a cricket match anywhere in the world was a 1922–23 match played as a benefit for Charles Bannerman, from which he received £490.

The first FA Cup final to feature numbered shirts was in 1933.

The first football World Cup final to feature numbered shirts was in 1938.

England footballers first wore their names on the back of their shirts during the 1992 European Championships.

In golf, the word 'par' means the target or regulation number of shots for a hole or for a course. So the typical hole is either par 3, par 4 or par 5 while par for most golf courses ranges from 70 to 72. Par was first adopted in 1912.

In football, the two handed throw-in was first made compulsory in 1883, while goal nets were first used in 1891. In the same year, the penalty kick was introduced into the game. The first ever penalty kick was awarded to Wolverhampton Wanderers in their game against Accrington Stanley on 14 September 1891. The penalty was taken and scored by a man named John Heath.

Lincoln was the first club to add 'City' to their name – in 1892.

The first FA Cup final to go to extra time was the 1875 game between the Royal Engineers and the Old Etonians. However, even after 120 minutes the two teams couldn't be separated and the match finished 1–1. Three days later, the Engineers won the replay 2–0 – not least because some of the Old Etonian team couldn't make the game because of other commitments.

Cricket was the first sport to enclose its venues and charge for admission. The first time this happened was in 1731 when the playing area on Kennington Common was staked out and roped off – so enabling the people running the game to charge people to watch it.

The first woman to play golf at St. Andrew's Golf Club in Scotland was Mary, Queen of Scots, in 1552. She was the club's founder.

The first Australian cricket tour of England took place in 1868. The touring party was made up entirely of Aborigines (native Australians) and the players wore caps of different colours so that the spectators could identify them. The team played 47 matches against various teams of which they won 14, lost 14 and drew the rest. Apart from playing cricket the Aborigines demonstrated a number of unique sports and activities, including boomerang throwing, the backwards race and cricket ball dodging.

The first Paralympic Games were held in 1948. People – mistakenly – think that the world 'Paralympic' is derived from the words 'paralysed' and 'olympics'. In fact, that's only half-right: it comes from the words 'Parallel' and 'Olympics' (i.e. the Paralympics are held in parallel with the Olympics).

The first time a boxer won the world heavyweight championship from the canvas (i.e. the floor) was in 1930 when Germany's Max Schmeling was awarded the fight because of a low blow (i.e. one below the belt) from Jack Sharkey.

The first football team to wear shinguards were Nottingham Forest, in 1874. They were invented by their centre forward Sam Widdowson, who wore them outside his socks.

The first British club to enter the European Cup was Hibernian in 1955.

The first twins to play in the same cricket test match weren't Steve and Mark Waugh of Australia, but Rosemary and Elizabeth Signal of New Zealand in a women's Test against England in 1984. Talking of the Waugh brothers, Steve made his debut first. When Mark first played for his country, it was Steve who was dropped to make room for him (with Steve being given the job of telling Mark.

Croquet was the first sport to embrace equality with both sexes allowed to play the game on an equal footing.

In 2006, Switzerland became the first team to be eliminated from the World Cup Finals without conceding a goal.

ROLES THAT WERE TURNED DOWN

Al Pacino's role in *The Godfather* – Warren Beatty

Michael Douglas's role in *Traffic* – Harrison Ford

Olivia Newton-John's role in *Grease* – Susan Dey

Richard Gere's role in *Pretty Woman* – Al Pacino

Harrison Ford's role in *Star Wars* – Al Pacino

Christina Ricci's role in *The Ice Storm* – Natalie Portman

Mena Suvari's role in *American Beauty* – Kirsten Dunst

Glenn Close's role in *Fatal Attraction* – Miranda Richardson

Harrison Ford's role in *Witness* – Paul Newman and Tom Selleck

Harrison Ford's role in *Raiders of the Lost Ark* – Tom Selleck

Keanu Reeves's role in *Speed* – Stephen Baldwin

Sandra Bullock's role in *Speed* – Halle Berry

Clint Eastwood's role in *Dirty Harry* – Paul Newman and
Robert Mitchum

NEXT!

Peter O'Toole's role in *Lawrence of Arabia* – Albert Finney (because it would have required him to sign a 5-year contract)

Cary Grant's role in *Arsenic and Old Lace* – Bob Hope

Christopher Reeve's role in *Superman* – Robert Redford, Steve McQueen and Paul Newman

Julia Roberts's role in *Pretty Woman* – Meg Ryan

Jodie Foster's role in *Silence of the Lambs* – Meg Ryan ('I felt it was too dark for me')

Jack Lemmon's role in *Some Like It Hot* – Frank Sinatra

Uma Thurman's role in *The Avengers* – Gwyneth Paltrow

Patrick Swayze's role in *Ghost* – Bruce Willis ('I passed on it. Another one of my smarter moves')

COUPLES WHO DIDN'T HAVE SEX ON THEIR WEDDING NIGHTS

Elizabeth Taylor & Nicky Hilton (she was a virgin when they married but they didn't actually have sex until their third night of marriage)

Richard Gere & Cindy Crawford

Brian Aherne & Joan Fontaine

Liza Minnelli & Peter Allen

Walt Disney & Lillian Bounds (Walt had toothache)

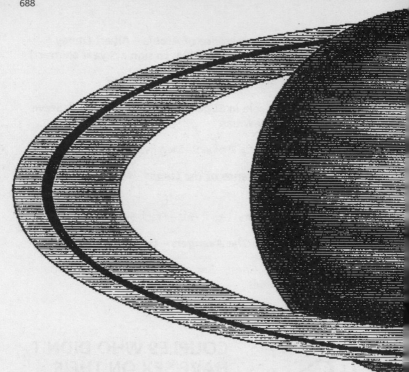

ASTRONAUTS

The first astronauts to go to the moon trained in Iceland because the terrain there was reckoned to be similar to the moon's surface.

The heart of an astronaut actually gets smaller when in outer space.

In 1971, astronaut Alan Shepard hit two golf balls on the lunar surface. Despite thick gloves and a spacesuit which forced him to swing the club with just one hand, Shepard struck two golf balls, driving the second 'miles and miles and miles'.

Astronauts can't burp in Space: there's no gravity to separate liquid from gas in their stomachs.

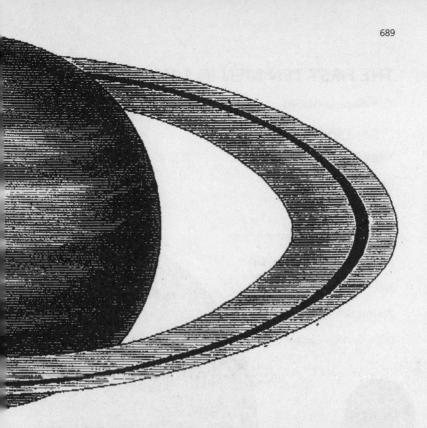

While astronauts might feel upset in space, lack of gravity will prevent their tears from rolling down their face.

Astronauts put mirrors on the moon. They wanted to bounce laser beams off them, so that the distance to the moon could be measured.

Astronauts lose their sense of smell in space because there is no gravity to move smells around. It also means that the fluid in their sinuses doesn't drain away automatically but remains there while they're on their missions. As for snoring, the word is that if they snore on Earth – they snore in Space too.

Neil Armstrong and Buzz Aldrin ate turkey in foil packets as the first meal on the moon.

THE FIRST TEN MEN IN SPACE

Yuri Gagarin (USSR)

Alan B. Shepard (USA)

Virgil ('Gus') Grissom (USA)

Gherman Titov (USSR)

John Glenn (USA)

Malcolm Scott Carpenter (USA)

Andrian Nikolayev (USSR)

Pavel Popovich (USSR)

Walter Schirra (US)

Leroy Gordon Cooper (US)

THE ONLY TWELVE MEN WHO HAVE WALKED ON THE MOON

Neil Armstrong (20 July 1969)

Edwin 'Buzz' Aldrin (20 July 1969)

Pete Conrad (19–20 November 1969)

Alan Bean (19–20 November 1969)

Alan Shepard (5–6 February 1971)

Edgar Mitchell (5–6 February 1971)

David Scott (31 July – 2 August 1971)

James Irwin (31 July – 2 August 1971)

Charles Duke (21–23 April 1972)

John Young (21–23 April 1972)

Eugene Cernan (11–14 December 1972)

Harrison Schmitt (11–14 December 1972)

WHALES

The killer whale is the fastest sea mammal. It can reach speeds up to 34 miles per hour (56 kilometers per hour) in pursuit of prey.

Many large whales have a blowhole crest. This is an elevated area in front of their blowholes that stops water getting in while they're breathing.

At birth, the white whale is black.

The blue whale, the world's largest mammal, weighs 50 tons at birth. Fully grown, it weighs as much as 150 tons.

Grey whales migrate 12,000 miles each year.

A sperm whale's tooth is the size of a big peanut-butter jar.

Whales can die from pneumonia.

The grey whale has a series of up to 180 fringed overlapping plates hanging from each side of its upper jaw. This is where teeth would be located if the creature had any.

The low frequency call of the humpback whale is the loudest noise made by a living creature. It can be heard from over three hundred miles away.

Female whales live twice as long as male whales.

Whales die if their echo system fails.

A baby blue whale is 7.5 metres long at birth.

Humpback whales have an underwater song that evolves from year to year. They use hierarchical language involving syntax and grammar in the songs they sing.

Killer whales have individual songs which they rarely, if ever, change.

A baby baleen whale depends on a mother's milk diet for at least six months. Every day, a baby grey whale drinks enough milk to fill more than two thousand baby bottles.

Whales sometimes rub up against the hulls of passing ships to get rid of parasites on their skin.

South Georgia was once the whaling capital of the southern world; it is now a whale sanctuary.

TV SHOWS THAT STARTED AS RADIO SHOWS

What's My Line?

This Is Your Life

Dragnet

Perry Mason

Gunsmoke

The Lone Ranger

Little Britain

Dead Ringers

FILMS THAT BECAME TV SERIES

Lock, Stock And Two Smoking Barrels

Doctor Kildare

Casablanca

In The Heat of The Night

The Third Man

The Saint

The Prime of Miss Jean Brodie

Quiller (from The Quiller Memorandom)

Man at the Top (from *Room At The Top*)

Mildred Pierce

SITCOMS THAT WERE SPIN-OFFS FROM OTHER SITCOMS

Frasier (Cheers)

Empty Nest (The Golden Girls)

Laverne And Shirley (Happy Days)

Rhoda (The Mary Tyler Moore Show)

Tabitha (Bewitched)

Joey (Friends)

DRUMMERS

Jeremy Vine (Flared Generation)

Steve Tyler (Aerosmith)

Simon Pegg (God's Third Leg)

Ben Stiller (Capital Punishment)

Eddie Jordan (Eddie & The Robbers)

John Thomson

Jeff Rawle

Matthew McConaughey

Max Beesley

Nancy Sorrell

Rowland Rivron

Shia LaBeouf

Al Murray

US PRESIDENTS

In 1845, President Andrew Jackson's pet parrot was removed from his funeral for swearing.

James Buchanan (1857–61) was the first – and so far only – bachelor to become president.

Herbert Hoover is the only US President to turn over his entire annual salary to charity.

No (former) American President has ever died in the month of May.

Prior to World War 2, when guards were posted at the fence, anyone could wander right up to the front door of the White House – the US President's residence.

More than half of all US Presidents have been qualified lawyers.

James Garfield (1881), who lived in the White House with his mother, often gave campaign speeches in German.

In 1881, President Garfield was shot twice by Charles Guiteau. One bullet grazed Garfield's arm but the second bullet was lodged somewhere in his spine and couldn't be found.

Over the next 80 days, he was attended by several doctors – some of whom poked their unwashed hands into his wounds. Meanwhile, Alexander Graham Bell devised a metal detector to find the bullet, but the metal bed frame Garfield was lying on caused the metal detector to go completely haywire. It never occurred to anyone to take the

President off the metal bed – probably because metal beds were so rare at the time.

President Garfield developed blood poisoning followed by bronchial pneumonia and then, 80 days after the shooting, a massive heart attack. He died precisely two months short of his fiftieth birthday. If his doctors had washed their hands and used sterile instruments, he probably would have recovered.

Theodore Roosevelt (1901–1909) was the first President to go underwater in a submarine.

Calvin Coolidge's (1923–9) pets included a goose, a wallaby, a donkey, a lion cub, two cats and twelve dogs. He was sworn into office by his own father.

Grover Cleveland (1893–97) answered the White House phone personally. He also worked briefly as an executioner before becoming President and hanged at least two convicted criminals.

Warren Harding (1921–23) was the first US President who could drive a car.

There are lots of photographs of Abraham Lincoln (1861–65) but not a single one of him smiling.

Franklin D. Roosevelt (1933–45) is the only US President to have had a Parisian Metro (underground) station named after him.

Richard Nixon (1969–74) is the only US President to have served two terms as Vice President and then to be elected to two terms as President.

Jimmy Carter (1977–81) was the first President to have been born in a hospital.

Abraham Lincoln held an alcohol licence and ran several taverns.

In 1965, Congress authorized the Secret Service to protect former presidents and their spouses for their lifetime, unless they declined the protection. Subsequently, Congress limited the protection of former presidents and their spouses (elected after 1 January 1997) to ten years after leaving office. President Clinton, who was elected in 1996, will be the last president to receive lifelong protection from the Secret Service.

THE AGE AT WHICH THEY LOST THEIR VIRGINITY

13
Kendra Wilkinson, P. Diddy, Anthony Kiedis (13 – the Red Hot Chili Peppers frontman did it with his father's 18-year-old girlfriend while his father watched)

14
Trevor Sorbie, Phillip Schofield

15
Burt Reynolds, Mike Stock, Steve Tyler (with a prostitute after three of his friends had had her first)

16
Daniel Radcliffe, Sienna Miller, Scott Baio (with Erin Moran)

17
Martina Navratilova, Russell Brand (with a prostitute in Hong Kong paid for by his father)

18
Duncan James

19
King Edward VII

20
Toyah Willcox

21
Yazz

22
The Duke of Windsor

26
Jimmy Carr

27
Anita Harris

31
Paul Potts

GENUINE THINGS WRITTEN BY DRIVERS ON INSURANCE COMPANY FORMS

'My car was legally parked as it backed into the other vehicle.'

'I told the police I was not injured, but upon removing my hair, I found that I had a fractured skull.'

'I was sure the old fellow would never make it to the other side of the road when I struck him.'

'The indirect cause of the accident was a little guy in a small car with a big mouth.'

'Question: Could either driver have done anything to avoid the accident? Answer: Travelled by bus?'

'There was no damage to the car, as the gatepost will testify.'

'A bull was standing near and the fly must have tickled him as he gored my car.'

'I had to turn the car sharper than was necessary owing to an invisible lorry.'

'First car stopped suddenly, second car hit first car and a haggis ran into the rear of second car.'

'The accident occurred when I was attempting to bring my car out of a skid by steering it into the other vehicle.'

'A dog on the road braked, causing a skid.'

'Wilful damage was done to the upholstery by rats.'

'I unfortunately ran over a pedestrian and the old gentleman was taken to hospital much regretting the circumstances.'

'Cow wandered into my car. I was afterwards informed that the cow was half-witted.'

'I ran into a shop window and sustained injuries to my wife.'

'As I approached the intersection a sign suddenly appeared in a place where no sign had ever appeared before, making me unable to avoid the accident.'

'The telephone pole was approaching. I was attempting to swerve out of the way when I struck the front end.'

'I knew the dog was possessive about the car but I would not have asked her to drive it if I had thought there was any risk.'

'When I saw I could not avoid a collision I stepped on the gas and crashed into the other car.'

'The accident happened when the right front door of a car came round the corner without giving a signal.'

'The accident was due to another man narrowly missing me.'

'The car occupants were stalking deer on the hillside.'

'The water in my radiator accidentally froze at midnight.'

'The other man altered his mind so I had to run into him.'

'She suddenly saw me, lost her head, and we met.'

'I misjudged a lady crossing the street.'

DIED ON PRECISELY THE SAME DAY AS ANOTHER CELEBRITY

Jack Lemmon & Joan Sims (28.6.2001)

Michelangelo Antonioni & Ingmar Bergman (30.7.2007)

Dame Anita Roddick & Jane Wyman (10.9.2007)

Jeremy Beadle & Miles Kington (30.1.2008)

Sir Arthur C. Clarke & Paul Scofield (19.3.2008)

Mel Ferrer & Bo Diddley (2.6.2008)

Bill Frindall & John Martyn (29.1.2009)

Farrah Fawcett & Michael Jackson (25.6.2009)

Karl Malden & Mollie Sugden (1.7.2009)

Keith Floyd & Patrick Swayze (14.9.2009)

Abel Muzorewa & Malcolm McLaren (8.4.2010)

Malcolm Allison & Simon MacCorkindale (14.10.2010)

Susannah York & Nat Lofthouse (15.1.2011)

Dame Elizabeth Taylor & Fred Titmus (23.3.2011)

Sir Henry Cooper & Ted Lowe (1.5.2011)

Severiano Ballesteros & John Walker (of The Walker Brothers) (7.5.2011)

HISTORY (2)

In 1358 there were only four public toilets in the whole of London. The largest was on London Bridge and it emptied straight into the river Thames.

In the early 1920s the Italian fascists used to intimidate their socialist enemies by feeding them large amounts of castor oil (a laxative) and then tying them to a lamp post so that they couldn't move away.

During the Great Fire of London, the diarist Samuel Pepys buried his precious cheese in the garden to try to save it from the flames.

The seventeenth century Italian astronomer Galileo Galilei spent so much time looking at the sun with his telescope that he was blind for the last four years of his life.

Shaka, leader of the South African Zulu tribe from 1818 to 1828, didn't trust his witch-finders, so he set them a test. He smeared blood on his own house and told them to find the witch who did it. When they found 300 'guilty' people, Shaka had the witch-finder put to death.

The remains of Alexander the Great were preserved in a huge vat of honey.

In the Middle Ages, sewage from public latrines ran directly into the river or the sea.

In 1531, the Bishop of Rochester's chef was sentenced to death for poisoning members of the bishop's household. He was taken to the town square where he was put into a pot of cold water hanging over a fire. It took two hours for the water to boil and kill him.

In 882, Pope John VIII was poisoned and then clubbed to death.

Genghis Khan's cavalry rode female horses so soldiers could drink their milk.

The French used to use a form of torture which involved a goat licking salt off a person's feet. Over a period of time, what started as something not too unpleasant would result in skin being removed from the feet.

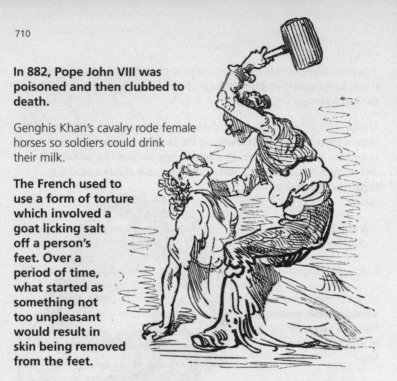

When, later in her reign, Queen Elizabeth I had lost all her teeth, she filled her mouth with cloth whenever she went out in public.

When the sixteenth century Danish astronomer Tycho Brahe lost the tip of his nose in a duel (during his student days) he replaced it with one made of a mixture of silver and gold.

In the days before toilet paper became readily available, people just had to use whatever came to hand. In the US of the late nineteenth century, the Sears Catalogue was very popular because it was printed on soft paper. When Sears switched to hard, shiny paper, sales of the catalogue went down.

Toilet paper shortages aren't just a matter of ancient history. As recently as 1994, there was a severe shortage in communist Cuba. After everyone had used up their newspapers, magazines and telephone directories, they started stealing books – even rare ones – from libraries.

When Marie Antoinette became pregnant, all the fashionable women of Paris started wearing padding over their stomachs. As her pregnancy developed, the women wore thicker and thicker pads. When her baby was born, the women's fashions returned to normal.

Christopher Columbus managed to avoid a battle against the people of Jamaica by convincing them he was a god. He 'predicted' the lunar eclipse of 29 February 1504, that he had read about in his almanac.

King Henry VIII suffered from scurvy because in the sixteenth century, wealthy people ate meat; vegetables were supposedly for peasants. And so Henry got scurvy.

Kings and queens always had food-tasters but King Charles VIII of France was so terrified by the thought of being poisoned that he wouldn't rely on them and simply stopped eating and drinking. Eventually, he died – not from poison but from malnutrition.

When the Byzantine emperor Justinian II was deposed in 695 AD, his enemies slit his nose and tongue on the basis that he would never be able to rule again if he were disfigured. Ten years later, Justinian The Slit-Nosed returned to power and paraded his enemies through the streets before killing them.

Vlad the Impaler – the ruler of Wallachia (present-day Romania) from 1456 to 1462 – was infamous for his cruelty. When 55 Turkish ambassadors refused to remove their hats in his presence he had their hats nailed to their heads.

The Aztecs believed that the tears of children would make the rains come and improve their harvest, so they put children in mountain caves to make them cry – sometimes letting them starve to death.

The Aztecs also had a festival – the flaying of men – in which a victim was skinned alive and a warrior would 'wear' his skin.

Many old Celtic graves contain the bodies of an old person and several younger people. Archaeologists think that the younger people were killed as a sacrifice to keep the old person company in the next life.

Saxon wives were sometimes buried alive with their husbands to keep them company in the afterlife.

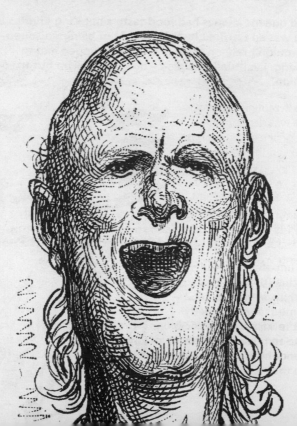

New Scythian soldiers had to drink the blood of the first (enemy) soldier they killed. They also had to collect the scalps of the people they killed in order to claim a share of the loot after a battle. The more scalps, the more loot.

When Genghis Khan died in 1227, he was buried beneath a tree near his birthplace. His soldiers killed all witnesses to the funeral (including animals) then killed themselves so that no living being would know where he was buried.

In the late eighteenth century, Poland was the second biggest country in Europe (after Russia).

In 1325, the Italian cities of Bologna and Modena went to war over a stolen bucket. The Battle of Zappolino – which was won by the Modenese – is also known as The War Of The Oaken Bucket.

The British handed Suriname over to the Dutch in return for New Amsterdam – which they renamed New York.

Between the two World Wars, France had 40 different governments.

As late as 1876 there were over a million slaves in Brazil. This amounted to 15 per cent of the Brazilian population.

The Swiss Guard is the world's oldest army. The earliest detachment was in 1497 and the Papal Swiss Guard in the Vatican (established in 1506) still exists today. The uniform worn by the Swiss Guard was designed by Michelangelo.

Pitcairn was settled in 1790 by British mutineers from the ship *Bounty* led by Fletcher Christian who had led the mutiny against the captain, William Bligh.

King Philip II of Spain had a palace with 2,673 doors.

A young Horatio Nelson was stationed in Antigua in the 1780s. He tried to stop trade with the newly-formed US. The Antiguans depended on this trade so Nelson was terribly unpopular on the island.

Zimbabwe was a mighty empire in the Middle Ages.

King Richard II died in 1400. A hole was left in the side of his tomb so people could touch his royal head, but 376 years later someone stole his jawbone.

When Florence Nightingale first went to work as a nurse during the Crimean War, she was shocked to discover that soldiers' amputated limbs were left outside for the pigs to eat.

During Sweden's great expansion in the seventeenth century, the country founded a short-lived colony in what is now Delaware in the US.

King George I could not speak English.

LASTS

The **last** execution in the Tower of London took place on Thursday, 14 August 1941, when Josef Jakobs, a German spy, was shot by an eight-man firing squad.

When Thomas Edison died in 1941, Henry Ford captured his **last** dying breath in a bottle.

The **last** Olympics in which the gold medals were made entirely from gold were in 1912.

The guillotine was **last** used in France publicly in 1939 and non-publicly in 1977.

The **last** American Civil War veteran to die was John Salling, a Confederate soldier, who died in 1958 aged 112.

In 1789, Catherine Murphy officially became the **last** British woman to be executed by burning. Except she wasn't actually burned. Let me explain. Catherine Murphy was convicted of making counterfeit coins – along with a lot of other people including her husband. But because they were all men, they were sentenced to hang; as a woman, she was sentenced to be burnt at the stake. Here's what happened though. She was brought out past the hanging bodies of her co-defendants and made to stand on a small platform in front of the stake, where she was secured with ropes. At this point she was meant to be burned but, according to witnesses, she was hanged instead. The next year, burning as a method of execution was abolished.

Similarly, the **last** British man to be hanged, drawn and quartered...
also wasn't hanged, drawn and quartered. In 1803, Edward Despard
was found guilty of high treason. Despite Lord Horatio Nelson
appearing in court as a character witness on his behalf, Despard was
sentenced to be hanged, drawn and quartered. This would have
meant him being hanged by the neck but taken down before he
was dead. Then he would have had his entrails (his inner body parts)
'drawn' from his body and burned in front of him – if he hadn't
already died from the shock of it all. Finally, he would have been
beheaded and his body would have been 'quartered' into pieces.
This was the very punishment meted out to Sir William Wallace, the
Scottish rebel leader, five hundred years earlier. However, in Despard's
case, the authorities were worried that the public might protest if he
got the full h., d. and q. treatment and so he was 'merely' hanged and
then beheaded – in front of a crowd of at least 20,000 people.

The **last** dodo bird died in 1681.

The Beatles **last** concert was at Candlestick Park, San Francisco, on 29 August 1966. The last song they played was *Long Tall Sally*.

The Beatles recorded their **last** song together *I Me Mine* in 1970.

The **last** song that Elvis ever performed publicly was *Bridge Over Troubled Water*, at his last concert in Indianapolis, in June 1977.

George Washington died on the **last** hour of the **last** day of the **last** week of the **last** month of the **last** year of the eighteenth century.

In 1999, Bhutan became the **last** country in the world to introduce television.

Pitcairn Island is the **last** British territory in the Pacific.

Zimbabwe comes **last** in the World Happiness Rankings.